Humiliation in International Relations

In international relations (IR), often some states deny the legal status of others, stigmatising their practices or even their culture. Such acts of deliberate humiliation at the diplomatic level are common occurrences in modern diplomacy. In the period following the breakup of the famous 'Concert of Europe', many kinds of club-based diplomacy have been tried, all falling short of anything like inclusive multilateralism. Examples of this effort include the G7, G8, G20 and even the P5. Such 'contact groups' are put forward as if they were actual ruling institutions, endowed with the power to exclude and marginalise.

Today, the effect of such acts of humiliation is to reveal the international system's limits and its lack of diplomatic effectiveness. The use of humiliation as a regular diplomatic action steadily erodes the power of the international system. These actions appear to be the result of a botched mixture of a colonial past, a failed decolonisation, a mistaken vision of globalisation and a very dangerous post-bipolar reconstruction.

Although this book primarily takes a social psychology approach to IR, it also mobilizes the resources of the French sociological tradition, mainly inspired by Emile Durkheim. It is translated from *Le temps des humiliés. Pathologie des relations internationales* (Paris, Odile Jacob, 2014).

Volume 6 in the series French Studies in International Law

French Studies in International Law

General Editor: Emmanuelle Jouannet (Sorbonne Law School)

French Studies in International Law is a unique new series which aims to bring to the attention of an English-speaking audience the most important modern works by leading French and French-speaking scholars of international law. The books which appear in this series were selected by Professor Emmanuelle Jouannet of the University of Paris 1 (Sorbonne Law School). French Studies in International Law is a books collection of the CERDIN Paris 1 Sorbonne Law School (The Centre of Studies and Research on International Law). The CERDIN is the largest French research centre in international law comprising 11 professors, 3 lecturers, 21 research professors and researchers, and 188 PhD students. CERDIN follows an active policy of collective work around several fields of key research, including: general international law, law of the United Nations, international disputes, international economic and finance law (in particular WTO), international human rights law, theory, philosophy and history of international law and foreign doctrines, international air space law, and the law of the sea.

Volume 1: Ordering Pluralism: A Conceptual Framework for Understanding the Transnational Legal World *Mireille Delmas-Marty translated by Naomi Norberg*

Volume 2: International Law, Power, Security and Justice: Essays on International Law and Relations *Serge Sur*

Volume 3: The Advancement of International Law *Charles Leben*

Volume 4: The Law against War: The Prohibition on the Use of Force in Contemporary International Law *Olivier Corten* (translated by Christopher Sutcliffe)

Volume 5: What is a Fair International Society? International Law Between Development and Recognition *Emmanuelle Tourme-Jouannet*

Humiliation in International Relations

A Pathology of Contemporary International Systems

Bertrand Badie

Translated by Jeff Lewis

•HART•

OXFORD • LONDON • NEW YORK • NEW DELHI • SYDNEY

HART PUBLISHING
Bloomsbury Publishing Plc
Kemp House, Chawley Park, Cumnor Hill, Oxford, OX2 9PH, UK

HART PUBLISHING, the Hart/Stag logo, BLOOMSBURY and the Diana logo are trademarks of Bloomsbury Publishing Plc

First published in hardback, 2017
Paperback edition, 2019

A catalogue record for this book is available from the British Library.

Library of Congress Cataloging-in-Publication data

ISBN: HB: 978-1-78225-619-9
PB: 978-1-50993-466-9
ePDF: 978-1-50990-116-6
ePub: 978-1-50990-117-3

Typeset by Compuscript Ltd, Shannon

To find out more about our authors and books visit www.hartpublishing.co.uk. Here you will find extracts, author information, details of forthcoming events and the option to sign up for our newsletters.

Preface to the English edition

Humiliation is a key concept of psychology, but is used only as an ordinary word in political science, and particularly in international relations. However, the word is nowadays becoming more and more frequent in academic commentary as well as in political rhetoric. Unquestionably, two threads must be considered: as a concept, humiliation is increasingly referenced in explaining the transformations inside the international arena; and as a practice, it is playing an increasing role in shaping diplomacies and foreign policies. Humiliation has become a real instrument of domination, and also a pretext for contesting hegemony and producing a deviant diplomacy. This change is beyond crucial: it is at the heart of one of the most important sources of violence in our contemporary world, but it is also triggering a deep transformation within the discipline of international relations. From this perspective, we can say that international relations took an initial academic shape in 1945 under the auspices of Max Weber and his science of power, probably now about to be reborn under the authority of Emile Durkheim and his science of social integration.

Nowadays, the main pitfall on the road of international relations would be to consider power as the key solution to all the problems that are at stake. The point was progressively made in European domestic politics, when governments faced an increasing request for political participation from society itself. Democracy was then developed, as a way of suspending—or at least balancing—power when its use became too risky. As a practice and as a science, international relations remained, quite the contrary, exclusively based on power without even imagining new ways of action. In spite of Wilson's dream and the first attempts of creating a new multilateralism, power could always recapture its own position in all the parts of the international arena. This contradiction would be unbearable in any kind of social system: it became totally untenable as and when the international system became global, active and socially mobilised. Power was increasingly received and endured as a humiliation, while those who exercised the power went on using it blindly as a means of keeping their threatened status. Power was no longer an instrument for reaching a target, but a means of continuing to exist. The adventure starts here: in the short term, humiliation became a strategy; in the medium term, it shaped a new international system; in the long term it fed a large well-spring of revenge and the new transnational violence that we now observe. In short, humiliation became a major concept in the discipline of international relations: this is precisely what I have tried to establish in this book.

Is it always and everywhere that truth belongs to the humiliated and error belongs to those who humiliate? Certainly not: humiliation is wrong in its method, but not necessarily in its ends. This confusion is certainly at the core of many misunderstandings and deadlocks that presently affect international life, and sometimes even annihilate the great causes. It shows the humiliated government in the best light, even if it was wrong and cruel, while the humiliating force inevitably looks bad and guilty, even if its goals were generous. In this sense, humiliation, as an established practice, creates many pervasive and structuring effects on the international arena, which most frequently are neither visible nor conscious. For these reasons, I have attempted to demonstrate in the following pages that humiliation is deeply structuring the contemporary international system and that its underestimation explains many an *impasse* in international negotiations, as well as many aspects of new international conflicts.

The need to integrate humiliation into the theory of international relations sheds light on the strengths and limits of the realist theories that still dominate the literature on the subject. Humiliation validates the key argument of the classic theory: power is still striving to structure the competition among states, while the balance of powers can be considered as determining relations among the most powerful states. But in the meantime, the result is not what was expected: humiliation, as a mark of weakness, is also proactive, triggering reactions and violence and even, promptly and efficiently, setting the international agenda. For these reasons, the result anticipated by realists is less and less consistent with the present situation: conflicts are less and less a strength competition and more and more a challenge coming from the weakest actors. Weakness politics is progressively substituted for power politics. In addition, if we accept this new perspective, we must admit, in the meantime, that humiliation—as an active factor—breaks down the wall between the political sphere and society, between strategists, "cold monsters" on one hand and social actors, even mere individuals, on the other. Humiliation is definitely more social than political, and gives the major role to non-state actors. Realism explains how humiliation is borne, consciously or not, by the strategists, while the sociology of international relations explains how it is received and how it generates new conflicts.

When I wrote this book, three years ago, one question haunted me: why was humiliation playing such a role nowadays, when it had previously been marginal? Obviously, international relations were much more aristocratic in the old days and did not have the significant effect we see today. Globalisation, by activating social communication and visibility, is certainly a strong explanatory variable. But something crucial is currently forgotten: this "unified" international system—that is to say, this "one world system"—is certainly the most unequal that has ever been witnessed in the history of mankind. As such, it is clearly an outstanding frustration-making machine. It seems that local political actors in the dominated world scrutinise this dynamic (ie the frustration-making machine), to ensure that they can go on using it to their benefit. Since 2013 too many international tragic events have confirmed that this hypothesis is correct.

Paris, December 2016

Table of Contents

Preface to the English edition v

Introduction 1

Part One: Humiliation in the History of International Relations: The Discovery of a New Form of Social Pathology

1. **Pitfalls of the Ordinary Lives of People 11**
   Tectonics of Societies 11
   Lack of Integration 12
   The Uncertainties of Status 15
   The End of the Cold War and Beyond 19

2. **Humiliation, or Power without Rules 25**
   Power Against Humiliation 26
   How Power Goes Wrong 33

3. **Types of Humiliation and their Diplomacies 47**
   Constructing a Typology 47
   Type 1: Humiliation by Lowering of Status 50
   Type 2: Humiliation through Denial of Equality 53
   Type 3: Humiliation by Relegation 55
   Type 4: Humiliation through Stigmatisation 59

Part Two: An International System Fed by Humiliation

4. **Constitutive Inequality: The Colonial Past 67**
   Exceptions and Outrages 68
   Pathways of Humiliation 76
   New forms of Patronage 82

5. **Structural Inequality: To be Outside the Elite 87**
   The Broken Dream of the 'Middle Powers' 88
   Emergent Powers and the Bonds of Past Humiliations 93
   Small Countries' Narrow Range of Action 100

6. Functional Inequality: Being Excluded from Governance 105
Minilateralism 105
Oligarchic Pressure 110
A Certain Diplomatic Paternalism 116

Part Three: The Dangerous Repercussions that Follow Humiliation: Towards an Anti-System?

7. The Mediating Role of Societies 123
The International Mobilisation of Societies 123
Neo-Nationalism and Fundamentalism 129
The Insoluble Contradictions of the Arab Spring 134

8. Are there Anti-System Diplomacies? 139
Oppositional Diplomacies 140
Diplomacies of Deviance 147

9. Uncontrolled Violence 153
New Conflicts, New Violence 153
Violence and Social Integration 160

Conclusion 167

Introduction

WHO DOES NOT remember this image and the comments about it, which were reported worldwide? The events took place in Jakarta on 15 January 1998. The Indonesian president was bending over a document that he was about to sign, somewhat in the manner of a surrender. In fact it was a 50-point austerity plan that was being imposed on him by the IMF. There were restrictions that affected his country, but also restrictions on the man himself, Suharto, dictator, and on his family. Standing behind him, the director of the International Monetary Fund towered over the president, arms crossed, and everything in his attitude seemed to be part of humiliating Suharto.

Michel Camdessus has many times protested that he had only adopted that particular stance for the cameras, and that standing with arms crossed had been his habitual pose, since childhood. The explanation counted for little. The image continued to circulate, especially among the Indonesian press, who considered it a humiliation suffered by the entire Indonesian nation. There are some circumstances in which the play of international events does not resemble the cold-hearted monster described by 'realists', in which things that are perceived, experienced and felt carry more weight than parameters, numbers, relationships of force—and more weight than intentions or strategic choices. When an image 'goes viral', it has its own life, and its spread is not hindered by excuses, denials or other explanations. The commentator for Radio France believed he saw tears in the old strongman's eyes.

Let us go back in History a little (although we will remain in this same territory). In 1840, Great Britain decided to send a punitive expedition against China, intended to chastise the Emperor. He, regrettably, had ordered the destruction of cargoes of opium that Her Majesty's ships had delivered to the Middle Kingdom in order to balance out the British Empire's balance of payments deficit with India. In Queen Victoria's Speech at the opening of parliament in January 1840, she denounced the Chinese opium prohibition campaign as 'an assault upon [her] personal dignity', and the Prime Minister, Mr Palmerston, followed suit, announcing that Britain would administer 'a good beating' to the Chinese. It made no difference that the Emperor had lost three sons to opium addiction; it made no difference that opium had been denounced and forbidden by law in the West, by societies that already protected themselves against its dangers. A long history of humiliation was beginning in the Far East, including punitive expeditions, the sacking of cities, and one-sided treaties.

The first of these was signed on 29 August 1842, in the harbour of Nanjing (Nanking), on board a British ship, the *Cornwallis*. It merits inclusion in the introductory pages of a book on humiliation, because the case displays all the most salient features. A weakened Chinese empire ceded Hong Kong to the British, and was required to open five of its ports to international commerce, the very points of entry of evil; the Chinese were further required to pay twenty-one million dollars in fines for having had the temerity to oppose this beginning of the narco-trafficking business. Above all, this treaty marked the beginning of a regime of extra-territoriality that Beijing, like so many other countries, had to suffer under for almost a century. Foreign nobles, those who came from the West, would be given the privilege of immunity before Chinese courts; they would only be tried by courts made up of Englishmen. All the stigmata of humiliation that would eventually become a frequent part of international life were subtly combined in this masterpiece of unequal rights, so admirable otherwise that it was renewed in 1858 in the Treaty of Tianjin. Loss of sovereignty, inequality of humans and States, legalised territorial and financial rape, institutions brushed aside: everything was in place. Obviously China would remember such a thing for a long time and, consciously or unconsciously, this memory is still the basis of its foreign policy as a world power that has recovered its strength.

But China is far from having a monopoly on a past filled with humiliation. The Ottoman Empire suffered as badly, and the Turkey that would one day be born amid an inflamed nationalism still remembers the humiliation the Sublime Porte had to endure. As early as 1535, François I obtained concessions from Suleiman the Magnificent, such that the French consul had the sole right to judge French citizens upon Ottoman soil. This treaty was concluded in an amicable manner, which little resembled the atmosphere aboard the *Cornwallis* three hundred years later. It renewed a tradition of privilege that the Bayle of Venice (the traditional title of the Venetian ambassador to Constantinople) had already benefited from in his day. Nonetheless, to the extent that a European system was being constituted that in another century's time would become the Westphalian system, this treaty revealed its true colours, made up of concessions, hierarchies and unequal sovereignty. In 1580 the British monarchy obtained the same concessions as the French, and The Netherlands and Austria followed suit in 1609. Later, the pattern of demands and concessions extended to Egypt, Persia, Siam, and even Japan, for a time. A new face of humiliation entered the lists: some foreigners are more foreign than others, and some authorities were not able to submit to the sovereignty of a neighbour. But humiliation comes equipped with laws, treaties and principles; it is not only a matter of individual acts, but also of norms. It is not limited to one relationship, but quickly becomes system-wide.

Humiliation becomes commonplace in standard diplomatic practice. How can we forget things like the 'embassies of expiation' imposed upon Imperial Chinese authorities when they committed 'mistakes'?[1] How can we hide the colonial regimes that, as they built colonialism, allowed special laws to be instituted, attributing to the dominated people various legal duties and obligations from which the dominators were set free? France soon showed its diligence in this area, especially in the conquest of Algeria. Officials made up crimes and violations that could only be committed by members of the subjected people; this expedient was particularly likely to be used against those who attempted to break free of their chains. The image of Pham Van Dong arises naturally in this context: this son of a high dignitary of the Court of Hué was chained up in the jail of Poulo Condor, an event we were reminded of, at the very end of the 20th century, in a blockbuster movie. The daily humiliation experienced by one who had come from the Nguyen Palace and who would become prime minister of the Democratic Republic of Vietnam, was also experienced by many builders of States: Mandela, Ben Bella, Gandhi, Lumumba, Sukarno, Nkrumah, Modibo Keïta or Samora Machel—the list goes on. They may not all have been imprisoned, but they had all lived with humiliation, whether symbolic and material. Many of them were able to testify about this to their people, and many of their compatriots were able, even eager, to identify with what their heroes had suffered. Humiliation in international life is also a matter of trajectories and itineraries or biographies that little by little coalesce into a collective consciousness.

Proof of this can be found in the manner in which Patrice Lumumba, on the day of Congolese independence, chose to tell the story of the humiliations he had experienced in dealing with the colonial regime, thus livening up a speech that was not what the officials in attendance expected. 'We remember the ironies, the insults and the blows that we had to suffer morning, noon and night, because we were Blacks. Who can forget that to a Black, you say "tu" (the familiar form of address in French), not because he was a friend, but because the formal and honourable "vous" form was reserved for Whites only.' Humiliation is memory; it is collective narrative, and even more crucially, it is a founding narrative, which cannot be abolished by decree.

In contemporary histories, international humiliation appears as the glue that holds together the elements of individual tragedies. For example, the tragedy of the Palestinian woman, about to give birth, who was stopped at one of the 500 checkpoints set up by the Israeli army of occupation. One might also mention the deep feelings of an Afghani who viewed, on 13 January 2012, a video showing four American soldiers urinating on the

[1] J Gernet, *Le Monde Chinois* (Paris, Armand Colin, 1972) 507.

bodies of three dead Taliban soldiers, or the feelings in the heart of an Iraqi upon learning about the torture practised at the prison of Abu Ghraib. But we would certainly make mention of those in Africa, in Asia or in the Middle East who happen to see, in a report in the media, the unbearable sight of human beings who have been torn apart, or whose bodies are rotting, covered with flies, lying along the paths of war, while Western television stations remind us, on the occasion of some bloody tragedy in Europe or North America, that out of respect for the dignity of the victims, their bodies will not be shown. This daily construction of selected views of victims' injuries is another face of humiliation.

The diplomacy of States seems to show us a quite different face. But this face too can be humiliating, as it was for Malian citizens when President François Hollande announced from Paris that presidential elections would take place in Mali, made public the schedule for pulling French troops out of Mali, began—from the Elysée Palace—a dialogue with Tuareg separatists, and finally decided, all on his own, that there would be a 'truth and reconciliation commission'. As he stated on 28 March 2013, 'We want there to be elections in Mali at the end of July, and we will insist upon this'.[2] He repeated this statement at a meeting of UNESCO on 5 June 2013: 'Elections will take place on the announced date, and at Kidal'. The organisation of an important election, its scheduling and its terms, being decided on by another State, a former colonial power, without the interested parties even being allowed to come forward to make the formal announcement: this is the kind of institutional humiliation that every day deepens the gulf between North and South.

The cumulative effect of these humiliations is considerable. This should not come as a surprise; it is the gradual installation of an international system that intends to be universal, and defines itself as egalitarian, just like the globalisation that pushes people to compare themselves to others through an ever-increasing number of exchanges; indeed these things dramatise humiliations and make them unbearable. Overtly or implicitly, humiliation is an item on the international agenda. It is part of the daily experience of social behaviours that impact the international sphere in some way, something that happens more frequently all the time. Above all, incidents of humiliation shape policies and contribute to the search for new forms of confrontation, given that classical international relations theory places only two characters on stage, with equal powers and comparable resources.

This international display or sharing of humiliation is visible everywhere, perhaps most particularly in Asia. In China, 18 September was proclaimed as a 'Day of National Humiliation' and was accompanied by flag-raising

[2] *Nouvel Observateur.com*, 14 May 2013.

ceremonies in commemoration of the Mukden Incident (1931) that served as a pretext for the Japanese invasion of Manchuria. The same title was given to 28 April in Okinawa, to commemorate the day in 1952 when sovereignty over the little archipelago was returned to Japan. Similarly, 3 December 1997, was styled a Day of Humiliation by the Korean opposition to mark the date of an agreement concluded with the IMF—an action some found as ominous as the date in 1910 when Japan annexed Korea. Oddly enough, the Sino-Korean community chose the same day as Canada Day (1 July) as a 'Day of Humiliation', because in 1923 Canada stopped accepting Asian immigrants on that day.

There is no argument: the idea makes its own way, and in the diversity of its appearances humiliation has become a standard parameter of international relations. The cases we have mentioned involve individual actors at times, but other cases concern whole peoples or nations. They constitute attacks on sovereignty, the founding principle of our international lives, an often fictitious guarantee of equality between states, not formally negotiable; but they are also attacks upon the dignity, reputation and honour of individuals and peoples—qualities that in the same moment appear, with greater frequency than ever, at the centre of symbolic battles disputed in an international arena. They always imply violence, whether symbolic or physical. They all have this in common: someone acts so as to force a partner to accept a lowering of status, in complete contradiction to the norms and values upon which international life is based.

This struggle for status—and for values that give it meaning—only deepens involvement with the international sphere as part of an ordinary social identity. Struggling for status, an international actor accomplishes this in accordance with a banal social game, whether at the level of the individual, group, institution or any kind of community. These are the actual circumstances of the international production of humiliation, in which the 'tectonics' of societies, their reciprocal impact, plays a key role. And in this context we see highlighted the *objectivation* of humiliation, that is, its being translated into a concrete diplomatic act, in which a game of oligarchs substitutes itself, in a critical way, for that which searches for a balance of powers, and this opens the way to an entire series of novel and reactive diplomatic moves.

Let us then retain, as a definition of international humiliation, any authoritarian assignment of a status that is inferior to the desired status, in a manner that does not conform to defined norms. In so doing we understand that at least three aspects of the sociology of international relations are directly concerned: there is a problem of the *status* claimed by international actors, a claim they make within a universe of limited competition; a problem of the *use*, on the part of those who have the resources of authority, of symbols that allow them to push people who do not have the right symbols down to lower ranks; and a problem of the *subjectivity* that constructs the perception and the reception by each actor of the practices that directly affect them.

In other words, humiliation is not considered by us to be a psychological characteristic, but an *effect* of the international system upon some of the entities that are included in it. It appears, objectively, as a form of dehumanisation affecting a system that has been constructed as human. An excellent example is this trenchant passage from Camus, published in *Combat* on 10 May 1947, addressing the first repressive actions in Algeria and Madagascar: 'If today the French hear about the methods that other French people sometimes use against Algerians or the Malagasy people without protesting, that means they live lives based upon the unconscious certainty that we are superior in some way to these peoples, and so the choice of a means of illustrating this superiority matters little'.

This constructed superiority, which is the motivation for humiliation in international relations, is no more dominant today within consciences than it used to be—far from it. Those who entertain this idea may be acting in good faith sometimes, and become irritated that they could be accused of such a thing. And that is the proof that we are dealing with something that goes beyond individual choice; something quite different that is carried forward by the international system itself, which we need to identify. Thus we distinguish humiliation from *shame*, which is only a feeling, and is not necessarily a component of the relationship with authority. And we also distinguish it from *trauma*, which has to do with violence and the impact it has on individuals. When trauma is associated with the most tragic forms of violence, it is far worse than humiliation. This is the case with genocides, which obviously cause humiliation, but which involve a desire for total destruction; because of this, a different and separate approach is justified.

Similarly, humiliation cannot be thought in terms of *resentment*. The analyses of Nietzsche on this subject, and the subsequent work by the German philosopher Max Scheler[3] construct resentment as passivity in the face of experienced humiliation. Nietzsche thinks of it as the attitude of people 'who do not love themselves as they are, but to whom a true reaction, that is, action, is forbidden'. In this regard resentment is similar to self-hatred. Scheler calls this a form of 'envy that is powerless', which can only overcome frustration by speaking in derogatory terms about the dominant group. We are in the realms of the 'slave morality' described by Nietzsche.

This 'falsification of the scale of values' (Scheler) is certainly to be found in international relations. Resentment and its rhetoric made up of slogans, curses and powerlessness are often presented as common characteristics of

[3] F Nietzsche, *Généalogie de la morale* (Paris, Gallimard, 'Folio', 1985 (1887)) Part III; M Scheler, *L'Homme du ressentiment* (Paris, Gallimard, 1970 (1912)).

dominated people, who are denounced or even mocked for being what they are. But this notion is a long way from covering the entire ground of the discussion. All humiliation does not end up turning into impotence, and the response is not necessarily just a matter of words. Just because someone is being dominated does not mean that they have ceded completely to a slave morality. In the face of humiliation, there is more than one international stance or position, and the variety of responses has probably increased. We have only to recall the wars of decolonisation or, nearer to us in time, the Arab Spring, a pure hymn to human dignity (*karama*) reconquered, in order to convince ourselves that humiliation and resentment are not equivalent.

From many points of view, humiliation in international relations goes beyond social psychology, which was the first discipline to engage in this type of research. Social psychology would show us that psychological predispositions, when they are shared among a social collective, can generate social events, particularly serious forms of violence.

What we are trying here is a different approach: we are trying to show how an international system, that is, the arrangement of a set of international norms and practices, identifiable at a moment in history, can generate humiliation and thus provoke the emergence of reactive diplomacies of various kinds, which we shall be at pains to identify. We begin with the basic premise that this dynamic, overlooked during the times of triumphant realism, today takes on major importance, and is in fact decisive as concerns the understanding of contemporary international relations. Our hypothesis suggests that the disorders that today affect power relationships are giving rise to new forms of humiliations, more varied and more frequent, and these forms inflame or aggravate the hostile perceptions held by those who are the victims (or who believe themselves to be such), and which leads them, in return, to produce new (though often dysfunctional) forms of diplomacy.

This orientation towards the matter does not cut us off from other research. The bulk of this does come from social psychology, and in this area the work of Evelin G. Lindner is particularly influential.[4] Lindner presents humiliation as a place where 'violent conflict ferments', and proceeds by means of inquiries and interviews carried out in Germany, Somalia and Rwanda, demonstrating the perverse effects of using humiliation as a mode of the exercise of power. This research continues the line followed by Thomas Scheff,[5] making a connection between emotion and nationalistic

[4] EG Lindner, *Making Enemies: Humiliation and International Conflicts* (London, Greenwood, 2006).

[5] T Scheff, *Bloody Revenge: Emotions, Nationalism and War* (Chicago, University of Chicago Press, 1990).

mobilisation, and by Ervin Staub, writing on the roots of murderous violence.[6]

Undoubtedly these authors have the great merit of having increased our understanding of the sources of violence, by recognising the conflict-generating nature of humiliation. Their theses are echoed in works by American political scientists such as James Davies, Ted Gurr, and many others. These authors grasp in a timely manner the much more active forms that social frustration takes today, when humiliation attacks one's self-image directly. Evelin Lindner is undoubtedly correct to emphasise the importance of the phenomenon in the context of globalisation. In order not to be explosive, as Lindner rightly maintains, globalisation must promote a real form of '*globequalisation*' that can satisfy all concerned, protecting some from humiliation, and others from the reactive violence that humiliation always tends to generate. Undoubtedly, we are encouraged to find the (otherwise still obscure) foundation of a new international politics in these researches.

Even a vision such as this cannot satisfy the true internationalist. Seen from a social psychology perspective, humiliation seems somehow truncated. We cannot today limit our consideration to human relations, making humiliation just an affair of individual actors. In order to understand humiliation as an international event, first let us construct it in its historical context, which will develop over time, showing the creative force of various contexts, and the plurality of types that appear as a result. We are then able to define this pathology in its contemporary guise, through the most important factors that establish it and assure its continuation, and which gives our current international system a capacity for humiliation like no other. Finally, we will be able to evaluate the dangerous reactions that result, made out of new conflicts, radicalisms and fundamentalisms of various types, and perhaps new types of mobilisation. Thus we may understand the obstacles that complicate international life, which cannot be reduced to the classical categories of political science.

[6] E Staub, *The Roots of Evil: The Origins of Genocide and Other Group Violence* (Cambridge, Cambridge University Press, 1989).

Part One

Humiliation in the History of International Relations: The Discovery of a New Form of Social Pathology

CONSIDERED AS A mere human relationship, humiliation belongs to what is universal, as much as to what is eternal. Throughout all history, individuals of every kind have been tempted to belittle others for the satisfaction of doing so, or in order to dominate, or to gratify their egos, perhaps even their perversions. Continuing down this line, let us imagine that the game of competition and individualisation, which increasingly affects social relations, should accelerate, and bring these tendencies dramatically into sharp relief. Inevitably, there is a relation between humiliation and modernity.[1] We understand too that the disruption of the logic of authority causes frustration, and therefore humiliation; it causes revolt just as mechanically. The plebeians of Rome, measuring their own increasing importance to the economy of the city, and to its army, already knew how to respond to the humiliation they felt, which was worsening. They moved back across the Aventine, cut themselves off from the city, created their own council and forced the aristocracy to recognise it.

Could History be repeating itself on a different scale, at a different level? Suppose that within this sketch of Roman history, we could recognise the diplomacy of the plebeian states of the contemporary international system, whose great council in this sense took place at the Bandung Conference in 1955, a first meeting bringing together what would be called the non-aligned states? And suppose further that this movement continued to create itself, from the G77 to the BRICS, to the extent that the humiliated ones, old and new, were gaining power? And what if we encountered once again the temptation to oppose the system simply because it is the system, once again the predilection for diplomatic contestation, the same temptation to deviate, and (all things considered) the same negative reaction from the aristocratic G7?

[1] Dennis Smith established a strong connection between globalisation and humiliation, *cf* D Smith, *Globalization: The Hidden Agenda* (Cambridge, Polity Press, 2006).

In reality, the question brings us back to the present day. The question cannot be easily transposed, or made to apply to international life in the most distant past. Until the end of the 18th century, war possessed its own rituals, perfectly internalised, as would be the case in a consensual game, a top-level political tournament, distinguishing the winner from the loser in perfect fairness. The loser had to accept the law of might, and even participate in the triumph of the one who defeated him. From ancient times, the notion of 'woe to the vanquished' (Brennus) expressed perfectly the law of war, so perfectly that the one who is defeated according to that law agrees that everything took place in accordance with applicable norms. A suicide might possibly be exempt from participating in the triumph of his vanquisher, but in Rome, everything was done to remind the victor that he was only a mortal, and was obliged to restrain his *hubris*. Better still, the rite of triumph included comedians who made fun of the general being honoured, so that he would not begin to think of himself as anything but human, lest he rise and crush those around him by his scorn.

In Westphalian times, peace was understood as a way of coldly and mechanically adjusting the relations of power, even of deciding to begin a new dynastic alliance. At all events, the game was coded, involving in most cases members of the elite, and leaving out the bulk of society, those upon whom the weight of humiliation habitually fell. The progressive destruction of this code, and the increasing involvement of whole societies in the international game, gradually rendered humiliation a commonplace form of suffering with regard to international relations. To the extent that these relations were bound up with the ordinary lives of various peoples, to the extent that war changed history, new forms of humiliation gave rise to new forms of diplomacy.

1

Pitfalls of the Ordinary Lives of People

WHY WOULD INTERNATIONAL life have stood forever as an exception? Why would it not, why would it never, become a type of social life like any other? Realists still think it is exceptional, exempt, but why? Because those who are controlling it are 'cold-hearted monsters'? But do they have the appearance of monsters? Because those who manage it form a very small oligarchy, and the vast majority of society is left outside? But is that still true today, given that public opinion in all its forms is visible, is present in more and more ways? The pages in newspapers devoted to 'international news' also speak, more and more often, about social movements, tumultuous movements of people that are reported on and thus reveal society to itself; revolts turn into civil wars—all these phenomena that are flaring up on the international scene.

Tectonics of Societies

We are getting nearer to the main problem: the international arena is becoming more social than political, and more and more looks like a tectonic change in societal structure, thus depriving the political elites of the monopoly they had in this 'arena of gladiators' (Hobbes), in which States confronted one another, while ignoring the social substrate of the other. How would that still be possible today? Given, that is, the incredible intensification of world trade, the multiplication of forms of exchange of all kinds, and above all the revolution in communications, which abolishes long distances and breaks down all borders, putting the entire world in contact with the entire world, even if the intensity of those relations remains unequal here and there. In fact, international life has gone global, that is, more and more lacking in State intervention. That which once occurred among nations now takes place on a planetary scale, certainly in a different way, but such that there is an end of enclave-making, of reciprocal ignorance and walls separating communities. Everyone depends on everyone else, as regards riches, security, suffering, hope, constraints, even feelings. This is particularly fertile soil for humiliation, a social phenomenon if ever there was one.

It is fertile terrain for the sociologist as well. This worldwide social space, unseen yesterday, not even conceivable before then, raises the question that Émile Durkheim once asked concerning the nation: where does this social order come from? How was it put in place? Without doubt, the answer is the same if we are referring to the level of the whole world, or almost the same: it was put in place by a continuous reinforcement of the volume of social interactions and their diversity, by the increasing density of exchanges, interactions and communications. How many international acts (or more specifically, world-level acts) do we perform each day, in the ordinary course of our activities, our routines? How many, as we consume, as we consume news, as we consume entertainment? And how many such acts did our ancestors perform or accomplish in the 19th century, or in any century before then? Why should this reinforced social density be an exception to the grammatical rules of the sociologists? And why would it not lead to particular social behaviours? Why would these behaviours not affect governments and their foreign policies, both limiting their actions as well as empowering them? Some may resist with all their might, but some may act to promote the growth of these new transnational populisms.

Lack of Integration

Let us go back to Durkheim and the answers he arrived at in his time. As he watched the development of industrial society, and the upheavals caused by its growth, he saw the risk of conflict that Marx had warned of, and the sociologist was thus led to question the very foundations of the social order—this mysterious paradox that was able to unite complexity and integration. The question is no less pressing today, and an internationalist cannot ignore it: space has become world space, while continuing to be broken up into smaller pieces; conflicts are renewed, or continue, but violence never goes away—and yet the hypothesis of an international order persists. Contrary to some views, international life is not as chaotic as some like to say, sometimes no more so than it was at the end of the 19th century, when Durkheim observed nations becoming industrialised. A minimum number of rules guarantees the minimum required for the international order to be maintained.

The key question asked by the author of *La Division du Travail Social*, in the preface of the first edition of his book, can function as a reference point for the shared reflections of an 'internalist' and an 'internationalist'. 'Comment se fait-il que, tout en devenant plus autonome, l'individu dépende plus étroitement de la société ? Comment peut-il être à la fois plus personnel et plus solidaire?'[1] (How does it come about that the individual,

[1] E Durkheim, *De la division du travail social* (Paris, PUF, 1973) XLIII.

whilst becoming more autonomous, depends ever more closely upon society? How can he become at the same time more of an individual and yet more linked to society?)[2] The translation from one field to the other in fact takes place on two different levels: on the level of a world space in which individuals affirm their individuality, while becoming more and more closely interwoven into a globalised interdependence; and on the level of an international system in which States are more and more dependent upon each other, all while claiming that they are maintaining, and even strengthening, their sovereignty.

In his day, Durkheim knew how to investigate the contradiction he observed in reflecting on the difficulties of people's life together in societies. At the very core of his thinking on the matter, he showed how such a tension was related to the various modes in which the division of work in society was arranged, the very work that divided and separated individuals, all while making them much more interdependent. Today, globalisation works in a similar way, on the largest scale: dividing and reuniting, including and distinguishing, proclaiming equality in its principles, destroying it through its practices—all the ingredients necessary to sharpen humiliation as much as possible, in the privacy of each international fact.

Durkheim based what was probably the most important part of his sociology upon a disturbing observation: 'Normally the division of labour produces social solidarity, but sometimes the results are different and even the opposite (of what was expected) [...] Pathology, in these and in other cases, is a valuable help to physiology'.[3] This social pathology can lead either to anomie, resignation to an absence of social rules that are commonly accepted, or to different kinds of constraint that cause frustration: 'Constraint only begins when regulation no longer corresponds to the true nature of things, and since (it is) without a foundation in morality, (it) can only be maintained by force'.[4]

Both these situations are becoming more and more familiar to the internationalist. The first leads to tensions that the international system is not capable of controlling. Long-lasting dissatisfaction on the part of those who are dominated begins to appear, and these people are cut off from the modes of governance of everyday life. Africa today is full of conflicts that embody this tragic condition: this translates into a lack of integration, as much material as symbolic, which weighs down the operation of our global space. The second situation reflects the abusive use of norms as a means of maintaining by force a particular state of the international system,

[2] E Durkheim, *The Division of Labour in Society* (New York, Free Press, 1984; Eng. Trans. by WD Halls) with thanks to Rob Aken and the staff of the Young Library at the University of Kentucky for providing this material.

[3] E Durkheim, *De la division du travail social* (Paris, PUF, 1973).

[4] ibid 370.

despite the change in the expectations of different groups of people, and the objective transformations of the global space. The existence of tremendous gaps between modes of governance locked into an older way of doing things, and the present reality of globalisation, attest to this.

With its blockages, its inequalities, and the gaps left after the disappearance of bipolarity, the international system alternates rather dramatically between the anomic division of labour and the constrained division of labour, that is, between two pathologies that were remarked on by Durkheim, when he observed them occurring in European nations. In other words, international life appears to be hostage to an eternal dilemma, a choice between authoritarianism and disorder.

Torn between an over-accumulation of power and an increasing ineffectiveness of that same power, the international system intermingles the effects of anomie and constraint. It eventually takes on a novel form, one in which power leads to impotence, where conflicts no longer occur because of rivalry, but because of inequality, where governance tries to recycle oligarchies, exactly at the point where it should demand the inclusion of every group. These are pathologies in which the dialectic of arrogance and humiliation affects the tonality, so to speak, of the clashes of all these opposites. This new game is substituted for the one that governed the ordinary condition of classical power rivalries in the Westphalian period, in which opponents were equals who recognised each other as having the right to manage, together, a much more compact international scene. Things were restricted to a juxtaposition of entities that mutually confirmed each other's sovereignty, as if individuals had entered into a consensual relationship. This is an order of things that Durkheim would have considered mechanical.

The practice of humiliation thus became the sign of one of the major pathologies afflicting the contemporary international system. It spread and became more complex, to the extent that the system separated from the Westphalian conformism that had operated in Europe since 1648, conceived of as the coexistence of sovereignties at the level of the state or nation. This system was based on a self-oriented vision that reduced the dangers of ordinary life by limiting the number of similar—if not quite equal—powers, themselves connected through familial and dynastic relationships that locked them together in solidarity.[5] Then things opened up towards the world and towards difference, towards large numbers and inequality; the international system was incapable of, or reluctant to, produce rules acceptable to everyone; worse, the system was obliged quite often to impose older, ineffective norms of doubtful applicability upon the very people who did not recognise them. Thus, humiliation begins to be a mode of international conduct, consciously or unconsciously, even being expressed in forms of

[5] B Badie, *The Diplomacy of Connivance* (Basingstoke, Palgrave, 2012).

diplomacy that are almost institutional, mere functions, routines, ways of being and doing that are held to be natural, unavoidable and necessary: for example, one announces from Paris that there will be an election in Mali, or one prohibits a nation from possessing nuclear weapons, while accepting the fact that some other nations possess them, or one mocks the attempts of an emergent power to become involved in the resolution of a sensitive international question, such as that concerning Lula in Brazil, or Erdogan in Turkey becoming involved in matters relating to Iran in May 2010.

Clearly the question of humiliation leads us towards a history of missed chances at integration, to the inability of the modern international system to create solid and globalised social bonds, to the obsessively persistent, seemingly unchangeable mechanisms that continue to prefer Westphalian and sectorised alliances to cross-cutting alliances, that weave the strands of globalisation together, to the inability to generate the minimum level of solidarity required, faced with the international division of labour. The powers that make up the system are no longer performing this function, or they are performing it so badly that integration fails, forced to retreat when history would seem to demand that it advance. Its weak consistency at world level corresponds to its failure at a regional level, and its increasing fragility at a national level. The partial failure that comes from all this has to be managed by means of bastardised forms of violence, both coercive and symbolic, or by mechanisms that work to debase the other, below the level of the norms that fed the other's expectations. Thus humiliation gains its stripes as an adjunct to diplomacy.

Thus the question of integration substitutes itself for that of power, creating inevitable turbulence in the closed world of the internationalists. The pathologies we can learn about from them are no longer explained by reference to a test of strength, or to a rivalry between combatants, but in terms of the inability of these powers to integrate smaller ones, those of low grade, the uninvited, the little people on the international stage, and even worse, the upstarts. This means that integration is not a utopian discourse on the world order, but a reaction to the inability to produce links and solidarity, and appears as a substitute for strategies of *déclassement* (debasement). There is a great fear of China, distrust of Brazil (a nation some would like to limit to football and samba), and embarrassment faced with a global South that has no place apart from travel brochures touting white sand beaches. This failed integration is associated with the same risks that Durkheim anticipated, which affect the framework of nation-states.

The Uncertainties of Status

International life thus becomes a permanent battle for status. Its changing conditions give rise to new hopes and aspirations, and the confrontation is sharper than ever because the contexts change more rapidly, the diversity of the actors in those contexts becomes more noticeable, and long-held positions become more fragile. The foreign policy of each State normally becomes pretentious, presenting an image that is several notches above what it could reasonably expect (*overachieved diplomacy*).[6] This breakdown of international standards leads others to dispute what has been accomplished, in order to protect themselves from any risk of losing status: the humiliation machine gets to work.

The analytic framework we shall examine is part of the genesis of social philosophy. Rousseau, grasping the human being upon the point of leaving a state of nature, pointed out the perilous effects of building a lasting relationship with the other person. In his eyes, the entry of the human being into society spelled the end of that mixture of the instinct for self-preservation and pity that had marked the human up to that point. It then leads to vanity, arrogance, self-affirmation and a quest for prestige.[7] The internationalist is not diverted by this; all the traits that enable us to measure the performance of foreign policies are in direct competition with each other. These characteristics present what appears to be an iron law of increasing intersubjectivity in international relations, where your status comes to depend entirely upon someone else's perception of you, where one person's success is a function of that person's capacity to belittle someone else, where the power of the one is only protected by downgrading the other. Even if he did not think any of this was 'important', Hans J. Morgenthau, one of the founders of realism in international relations, admitted that international prestige corresponded to 'a desire for social recognition', and constituted a 'potent dynamic force'. He considered that '… it is only in the tribute others pay to a person's goodness, intelligence and power that the person becomes fully aware of, and can fully enjoy, what he deems to be his superior qualities.' Thus he underlined that the purpose of prestige was to 'impress other nations'. In his mind, 'diplomatic ceremonial' and 'displays of military force' were the best means for that.[8] Then he gave several examples of attacks on prestige, and thus of diplomatic humiliation: in 1946 a Soviet minister left a parade in Paris celebrating victory over the Nazis, because he was placed in the second rank of the march, while the other great powers led the way. How very many times has that scene been repeated, here and elsewhere.

[6] T Volgy, R Corbetta, KA Grant, RG Baird, 'Major power status in international politics' in T Volgy et al, *Major Powers and the Quest for Status in International Politics* (New York, Palgrave, 2011) 16.

[7] J-J Rousseau, *Discours sur l'origine et les fondements de l'inégalité parmi les hommes* (Paris, Gallimard 'Folio' 1996 (1755)); A Honneth, *The Struggle for Recognition: The Moral Grammar of Social Conflicts* (Polity Press, 1995 [1992]).

[8] H Morgenthau, *Politics among Nations. The Struggle for Power and Peace* (New York, A Knopf, 1964 (1948)) 73.

Morgenthau concluded the chapter by showing how the politics of prestige usually tends to slip towards corruption by making 'too much' of prestige, or 'not enough', or by permitting ostentation—like the Italians in Ethiopia—or by doing the opposite, excessively limiting one's scope of action.[9] Significantly, he turned away from the other face of corruption, which has to do with the asymmetry it generates. Prestige for him is only a competition over power, as in the anecdote about the downgrading of the Soviet minister, but never the humiliation of the weak. Mussolini was thought dangerously rash for sending an expedition into Africa, but the humiliation suffered by the Negus and the people of Ethiopia is never taken into consideration.

Thus the apprehension expressed by Rousseau in his day turns out to be well-founded. He feared seeing the appearance, in an uncontrolled game, of the roots of social inequality, which could be easily transposed to international life. The way traced by the philosopher is doubly significant for the understanding of our object. He suggests first of all that 'otherness', as long as it is not mastered, that is, contained within a set of rules that are accepted by all, leads States into a contest to see whose self-esteem is the biggest, and thus to arrogance. Arrogance can be considered an aggressive form of the corruption of prestige, which is limited to the capacity to force those who are standing before you to pay you respect. In this sense arrogance is a form of violence that expresses itself through humiliation.

Rousseau's contribution goes even further, when his work suggests to us that the quest for prestige can be a motivating force at the international level, a mechanical way of thinking of diplomatic activity, a sort of iron law making the humiliation of the other a strategy for conquest or survival. Being in a 'club', like the P5 or the G8, or any other 'group of friends', such as the international game is wont to generate, is also a way of affirming that others are not in the club, or are members only through the willingness, or the charity or generosity of those that are in already. Intervening on behalf of the others means reminding them that they will, following any intervention, owe you peace, respect, or the installation of a democratic government. Therefore only the shared will of the international community can erase the humiliation that the spirit of prestige brings into being. We can see the redemptive virtue of multilateralism in such a context, but in practical terms such a thing is a very long way off.

One can understand, under these conditions, why *recognition* is so important in international relations.[10] Having left Rousseau, we are now taking up a

[9] ibid 82.

[10] *Cf* T Lindemann, 'Peace through recognition: An interactionist interpretation of international crisis' (2011) 5 *International Political Sociology* 68–86; T Lindemann and J Saada, 'Les théories de la reconnaissance dans les relations internationales' (2012) 87 *Cultures et Conflits* 7–25.

Hegelian perspective in which the human condition is a struggle of each one for the recognition of the other. This principle is more evident in the international realm than anywhere else, because international law, something common to everyone but rejected by Hobbes (and denounced by his successors, theorists of sovereignty), has more difficulty in being obeyed and producing status by its authority in that realm, because there, competition is as normal as it is unregulated; because the sovereignty one aspires to is only real if it is justly *recognised* by the other.

Worse yet, recognition is easier to obtain within small groups than within large groups of similar people, much easier than it is from among a diverse group. It is easier to be recognised when all actors are wearing the same uniforms, than when they all come from different 'roots'. Among a small number of people who are similar, it is easy to obtain 'connivance', as happened in the days of the Concert of Europe, perhaps even after that.[11] Because of the difference of scale that characterises colonisation, and even more so decolonisation, the objective is more difficult to attain, and even today cannot be realised unless the small entity pays the price of its smallness by imitating the great. If the small one does not make this concession, recognition will be harder to obtain. But if the others add to their modest resources a claim to an identity other than that of a State, there will simply be no recognition at all. And even if the intrusion is a modest one, someone asking to be allowed to air an opinion, only a bare minimum of recognition is likely to be forthcoming.

We may observe in this moral retrogression all the complexity of the contemporary game of world governance, which classifies actors as a function of their proximity to the ideal-type of the State, placing them higher in the hierarchy of States if they can be classed as 'moderate'. This obscure title translates only the good mood of the one handing it out, and it has little value, on the material side of things, unless it is in conformity with dominant diplomacies.

All this points to the international importance of the 'denial of recognition' analysed by the German sociologist, Axel Honneth.[12] This is to deny the other the identity it demands and, in so doing, to deny the status that would have enabled that other to reach its objective or goal. The 'moral wound' thus inflicted becomes a dangerous diplomatic weapon. Levelled at the credibility (material or symbolic) of the one who is being denied, it causes *objective* humiliation, caused by one's being marginalised or excluded in the international game, and also a *subjective* humiliation related to being deemed inferior, or at least incapable. We are in agreement here with the thesis of Paul Ricœur, according to which recognition is the regard each of

[11] J-A de Sédouy, *Le Concert européen* (Paris, Fayard, 2009).
[12] A Honneth, *La Lutte pour la reconnaissance* (Paris, Le Cerf, 2000).

us has for his or her own capacities, compared with those of others.[13] So it was with the Ottoman Empire, at that time excluded from the Concert of Europe of the 19th century, and is now for Turkey, whose accession to the European Union may never take place, and the government of Erdogan, which is denied the right to negotiate about nuclear issues involving a neighbouring state (Iran), just as Lula in Brazil was denied an opportunity to negotiate with a neighbour over the same issue.

The international game thus becomes a gigantic competition for the acquisition of a status, which is more hotly contested because it is not governed (at least not between States) by any rule that could objectively define the capacities of one state or another, the exception being the sacrosanct principle of the sovereign equality of all States, as this is expressed in the United Nations Charter. Of course, apart from that, the competition for status is open and validation is carried by the judgment of the other. If the other has great resources and a recognised institutional position, then its judgment may be considered to be much more humiliating.

The 'competition for status' is becoming, little by little, the norm in the international game. Undoubtedly the end of bipolarity reinforced it considerably.[14] During the Cold War, status was a function of one's position in one of the two alliances that faced each other. An exit from the game, or alternatively, putting the prescriptive value of the game into question were hardly possible outcomes; indeed they were often considered improper. The spirit of Bandung was the first manifestation of this will to exit the game, and this quickly encountered its limits: the status of States emerging from colonisation and asking to be considered non-aligned quickly came to depend, by tacit agreement, upon what American or Russian protection could do for them. Pakistan and Sri Lanka chose the first, India and Egypt the second.

The End of the Cold War and Beyond

This bipolar dependence was certainly an incomplete means of recognition, and thus a humiliation. It continued to be moderate, because the system made it a rule to which everyone was equally exposed. Humiliation does not appear in all its intensity until bipolarity begins to be contested and indeed to break up as a result of the first individual defections. Such dissent was essentially based on hopes about co-management, hopes that may have existed on both sides, only to be dashed. There was a lack of recognition on the part of the Big Brother. General de Gaulle was humiliated by the fact that little attention was paid to his memorandum of September 1958,

[13] P Ricoeur, *Parcours de la reconnaissance* (Paris, Stock, 2004).

[14] Volgy et al, *Major Powers and the Quest for Status in International Politics* 20 ff.

in which he called for a directorate to govern NATO. The special agreements made between London and Washington in Bermuda (made between Eisenhower and Macmillan in March 1957, Kennedy and Macmillan in 1961), then in Nassau (between Kennedy and Macmillan again, in December 1962), establishing active nuclear cooperation between the two countries, were like a slap in the face to de Gaulle. Kennedy's declaration, on 17 May 1962, rejecting the idea of national strike forces, was made two days after a conference held at the Élysée Palace announcing a diametrically opposite French nuclear doctrine. It was the last straw. The policy of 'greatness' and 'national independence' was thus constructed as a first 'reconquest' in the face of the humiliation that had taken place.

The intransigence of Big Brother thus awakened the logic of humiliation within structured systems, which should nonetheless have been able to restrain it. The observation is the same in the East, as when Mao Zedong understood that the personal humiliation he would have to undergo during his visit to Stalin in 1950 would not earn him any compensation, neither on the politico-military level (during the Korean War or the Tibetan revolt in 1959), nor on the economic level. Humiliation in such contexts takes on its full value, when it is not compensated by the material or symbolic advantages that are spontaneously attributed to alliances.

The end of the Cold War and of bipolarity was a lightning liberalisation of the competition for status. Status from now on must be earned in a market that is free, or nearly so. For each one, claiming a status leads all others to set themselves up as *de facto* judges, taking no, or very little, account of the logic of the alliances. The search for recognition, from that point, is a search for validation of the status requested. Any refusal or impediment thus becomes a mark of humiliation that will be interpreted as a reaction on the part of the international system, that is, a response deriving almost mechanically from an arrangement of powers, values and institutions at a given point in time.

The American internationalist Robert Gilpin was aware of this before the Berlin Wall had ever fallen. He established that a divergent interpretation concerning the hierarchy of types of prestige was a non-negligible source of war.[15] We have no difficulty agreeing that such dissonance—and the long list of felt humiliations that come from it—was bound to become stronger if the codes associated with East-West confrontation disappeared. It is nonetheless true that the bipolar system, at this level, was quickly attacked on the periphery: most colonial wars resulted from a misapprehension on the part of the old powers, who denied, with reckless speed, any credible status to the insurgents facing them. Of course, once independence was acquired, the great powers craftily flattered the weakest among these, trying to persuade them to change sides.

[15] R Gilpin, *War and Change* (Cambridge, Cambridge University Press, 1981).

After 1989, almost the entire saga of international tensions was sucked into this dialectic of demanded recognition and inflicted humiliation. The phenomenon, however, did not develop along military lines (contrary to what Gilpin suggested). Modes of governance, negotiations, and diplomacy became hostages to this dialectic. Let the reader judge: Russia was in some ways the first victim. This country had lost its role as a co-manager of the world, a role it had taken pride in during the Cold War and during détente. After this loss, Russia never stopped trying to gain re-admittance to the new circle of world govenors or, failing that, to destabilise it. Its foreign policy since 1989 has been designed in terms of the quest for a new permanent status, and in terms of unsatisfied ambitions; public opinion in Russia is dangerously slanted in this sense.

Far from including the expiring USSR or the new Russia, the new order excluded and marginalised the Russians. Mikhaïl Gorbachev was humiliated at the G7 meeting in London in July 1991, when the aid that the oligarchs were to give Moscow was an item on the conference agenda. The weakened President had to wait long hours in the antechamber, while most of the heads of States and governments were meeting a few meters away, and agreeing to reserve the largest part of their financial support for his likely successor.[16] That was Boris Yeltsin. He was at the very centre of the debates held at the G7 at Naples (July 1994) and Denver (June 1997), but was not officially admitted until the Birmingham meeting (1998). Even so, this admission ticket was discounted somewhat by being styled an admission to the 'G7 + 1', and the 'old boys' were still able to meet as a group before the plenary meeting. This designation lasted until the meeting at Kananaskis (Canada 2002).[17]

Bill Clinton publicly recognised the *deal*, even the *linkage*: Russia was to be admitted into the club of the oligarchs and then also made a member of the World Trade Organization, on the condition that Boris Yeltsin should approve an extension of NATO to cover their former satellite nations, and even some former Soviet republics, for example the Baltic states.[18] The suspension of Russian participation in the G8 was for a long time a subject of internal political debate in the West, often taking the form of a denunciation of Russia's failure to be a democracy. John McCain and Joe Lieberman were noteworthy as zealous disciples who could on occasion turn into the bearers of punishment.

Admission to the G8 was supposed to enhance Russia's standing, but it ended up damaging it further. Moscow understood that in order to be

[16] R Dumas, with B Badie and G Minassian, *La Diplomatie sur le vif* (Paris, Presses de Sciences Po, 2013) 43.

[17] P Hajnal, *The G8 System and the G20* (Burlington, Aldershot, Ashgate, 2007) 41.

[18] ibid 42; W Clinton, *My Life* (New York, Vintage, 2005 (2004)) 750 ff, French translation *Ma vie* (Paris, Odile Jacob, 2004).

co-opted, it would have to give up wanting to be equal. The 'Charter of Paris for a New Europe' (November 1990) existed only in the form of appeals in favour of human rights and the rule of law, or as a grouping of long-time popular democracies in favour of Western constitutional standards. The Organisation for Security and Cooperation in Europe, set in motion by a Stability and Growth Pact (March 1995), kept up a minimal level of activity, leaving little place for Russia, from then on quite isolated. Like Ivan IV, defeated in his day in the war of Livonia and cut off from European waters, Russia was forced to look to the East, to the Shanghai Cooperation Organisation (created in 2001) and China, and later to the BRICS nations.

This margin of humiliation appeared all the more severe, since the international system had been de-structured and unregulated since 1989. 'Minilateralism', club diplomacy and free co-opting came in to replace the strict rules of bipolarity, and that was sufficient to throw the status of everyone into a state of chaos and confusion. As things stood, Russia had in its favour only one protection left that could limit the wobbles towards destabilisation that various trends might suggest: its seat among the five permanent members of the Security Council and the veto that comes with it. And Russia exercised this veto as a sort of last line of defence against the risk of extreme humiliation. The veto was used to dissuade the UN from undertaking a mandated intervention on Serbian soil (1999), and to block all action in Syria, although Western operations in Libya had seemed to relegate Russia to the status of an onlooker, something not compatible with Russian pretensions of influence in the Middle East. In an active mode, Russia contributed texts to major resolutions of the Security Council that indicated the limits of its ambitions: one example of this was Resolution 1244 (10 June 1999) concerning Kosovo, in which Moscow took an opportunity to remind everyone about 'the desire of all member States to preserve the sovereignty and the territorial integrity of the Federal Republic of Yugoslavia, and that of all other States in the region'.[19]

Obviously the overwhelming majority of States have no such advantage. Thus a major contradiction came to form part of today's situation. On one hand, the end of bipolarity set foreign policies free, giving as much encouragement to 'lone rider' attitudes as to group tendencies, opening up a range of action considerably wider than that associated with the patronage of the previous era, and putting a strain on military powers. Otherwise, a single event removed all guarantees from the status claimed by one or another group or nation, sealing the victory of unregulated agencies, and of clubs (like the G8) as opposed to institutionalised structures. Similarly, an

[19] N Lemay-Hébert, 'La situation au Kosovo' in M Albaret et al, *Les Grandes Résolutions du Conseil de sécurité des Nations unies* (Paris, Dalloz, 2012) 242–243.

exit from East-West rivalry marked the rise of the logic of inclusion and of interdependence over geopolitical divisions, as well as the absolute victory of the world level, as opposed to regional alliances. But at the same time the traditional powers experienced a rise in global tensions, as they did what they could to force the continuation of an oligarchical order.

This is not only a major, but a double contradiction, which sets loose all the possible uses of humiliation, by exacerbating the battle waged for the control and reassignment of the status of various self-proclaimed powers. This task is a meticulous one. One must resist the temptation to humiliate those who inflate their status insufferably, as long as there are some advantages for the major players: Qatar, whose diplomacy makes us think sometimes of the frog in Aesop's fable 'The Frog and the Ox', is tolerated, even encouraged in its recklessness. Saudi Arabia is seldom criticised, except in the critical context of September 2001.

At the same time this hypersensitivity of the question of status is caused by three factors that are particularly important today. First, there is a nationalism, necessarily rather intense, on the part of States that were liberated, most of them, from colonial oppression. Next, we have a world configuration that increases the influence of societies, precisely in regions where social pathologies are the most virulent, pushing states into audacious statements about the role they should play and the functions they should fulfil in the international arena. Finally, faced with the weakness of international instritutions, those who consider themselves victims obviously devote most of their energy to denouncing the informal arrangements that exist, along with various games at which others connive, initiatives of 'minilateralists' and oligarchs. All this is accomplished in a ready-to-wear fundamentalist or populist garb that is offered to clothe the destitute.

There are enough sources of tension to destabilise a fragile international system; enough elements that generate violence, where any competition for power is outclassed by a competition for status. Things would be rather commonplace if we stopped there, because the same configuration is identifiable in what is commonly called 'transition situations'. What is new, what has been put in place little by little since the 19th century, has to do with an interesting inversion: the quest for status is more likely to cause war as we go down in the rank of powers, until we reach, if not the weakest, at least those who we would like to contain within that class, who are more numerous today than ever.

However, one should say that peace has never depended so much on progress in the area of *respect*. We are thinking of the marvellous intuition of the philosopher Kant, who placed respect in the position of an imperative of Reason. But the entire history of international relations testifies to the murderous permanence of the adage that establishes that 'others' are not like me. Strongly implanted once, this maxim proved to be relatively functional. Today, its failures are daily and catastrophic. Kant, in agreement with

Rousseau, warned of the dangers of self-esteem without limits, conceiving of respect as the 'representation of a value that diminishes my self-love'.[20]

This Kantian vision of respect is completely modern: in thinking of respect as a means for arranging the increasing diversity of the global space, and as a means of regulating the tensions that stem from it, Kant comes close to stating the principles of an ideal diplomacy. He defines respect in terms of a controlled distance, which in fact leads us to value the other especially when that other is very different. In this regard, we touch upon the real social utility of respect, not just its ethical significance.

The mastery of self-esteem in international relations is the antechamber of true modernity. It passes through many stages: the knowledge of the other, a just place to be given to the culture of the other, the implementation of the other's international social integration, in material terms as well as symbolic, and the right of the other to be included, and to negotiate his or her status apart from all authoritarian prescription. Such a programme has affinities for the *solidarisme* of yesteryear and for contemporary multilateralism, free of its aches and pains, and free of its contradictions.

Such a route is another means of re-reading the story of contemporary international relations. It suggests somewhat the other side of this. Pascal considered that respect had to be earned, but that it was nonetheless subject to habits and traditions. These, indeed, bound humans with 'the cords of necessity' stemming from the use of force, or with 'the cords of imagination' that have an affinity for the spectacle of power, with its brilliant displays. We might imagine that we are in the international arena. The other side of the story is also about resistance and reconquest, an effort to move beyond the tension described by Pascal. But this is a story that may have gone wrong, because it is not able to maintain the old fetishisation of power in its classic form.

[20] E Kant, *Les Fondements de la métaphysique des mœurs* (Paris, Livre de Poche, 1993 (1785)); A Honneth, *The Struggle for Recognition: The Moral Grammar of Social Conflicts* (Polity Press, 1995 [1992]).

2

Humiliation, or Power without Rules

EUROPE'S INVENTION OF the international sphere was not as simple as one might think. Since we are all the direct inheritors of that invention, and since the entire world operates principally using that legacy, we have a tendency to forget how very original it all once was. The Old Continent was not only formed under the influence of war, but lived for centuries under its complete sway. The American political scientist Charles Tilly elegantly and convincingly showed this when he wrote about the intimate connection between 'state-making' and 'war-making'. War not only marked out the territories and drew the borders, but also arranged relations of authority and found the means of mobilising resources. Even more, war explains the extreme fragmentation of the continent, something pathological in itself, and that strange marquetry of States that makes necessary the range of colours used on maps. Nothing like this exists in Asia, or in America, except in the southern part, where there are some reminders of Spanish colonial heritage.

This means that the intimacy linking war and international relations in the memory of Europeans, just like the dialectic between war and negotiation, makes both of these the permanent matrix of regional equilibrium.[1] This also means that the fetishisation of this last notion is raised to the rank of a vital principle of our diplomacy. We could go further and express our astonishment that all the great Western thinkers have found virtues in war, associating it closely with the State in a positive way, apparently forgetting that this association can also take a turn for the worse. Machiavelli connected it to the fatality of infinite desire that belongs to every human, but he also considered it a sure way of avoiding civil war. The prince, before anyone else, needed war in order to survive and prosper, just as he needed to increase his military power. Kant himself only expected perpetual peace to be achieved after the necessary experience of war, and Rousseau connected this 'necessity' to the state of existence in society, a context of self-esteems mutually sharpened against each other.

[1] L Bély, 'Négocier la paix de Westphalie au temps des revolutions' in F Petiteville and D Placidi-Frot (eds), *Négociations internationales* (Paris, Presses de Sciences Po, 2013) 171–198.

Power Against Humiliation

Post-medieval European thought invented, for its own purposes, a functional war, and did not hesitate to dissolve the substance of international life in the order of aggression. No one at that time dreamed of the cooperation that could have been the norm for States in their gestation period and in their adolescence. We know that this martial vision—so difficult to give up today—is mainly the work of Thomas Hobbes. He experienced the horrors of the English civil war, and the Thirty Years' War was being fought not far away; the English philosopher quickly concluded that violence was the greatest challenge to society, politics was the only protection against it, and state sovereignty was the only instrument that had any chance of meeting the challenge. The author of *Leviathan*, vaunting the merits of a vigilant sovereign, could only imagine this sovereign and his peers as 'perpetual gladiators'. Sovereignty may be necessary for security, but no one knows how to reduce this need: gladiators fight endlessly, and their survival depends on their power and their ability to balance each other.

How can politics do without war? How could war appear as anything other than a perpetual homage to politics, to serve it, consolidate it, accomplish its aims? At this level, the international system is realised through power, and through a game that redefines, almost consensually, by a law of confrontation, the logic of relations and status between rival princes. Diplomacy is not necessary in order for humiliation to be produced: the law of war alone will decide who will be humbled within this small, limited circle. The game is deemed acceptable.

This functional mechanics finds its logical development in the 20th century in the work of the German jurist and philosopher Carl Schmitt. The root remains as before: humans are not necessarily good. As sinners, humans may evince at any moment a penchant for hatred of others. But as long as this hatred remains individual (*inimicus*), it is able to be pardoned. At the public level, this instinct towards hostility becomes fixed, on another hand, upon the enemy as *hostis*, and this enemy has the virtue of founding political communities. These communities need enemies in order to survive—indeed, they need them in order to continue to exist. In this, war is the founder of politics, the role of the State being to actualise this function by *deciding* who the *enemy* is, and who will bond the nation together[2]—the friend being confined to a secondary role, as the person who is not the enemy, while the enemy is the only true founder of politics.[3]

The enemy is so important that it can only exist by being known and recognised as such. This recognition, the turning point of our demonstration, is at its clearest in the Schmittian ideal. The syntax is clear: the enemy

[2] C Schmitt, *The Concept of the Political* (Chapel Hill, Rutgers University Press, 1927).
[3] ibid 165.

is declared head-on; it is the one you fight, but also the one with whom you negotiate and make peace. Let us pause at this very sensitive point in the analysis. Schmitt takes us to a situation of perfect confrontation, in which hostility appears to sweep away any collateral development. We have before our eyes the spectacle of the Cold War, in which, given the clarity of the opposition between two military forces and the idea of the balance of those forces, humiliation appears to play only a minimal, residual role. Nonetheless, the interest of this conception is to lead us along new pathways, where we find the real malfunctioning of power.

To begin with, what is the real extent of the idea of the enemy? Everything in the tradition following Hobbes indicates that the enemy can only be the equal, the double, the similar, ie another State and of *equivalent power*. What is the case in other situations, when the designated enemy is no longer a State? Caught in contradictions and absorbed by Nazi totalitarianism, Schmitt betrays himself while musing about the Jews faced with the Third Reich. Logically, everything falls apart: can a Leviathan be defied by a non-Leviathan, can a political community be defied by an 'other' who is not a community and does not have available to him the panoply of war? We are in the midst of this at the start of the third millenium: the 'asymmetry', which prolongs, in the current situation, the intellectual mechanism typical of Schmitt, and rapidly gives form and substance to the weapon of humiliation, holding that the new enemy (which is not a State) possesses lower status for that reason.

Schmitt, again marked by his times, was tempted to affirm, remaining faithful to his own intuitions, that war could not evolve, except by becoming total mobilisation of the capacities of each society; this is the 'total war' Ludendorff was talking about in 1935.[4] Thus he went beyond the opposition presented by Clausewitz, who distinguished 'real war' (where the violence was limited to soldiers) and 'absolute war' in which civilians and soldiers alike were involved.[5] The first is indeed what Hobbes spoke about, and conforms to what is required from war as an instrument, which places it at the service of politics. As for the second, predicted by Schmitt, does it not imply societies that carry conflict into the intimacy of the social pathologies and humiliations they feel? Has this not gradually multiplied as societies have entered into the *danses macabres* of war? The question of status, of recognition and of hate—has it not crystallised all humiliations? Is it not true to say that the *socialisation* of war, given these conditions, was the decisive turning point? Clausewitz saw the birth of a new type of war, the 'war of partisans' conducted in Spain against Napoleon, and he was probably prescient in refusing to equate partisan wars with wars between states.

[4] E Ludendorff, *La Guerre totale* (Paris, Perrin, 2010 (1935)); *Der totale krieg* (Munich, 1936).

[5] C von Clausewitz, *On War* (Princeton, Princeton University Press, 1989 (1832)).

In fact, the entire long history of wars tended to contain martial activity within limits that were meant to protect against humiliation. Feudal institutions distinguished between 'la guerre guerroyable' (orderly campaigns that respect the customs of war) and 'la guerre mortelle' (total war, as we would say today). The first sort was fought in conformity with honour and the customs of chivalry.[6] It was by moving away from this, opening the ranks to mercenaries, then later to popular wars, that this aristocratic form of war came undone. It had corresponded, even before the term existed, and better than anything else, to this genre, which could be applied only to relations between States without damaging society.

This early form of war made limited but tightly-controlled use of humiliation, as a codified and symbolic marker of the situation that the battlefield had produced. A close study of the myth of the 'Burghers of Calais' reveals something of this curious alchemy. As we may remember, the history books produced by the Third Republic taught that in August 1347, the King of England, Edward III, angered by the length (11 months) of a siege of the city of Calais, defended by Jean de Vienne, demanded as a token of surrender six men from the city, with shirts open and ropes around their necks, so that he might do with them whatever he wished. To show the merits of altruism and patriotism, Republican historiography tells us that Eustache de Saint-Pierre and five of his fellow citizens gave themselves up willingly, to suffer this cruel humiliation. The king's wife, Philippa of Hainaut, who was pregnant at the time, along with a few barons who pitied the hostages, managed to obtain mercy, and the humiliation came to an end.

Today it is known that this story was not true:[7] but that only makes the myth even more interesting. It is based on a rather biased narrative from Froissart, and suggests that the chronicles of that period prized a policy of magnanimity, and disapproved of humiliating actions, which were not considered true acts of war. Froissart even placed words in the mouth of one of the barons, Gautier de Maury, quoting him as saying that the only crime of these bourgeois had been 'to fight for their king', something that was not reprehensible but actually completely honourable. Philippa de Hainaut did not take much of a chance, because the chronicle tells that she had dinner served to the six heroes, and gave six gold coins to each of them.

But we can go further, beyond the false narrative, and note that the reality was probably different. No doubt, the scene constituted an act of 'public penance' that symbolically expressed the surrender of the city, as often happened at that time, in order to allow the victor to grant pardon and avoid demeaning the defeated partner. Those who had volunteered to be tied up were supposed to be acting a part in a drama, not risking their

[6] P Contamine, *La Guerre au Moyen Âge* (Paris, PUF, 1980) 458.
[7] J-M Moeglin, *Les Bourgeois de Calais* (Paris, Albin Michel, 2002).

lives. Thus war did not exclude humiliation; rather it codified it, set it in a frame, and strictly maintained it within the framework of relations of power, in order to show how the modification of that framework was expressed by a real change in domination. (It is not likely that this interpretation was in Rodin's mind, as he created no fewer than twelve versions of the scene in sculpture.)

The same significance was represented 300 years later when Diego Vélasquez in 1635 produced his famous painting, *The Surrender of Breda*. The painter took as his subject an episode of the Eighty Years' War, in which the Calvinist United Provinces fought against the kingdom of Spain. The city of Breda, defended by Justin of Nassau, was besieged by Ambroise Spinola on behalf of Philip IV, King of Spain. In surrendering, on 2 June 1625, Justin obtained the right to leave the city along with the surviving members of his garrison, and the inhabitants of the city received a guarantee that they would be shown clemency.

Unlike the romanticised account of the surrender of Calais, the representation made by Vélasquez conforms to the historical truth. The generous gesture of Spinola, as depicted by the Spanish master, is world famous. Here there is no public penance, but the continued presence, in the centre of the painting, of the symbol of power, manifested in this case by the keys to the city, which Justin is handing to the victor. By encouraging the vanquished to rise, and in looking straight into his eyes, Spinola shows that the game of power may dispense with all forms of humiliation. The physical characteristics of the arms carried on both sides indicate perfect equality of status. The physical pain of war is not even present. This resembles the action of Ferdinand of Aragon who, having defeated (in 1492) the last of the Moorish kings, Boabdil, refused even to force him to dismount.[8]

Obviously this is a very idealised representation of war; we see a game of pure power, from which one would like to erase all trace of physical and moral suffering. Everything is done in order to pretend that humiliation is not part of the game. Strength appears to be united to greatness of the soul, safe from all degradation. Once again, the desire to show this is not negligible, especially inasmuch as we know that the painting dignified the Salon des Royaumes in the Buen Retiro Palace of Philip IV. An act of propaganda? Certainly. Faithful to, or representative of practices of that period, of all such practices? Of course not. But it is in conformity with a conception of war, and what is more, with an international system in which State authoritarianism and a strict game of power dominated from the start. One held off the destabilising effect of social pressure, and the other guaranteed the simple effectiveness of a completely Hobbesian set of regulations. Taken together, they rejected and even prohibited any strategic abuse of the status of a defeated foe.

[8] www.clg-curie-etampes.ac.versailles.fr/spip.php.

In a game with only a few players, who are themselves represented by princes whose status is comparable, and who are often connected by familial ties, relationships have nothing so dramatic or complex at stake. By stabilising itself in this world of juxtaposed States, and in initiating the Westphalian era, Europe was headed in the direction of simplifying itself by gradually eliminating minor entities, as in the treaties of Münster and Osnabrück, which helped remove many small principalities. The problem now only arises at the margins of the Continent: humiliation can strike those who are made to feel they are not part of the 'club', not members of the House of Europe, whose destiny is in-fighting—but among members, between equals. The Ottoman Empire was regularly treated this way. At the limit, one might ally oneself with the Empire, as Louis XIV did during the War of the League of Augsburg, for want of a better solution; but one did not negotiate—one dictated. The Russians also were made to suffer, in accordance with an eternal story that places them neither quite inside nor quite outside. We may remember the humiliation of the Tsarina Elisabeth I and her minister, Alexis Bestuzhev-Ryumin, whose plenipotentiary was excluded from the negotiations at Aachen (1748) which ended the War of the Austrian Succession, and in which the Tsarina wished dearly to participate.[9]

As Westphalian values began to be put in place, international relations accomplished more and more in a game pure of power which was self-sufficient. Power was the perfect master of the relations between princes; it acted as a perfect regulator, understood and accepted by everyone, as long as they were part of the family. War took place regularly, and thus actualised the game in accordance with precise rules that actually prohibited ideological schisms, distinctions of regime, and even animosities and their attendant effects. The War of the League of Augsburg (1688–1697) was archetypal. Louis XIV affirmed his identity as the 'Sun King' at the end of the 17th century, placing his kingdom in the position of a hegemony. Little more was required to make all the other princes ally themselves against him—the Holy Roman Emperor, William III of Nassau, the King of Spain, the Duke of Savoy, Portugal, Sweden, Scotland, etc. Louis XIV was left with only the Sublime Porte and the Jacobites.

Here, power speaks only to another power. It is not certain that William III of Nassau, a protestant taking possession of England, had any affinity with Leopold I, the very Catholic Emperor of Austria. The coalition of protestant States created by William III nonetheless consistently sided with the Emperor and the King of Spain—all simply to contain French hegemony. Several decades later, France and Austria, at war for more than 200 years, had no scruples about signing the Treaty of Versailles (1 May 1756)

[9] FD Liechtenhan, *Élisabeth I*[re] (Paris, Fayard, 2007) 190.

that sealed their alliance, the sole aim of which was to counter the dramatic rise of Prussia. Mechanically, this pushed Prussia closer to England, and led directly to the Seven Years' War. This enchanted the realists, and was too beautiful for their philosophical master, Hans Morgenthau, who did not fail to emphasise the degree to which the Seven Years' War established 'the ideology of the balance of power'.[10]

The game permits at one and the same time an extreme flexibility of alliances and a certain inevitability of confrontations. For example, the War of the League of Augsburg shows that in order to maintain a hegemony, the strongest party must continue to expand. In a game about power, the status quo is almost impossible to maintain, beyond a provisional arrangement. The complexity of the established borders implied stabilisation and consolidation from the perspective of Louis XIV, similar to what had been done through the 'policy of Reunions', which had constructed every realm in Europe, acre by acre. Charles Tilly is quite right—since each treaty aimed at a compromise, each agreement rested upon some ambiguity, and this furnished a reason to prepare for a new war.

The desire to have more merged with the desire to exist. We already sense that this attitude will have its day, but only that; let the peoples, nations, societies or ideologies intervene, or let the regimes be placed in danger of not surviving, and the game will no longer be the same. The modifications of power will give way before the opposition of status. Having begun as an accessory, humiliation has now become an effect of the system, especially if powers emphasise it without guarding against it. That fracture would occur during the 19th century. For the moment, humiliation remained cold and contained. The negotiations that punctuated each of these wars turned out to be complex, heavy, and measured. The Treaty of the Pyrenees, signed by France and Spain in 1659, implied a negotiation that that lasted three years, while the Peace of Westphalia (1648) only appeared seven years after the beginning of preliminary negotiations. The ritual of these procedures served a complex function, that of precisely defining a new equilibrium, rather than the crushing of the other. The Treaty of Ryswick (1697) confirmed France's rights over Alsace, including Strasbourg, but re-established the Duke of Lorraine upon his territory, while conceding to the French Army the right to pass over that territory. The kingdom of France gave up its conquests on the right bank of the Rhine, and was obliged to destroy some of its fortresses. In order to conciliate the Spanish in advance of anticipated succession problems, Louis XIV gave some cities in Flanders to Spain. In order to have himself recognised as king of England by his French neighbour, William III limited his claims. In order that all might

[10] H Morgenthau, *Politics among Nations. The Struggle for Power and Peace* (New York, A Knopf, 1964 (1948)) 213–214.

be properly balanced, France received the western half of the island of Hispaniola (which would become Haiti and the Dominican Republic), plus some financial compensation for its rights over the Palatinate.

This pattern of quid pro quo occurs mechanically, almost every time. With the Treaty of the Pyrenees (1659), France gained Artois and some Flemish cities from Spain, but gave up the county of Barcelona. In order to improve the balance of this new division of lands, France gave its support to the Spanish crown against Portugal, all supplemented by a marriage contract between the future Louis XIV and the infant Marie-Thérèse. The Treaties of Nijmegen (1678) returned Franche-Comté to France, in return for France giving up its military conquests. The Treaty of Utrecht (1713) led Louis XIV to surrender cities he held beyond the Rhine (Brisach, Kehl, Fribourg) in order to obtain Orange and the valley of the Ubaye, and he ceded the Susa Valley, and also Furnes and Ypres, which became the property of the Habsburgs. Acadia passed into the hands of the English, along with the island of Saint-Christophe (now St Kitts). The grandson of Louis XIV was recognised as king of Spain, but renounced his rights to the crown of France.

There is incredible complexity, but a constant concern for balance. There is a sophisticated territorial game, but it is almost always amended through the game of governance and dynastic assignment. States are created, powers are calibrated, and the outline of each protagonist is redrawn. New wars are scheduled, and new hegemonies are drawn.

The act of re-establishing balance can prove exceptionally hard to manage. The Treaty of Paris (1763) put an end to the Seven Years' War (1756–1763), and its function of re-establishing balance has already been described. The military victories of Frederick II and England's naval superiority proved too much for the kingdom of France, which welcomed peace negotiations. The result was severe, and France might well have appeared humiliated after having lost its possessions in Canada, in Ohio, and on the left bank of the Mississippi—in particular Louisiana, virtually all its Indian lands, several of the Antilles islands and some *comptoirs* (French settlements) in Senegal. The readjustment of power also took place overseas. Here, there was little or no re-balancing: obtaining Saint-Pierre-et-Miquelon was not credible, any more than keeping, *in extremis*, fishing rights in Newfoundland or an English guarantee to respect Catholicism in Quebec.

The humiliation in the offing was exactly noted by Voltaire in the *Précis du siècle de Louis XV* (1763). The State lost 'the flower of its youth, more than half the money circulating in the country, its navy, its business,' and above all, 'its credit'. It would be necessary to start again, to reconstruct the State's power, in order to reconquer. This effect is commented on by realists who like to talk about a hegemony that makes itself and unmakes itself in order to remake itself. And it is a prelude to something else: from now on it is a question of commerce and empire; much more so than strongholds.

Perhaps this is the appearance of the end of a cycle of construction of States, and the first symptoms of power going wrong.

How Power Goes Wrong

Power, as we have just seen, appears to be an ideal, and from Hobbes to Schmitt, from the Peace of Westphalia to the Treaty of Paris that put an end to the Crimean War (1856), it was a real constitutive principle in international relations or, more precisely, a constitutive principle for the type of international relations that created Europe and a good portion of modernity. 'Power for power's sake', or more exactly, a perpetual search for the most precise equilibrium possible between powers, remains for Morgenthau the best possible approach to international reality.[11] We reach here the state of a historical novel about a bygone era: a time that had its own mechanical processes, which ran almost by themselves; a time that did not stop for humiliation, which had no need of it.

Things took a slight upturn in the 18th century, before quickly worsening. In the main, three factors were able to derail this well-oiled machine. The first is very old, but often dormant at the strongest moments of Westphalian realism: the idea of a *just war* which exploits power, and which thus orients it and domesticates it. The second factor preoccupied the entire 19th century, and has not receded since: the encounter with *social constructions* that weigh upon States, which through national movements and the greatest diversity of social expressions gain an importance that undermines and then reshapes power. The third factor came to prominence a few decades later, and has never stopped growing in importance: the discovery of the distant *other* that made possible an exit from the club, something that went beyond being equal.

A just war obviously disturbs power in exploiting it. As soon as force is placed in service to the just or the true, it breaks with the principles of equality and symmetry that gave meaning to the actions of Hobbes' gladiators. Suddenly the enemy, who was not the object of hatred before, becomes stigmatised and criminalised by definition. War is not at the service of power, but rather destined to re-establish the good. The use of force is no longer a matter of the mechanics of political bodies, but the duty of aiding someone faced with an unjust aggressor, according to the formula of St Ambrose. We easily understand why the thesis was refuted by Schmitt, who would not even hear the subject discussed. We easily surmise why the thesis was accepted by Christianity, especially during the Middle Ages, but rejected by the Renaissance. It was rejected by Machiavelli, who only cared about what war could gain for the State, and left it to the State to

[11] ibid 8.

determine a war's legitimacy or licit character: 'War is just, for those who find it necessary'. And also by Luther, who held all wars to be necessarily unjust, and by Erasmus.

When the idea of a just war was reframed by religious people in order to meet such arguments, it was more precise and thus more incisive. In the 16th century the Dominican Francisco de Vitoria had spoken in this way about causes that had a duty to be just (to themselves, as it were), or authorities who, in order to conduct a just war, were obliged to act in conformity with what is just, and to employ means that are proportionate to the task. There lies the danger: rhetoric can establish such equivalences, and a prince will be able to act on them without restraint. The enemy will be shamed and humiliated, and the Crusader sanctified. The effects are all beneficial: the most cold-blooded realists understood this, since they were so familiar with contexts in which good and evil were referred to. This is how things were with Reinhold Niebuhr, protestant pastor and the inspiration for realism in this context; but the same is true of Morgenthau. The balance of power can be linked to a struggle between good and evil.[12]

The humiliation machine is in motion. Someone will film Saddam Hussein being hanged, he who was supposed to be the Hitler of the Middle East, and someone will decorate his statue with an American flag before pulling down the monument itself. Someone will film a bloody Gaddafi, just emerged from being impaled, and all TV viewers will be treated to the spectacle of his tortured body, as if they had filmed the final stage of the Tour de France. We are a very long way from the surrender of Breda. Terrorists, criminals, assassins, bandits: the new act of war is no longer intended to define power, but precisely to criminalise and thus to abolish and destroy the status of the other. This is the centre of our problem.

Often enough, the cause in itself is just, and the just war is welcome despite the abuses that are made of the notion; but too often the choice is arbitrary, disguised. We should all listen to Grotius in support of Isocrates, according to whom 'the most just war is fought against savage beasts and men who resemble savage beasts'.[13] But he quickly added, citing Plutarch, 'Wanting to lead barbarian nations towards more cultivated morals is a pretext under which we conceal our desire for what they have'.[14] He recalled further that so-called 'just' wars are likely to be unjust unless 'the crimes are quite atrocious and [the responsibility for them] very manifest'. He cited

[12] R Niebuhr, *Moral Man and Immoral Society* (New York, C Scribner's, 1947); Morgenthau, *Politics Among Nations* ch 15; on Morgenthau and morality, cf also WE Scheuerman, *Hans Morgenthau: Realism and Beyond* (Cambridge, Polity Press, 2009).

[13] H Grotius, *The Rights of War* (Indianapolis, Liberty Fund, 2005 (1625)) II, XX, XV, 2–3.

[14] ibid 492.

Mithridates: 'It is not the faults of kings that they pursue, but their power and their majesty'.[15]

A just war wanted by too many people, and spilling out of its planned course: examples are numerous, today or in the past. It is a war such as this that engenders rage, disgust and hatred among those who are associated with the target. It is a war that, in creating humiliation, also creates new violence.

An *encounter with the social* constitutes another source of disturbance or disruption, one that is different and more complex. The more that power comes into contact with the tissue of social existence, the more it loses the cold and mechanical characteristics we have described. Obviously, the more numerous and diverse the actors, the greater the chance that we will see multiple interpretations of power appear, mingling with the expectations and frustrations of the population most concerned. The social game has the virtue of reshaping and translating power so that it acquires a real sociological status. There are so many powerful sources of a kind of humiliation that becomes a defining parameter of the international system.

The wars of revolution and of empire contributed greatly to this work of conversion. We leave, for the first time, the sacred game: war was no longer a tournament between princes, but a means explicitly designed to overthrow them—first in the name of the people, and after that in the name of conquest: two reasons to implicate societies and to evolve slowly towards the 'total war'; two reasons, also, to connect these wars to the rise of national feeling, a first stage for this social conversion, the initial generator of humiliations, which has never ceased from this point.

Let us trace the route of Johann Fichte (1764–1814), who was deeply influenced by these twin reasons. He was born just after the Seven Years' War, and grew up in an atmosphere of Prussian power and ascension. He studied theology at Jena before teaching there. He encountered into the French Revolution, and adopted its ideas so thoroughly that he was hired as a preacher for the armies of the Year II. He acquired liberal convictions and a romantic sensibility. However, shocked by the Prussian defeat in Jena, his adopted home town, he discovered the idea of the German nation in the devastating effects of French power. A year later, he wrote his famed *Addresses to the German Nation* (1807). His pre-Hegelian philosophy, as expressed in the *Foundations of Natural Right*,[16] places in 'otherness', and the confrontation with the 'other', the essential source of the freedom which each person has within him- or herself. No one could better grasp the transformation of power, which could already be perceived: instead of maintaining a balance,

[15] ibid 493.

[16] J Fichte, *Foundations of Natural Right*, trans. Michael Baur; edited by Frederick Neuhouser (Cambridge, Cambridge University Press, 2000).

power will now nourish and display otherness, leading it to extremes, to hatred, humiliation, closed-mindedness and rejection.

The battle of Jena has often been presented as a turning point in intersocial history, and it very probably was one, at least as concerns the history of the German national movement. In the same year, in occupied Nuremberg, a pamphlet appeared with a very clearly expressed title: *Germany and its Humiliation*. People were not sure who the author was, but the publisher was quickly identified as the bookseller Johann Philipp Palm. The booklet spoke of resistance, and also denounced the French occupier, who in the end did not hesitate to shoot the unfortunate publisher.

So begins the story of a strange blend of humiliation and fascination, of which Fichte is very representative, and which opens up a long history still uninterrupted today, after having touched the Ottoman Empire, Africa, Asia, colonisation, decolonisation, Bandung and all the fundamentalisms. The dialectic of power and emancipation begins here, between violence from the top and violence rising from the bottom. It is as if power had suddenly become a liberating factor with regard to social capacities; as if power, reacting to the rise and increased force of societies, gained revenge by becoming primarily a weapon used to lower the class status of peoples and cultures.

Illustrations of these changes can be found at any period of the relationship between France and Germany, up to 1945, as if the spectre of the *Erbfeind* (hereditary enemy) already dominated the situation. This transformation of power—which is equivalent here to a disturbance and loss of past virtues—explains this sudden social intimacy with the enemy, this *hostis* who from now on is also an *inimicus*, and is led to make humiliation a common weapon that speaks to a great number.

This 'socialisation' of war and international relations clearly opens the way to *xenophobia*, the stigmatisation of what is foreign, particularly all the social attributes of the foreigners, their culture, their morality and their customs, even their language or their religion. We are witnessing a sort of inversion: power tending to submit to a social game that—at an earlier time—it had itself provoked; and from now on, power is the partial hostage of this game. In fact, this social reorientation of power recalls that moral slippery slope that we observed in connection with the return of the just war.

This social engagement undoubtedly makes the task of the strategists more difficult, but in differing ways. Conscious of its importance, Chancellor Bismarck made concessions to its symbolism, and did not hesitate to use the emotional aspects of an event: he proclaimed the German Empire in the Hall of Mirrors at the Palace of Versailles on 18 January 1871. He was an aristocrat who had little interest in popular feelings, but as an obsessive realist he was able nonetheless to limit their development by coming very quickly to an agreement with Thiers and the provisional government, instead of profiting from the communard movement in order to cast the enemy headlong into anarchy.

The equation was already different with Clemenceau—uncompromising, radical, constructing patriotism through the virtue of collective mobilisation and as a type of natural synthesis of his options, republican and anti-socialist. His direct opposition to pacifist idealism, which was in 1918 represented by Wilson and John Maynard Keynes, and very popular then, led him back towards the realist camp; but realism was now to have the benefit of a social sensibility. The 'Tiger' Clemenceau, by carrying his demands to extremes, jeopardised the future, constructed a new international order that was uncertain and dangerous, mocked the sacrosanct principle of the balance of powers, and invented *strategic humiliation*, whereby the downgrading of the Other and the Other's dramatic loss of status count more than the mere redefining of relationships of power.

This policy of humiliation is archetypal. A conquered Germany, but still standing and in control of its own territory, suffered punishment at Versailles in a manner that had never been seen up to that time. German plenipotentiaries were not even invited to discussions, which was unheard of, especially if one remembers that France in 1815, having been invaded and bled dry, was still admitted in Vienna, just as Russia was in Paris in 1856. The negotiation was no longer a compromise, but the formulation of a diktat that required only the mutual agreement of the allies. The presentation of their decisions confirmed a symbolic orientation that had been begun in 1871: the Gallery of Mirrors was used again, as if one humiliation could erase another. The principal clauses converged upon the idea of *déclassement* (downgrading, humbling, lowering) and loss of status. The territorial amputation part remained in conformity with previous practices. But a disarmament scheme was added: Germany was to be permitted a land army limited to 100,000 men, a navy limited to 16,000 men, no heavy artillery, no battleships or aeroplanes, conscription was prohibited, there were demilitarised zones (up to 50km from the right bank of the Rhine), and these were even susceptible to being occupied (the left bank of the Rhine, Mayence, Cologne, Koblenz). Germany was to be forced to recognise the wrongs it had done, to deliver up its leaders to justice, most notably its Emperor, who would be declared a 'war criminal'. Germany was obliged to pay 269 billion gold marks, more than a year's worth of the nation's income, a figure whose outrageous size led Keynes to resign from his delegation. The method has changed; we simply march straight into humiliation.

Clearly, we are witnessing a new stage in international relations and in the conception of power. Vienna in 1815 and Paris, just after the Crimean War, put the defeated parties back into the game of European governance, while still punishing their defeat with territorial sanctions: thus the Czar in 1856 lost his hold over Moldavia and Wallachia, which had been protectorates; he was obliged to accept free navigation along the Danube, the neutrality of the Black Sea, and exclusive protection of the Christian subjects of the Sultan. Nonetheless, he found in these negotiations a basis for a future alliance with France, and even, later on, with England. Germany in 1919 encountered only the conditions of its exclusion from the new European order. It faced a completely different scenario from the one that appeared in 1871, when Bismarck was looking for a new balance of powers, with a France that was limited in its capacity for revenge but still present. Here, there was no question of the new balance of powers, not even in a Wilsonian order.

This dynamic of humiliation quickly structured a new type of international relations and diplomatic action. It is quite true to say that in its wake German nationalism was brought to a fever pitch and radicalised, which took the form of the concept of *Lebensraum* (room for Germans to live). In response to stigmatisation, an echo arose, that was the pretense of exceptionalism and superiority, pushed to the point of a discourse on race that quickly became racist. Other echoes carried conspiracy theories, themselves pushed to the point of caricature. Humiliation did not create the most extreme posturing, but it served as a support for it. The same logic determined the agenda of German diplomacy, and things were actually made easier because what was supposed to be a new international order turned out to be based on the punishment of the loser. Versailles paid very little attention to the Wilsonian principle of nationalities, and many different peoples still had to beg to be recognised. The brand new League of Nations refused to grant the status of founding member to the countries that had sided with the losers. Strangely enough, the criterion of full sovereignty was not retained, which permitted India, and dominions and certain colonies to become members. Argentina proposed in 1920 that all States should be considered *ipso facto* members, but only a minority agreed. Sovereign equality bowed before constituent inequality.

Germany was admitted to the League of Nations in 1926, and withdrew in 1933. There followed a whole series of diplomatic and aggressive actions, which had been forged by the dynamic of humiliation: the denunciation by the Reich of the clauses on disarmament, the reconstitution of a Luftwaffe, the reestablishment of conscription (1935) and the remilitarisation of the Rhineland (1936). The Second World War was approaching, bearing a dialectic of humiliation and revenge.

This observation was undoubtedly present in the mind of the victors in 1945. It had not been completely corrected. Certainly, these conquerors were better at denouncing regimes and ideologies, without saying as much about peoples. They were careful to leave civil society in Germany and Japan a space of autonomy that made their reconstruction possible, and made it possible for them to manage their own status, which otherwise was quickly consolidated by economic success, and in the case of Germany, integration into Europe, a bulwark to the risk of humiliation. They decided, finally, to maintain essential parts of political institutions, particularly the imperial institution in Japan. At the same time, the declaration of Berlin (5 June 1945), the Potsdam conference (August 1945), the London conferences (1948) for Germany, the Treaty of San Francisco (1951) for Japan, all had the effect of creating 'political dwarves' who were also vassals of the United States, at least during the time of the Cold War. In addition, the multilateralism that was reconstituted and reinforced through the creation of the United Nations presented more than ever the figure of a club of victors, excluding those who had been defeated, and offering the winners seats as permanent members of a Security Council, additionally provided with a right of veto. Humiliation was contained within limits, but strong nonetheless; its effects were very probably attenuated by the rigour of bipolarity and the solidarity that is proper for a game of alliances, one that absorbed Germany in less than ten years.

Thus disrupted and rattled by social pressure, power was further disrupted by the gradual discovery of the *distant other*, issuing mainly from the South. This time the gladiator did not encounter his double, but a partner he had constructed as inferior, lacking substance measured by the standards of civilisation, unable to perpetuate the old aristocratic war. Power encountered infra-power in accordance with a Messianic interpretation, stemming from Christian thought as well as the Enlightenment, leading only to conversion. The balance of power thus lost its meaning in favour of a *postulated imbalance* of power. The act towards the other can only concretise superiority, and through this, the breaking of common rules.

The one nearest was the first one touched, obviously. The Ottoman Empire was a permanent laboratory for the violation of equality, to the extent that Westphalian modernity was in the process of being constructed. Islam quickly served as a catalyst, while the geographical proximity of the Porte was able to sweeten the game: the sultan, inasmuch as he had lost his offensive powers since the disappearance of Suleiman the Magnificent (1566), was yet able to insert himself into complex coalitions that made him seem likable in the eyes of certain persons.

Since the 16th century we have seen non-egalitarian diplomatic practices come into common use, practices quickly categorised as capitulations. The exemptions that these offered to the citizens of European realms were all the more humiliating because they had to be renewed every time one sultan succeeded another. The pressure was heavier, since the continuity of the Empire was denied in favour of new relationships established with a young prince who was more or less experienced, and who had to renegotiate everything in order to secure acceptance. The game consisted of accompanying new capitulations with a whole set of 'commands of the sultan' that amounted to so many limits placed on sovereignty, and certain agreed concessions (especially in regard to taxes) made to a whole list of foreign residents.[17] The Abbé de Mably, who was suspicious of Turks (whom he held to be completely untrustworthy) even claimed that there should have been more capitulations, if they had not run up against the 'monstrous ignorance of the Porte'.[18]

This systematic policy of imbalance became, in the 19th century, the daily basis of relations between Europe and Ottoman Turkey, cheerily described by Czar Nicholas I as the 'sick man of Europe'. The Crimean War allowed the Russian intervention to be contained within the Empire, and the Treaty of Paris sealed the Czar's defeat. Nonetheless, it mandated in its Article 9 a constitutional reform that the Sublime Porte was obliged to implement. Formally 'granted' by the sultan's decree, this reform was aimed at promoting equality before the law for Muslims and Christians, according to modalities directly intended, defined and dictated by the powers. These same powers did not wait long before calling the Grand Vizier to order in a memorandum dated 5 October 1859, regretting that these arrangements had not been carried out; while the English ambassador, Sir Henry Bulwer, after having consulted with his consuls in the Empire, noted that 'Muslim fanaticism […] does not break out into violence unless encouraged to do so by dispositions of agents of the public authority'.[19]

Unable to meet the Western armies, the Porte had to appeal to military counsellors from France or Prussia. Strongly challenged by commerce from the West, it had to adopt the commercial code. In competition with European science, it had to open itself up to the universities that produced it. Indebted to States on the Continent, it was obliged to meet the demands of its creditors, and accept the institutional reforms they required.[20] Over the course of the 19th century, Euro-Ottoman relations invented the diplomacy of a forced political conversion. The memory of this now returns in the warning signs of the new strategy of Ahmet Davutoglu, the foreign minister of Turkey under the AKP party.

This approach became normal to the extent that Europe discovered the Muslim world, particularly through the conquest of Algeria. The indigenous people were described in current terms, notably by Tocqueville.[21] His views were quickly generalised over the entire 'South': the author of *Democracy in America* thought that 'Hindoos' ('Indous') were 'beasts as brutal as they are ferocious'[22] and that China had a government that was 'imbecilic and barbarous'.[23] John Stuart Mill accordingly held that

[17] G Poumarède, 'Négocier près la Sublime Porte' in L Bély (ed), *L'Invention de la diplomatie* (Paris, PUF, 1998) 71–85, particularly 81.

[18] Abbé de Mably, *Collection complète des œuvres* (Paris, Desbrière, 1794) vol 6, 37.

[19] E Engelhardt, *La Turquie et le Tanzimat* (A. Cotillon, 1882) vol 1, 170–172.

[20] *cf* B Badie, *The Imported State* (Stanford University Press, 2000).

[21] D Losurdo, *Contre-histoire du libéralisme* (Paris, La Découverte, 2013) 262 ff.

[22] ibid 281.

[23] ibid 349.

despotism was 'a legitimate mode of government when one is dealing with barbarians'.[24] Algernon Sydney spoke of Asiatics as 'cowardly and effeminate people'[25] and Franklin spoke of a 'pyramid of peoples'. The liberals banded together in order to substitute for Westphalian international relations a relation of inequality that would now authorise what the first prohibited. Mill characterised the opium wars as 'a crusade for liberty of commerce and for liberty as such'.[26] Such a stain would prove difficult to wash out, and would weigh heavily upon the international system for a long time. And then the rhetoric began, about the people of God 'who make fertile the forbidding desert', a reference to America, involved in a war against 'redskins'.[27]

It is no accident that China has made the 19th century into a symbol of national humiliation (*bainion guochi*).[28] Some people extend the period all the way to 1949, the date of the proclamation of the Peoples' Republic of China, or even up to 1997, the date of the retrocession of Hong Kong. This cursed century was one of many contradictions. China was one of the oldest empires on Earth, and the importance of its inventions, its culture and its art were well known to everyone, at least in principle. At the same time, its resistance to opening up to the world remained very strong, as was confirmed when China's neighbour Japan opened up to the West in the Meiji era. In a way, the Western plenipotentiaries could have felt humiliated about having been evicted so many times by the Manchu emperor, like the members of the Macartney mission, sent by King George III in 1733, who entered Beijing 'as beggars, [and lived there] like prisoners, [and left again] like thieves'. The Jesuits who arrived in the 17th century had almost disappeared: the adventurers and merchants who knocked on the door had neither culture nor finesse.[29]

This is really where the new History begins. It was not so much a matter of widening European international relations with a world that had appeared, as it was about redressing a balance of payments deficit: an old story. Westerners valued the silk and tea produced in China, but China had little interest in buying anything from the Westerners. A conclusion was quickly drawn: the Empire was not interested in modernity and therefore, as Hegel claimed in 1822, 'no progress can take place in China'. The objective reality of this state of being closed off from the outside world is difficult to argue with: but the simplistic meaning it has been given, its characterisation as a refusal of all modernisation or as a manifestation of the fearful passivity of the peasantry (the vast majority of which never saw

[24] ibid 253.
[25] ibid 114.
[26] ibid 280.
[27] ibid 259.
[28] W Callahan, *China: The Pessoptimist Nation* (Oxford, Oxford University Press, 2010).
[29] J Gernet, *Le Monde Chinois* (Paris, Armand Colin, 1972) 505.

any of this), has been criticised in more recent times, especially in the work of Jane Elliott.[30]

Re-establishing a commercial balance required a reactivation of the opium trade, begun by the Portuguese, and continued by the Dutch despite a number of laws prohibiting it, not only European laws but also an edict from the Chinese Emperor Yongzheng (1729). However, drugs represented one seventh of the revenue from British India: the argument appeared conclusive.[31] The history that would subsequently be written involves a number of ethically risky premises: the opening to the other is not made on the basis of human considerations, or even diplomatic ones; it presupposes a principle of non-reciprocity (drugs are an evil for Europeans, but they may be something good if they are bought by people who live far away); force is used to assist the process of opening China to commerce; punishment is directed against any resistance to this force; the legal order that derives from this situation is based on inequality; this order stimulates competition between Western powers. This is an important and durable invention, for the most part; the meaning of the words in the principles may vary here and there. There we can find, often concealed, the inegalitarian root of contemporary diplomacy, burdened in extreme (though not exceptional) cases by the stench of common racism.

An opening is forced, or an illegal trade is forced on China: the first Opium War was caused by the Emperor Daoguang's order to destroy opium cargoes warehoused at Canton. Captain Charles Elliott, superintendent of British commerce at Canton, observed that foreigners who were established there did not have to obey Chinese laws. The imperial commissioner having no solution, Palmerston opted to administer a 'good thrashing' and organised an expeditionary force: victories to begin with, defeat and harassment afterward, the beginnings of resistance, and finally, the dispatch of an armada of 80 ships, so many that the emperor understood he could not withstand them.

The same thing happened 20 years later. Or, more exactly, the same logic of unequal war led the same Palmerston to react when the Chinese boarded a ship flying the British flag, and to stand alongside Napoleon III, who had deplored the death of a French missionary. But, this time, *punishment* would be the order of the day. Resistance would bring repression, demands for payment, and what they called 'embassies of expiation'. On 7 October 1860, shortly after their victory at Palikao, French troops, followed soon after by English troops, arrived at the Summer Palace of the Emperor and began to loot it. Often uncertain of the value of these unknown objects,

[30] JE Elliott, *Some Did It for Civilization, Some Did It for Their Country: A Revised View of the Boxer War* (Hong Kong, Chinese University Press, 2002).

[31] chine-ancienne.e-monsite.com/pages/la-premiere-guerrede-l-opium.html.

which were unfamiliar in European terms, the soldiers muddled around in a farce, attempting to sack the Palace, and mocking and deriding the staff of the Palace, if we are to believe the report of a witness.[32] The pillaging was done in a disorderly manner; many jewels were left in the Palace, collected up by peasants and were eventually recovered by the authorities. Other jewels ended up in the apartments of Queen Victoria, or in the rooms of the Empress Eugenie de Montijo, or in a museum built for such items at the Palace of Fontainebleau.

Learning that some of their fellows had been horribly tortured, the French and British troops set fire to the Palace a few days later, sparing only a few buildings. 40 years after, on 14 August 1900, at the time of the Boxer Rebellion and the new punitive expedition that followed it, the 13 buildings that had been saved were completely destroyed. Along with French and British troops, there were also Americans, Germans, Russians, Japanese, Austrians and finally Australians, all participants in this second sack of the Summer Palace: Europe's internal divisions were no longer of any significance; events were on another level.

Those events are being diplomatically distilled today in Beijing. In February 2009, just before the 150th anniversary of the first pillaging of the Summer Palace, the Chinese authorities launched an important campaign to search for the stolen items, sending a group of experts to visit Western museums. In October 2010, amid many different commemorative events, an exhibition of recovered sculptures was opened in Beijing. Discreet allusions were made, here and there, in a judicious manner.

Subsequent events were just as humiliating. The Treaty of Nanjing, cited above (29 August 1842) and the Treaty of Beijing, which concluded the second Opium War (24 October 1860), were classic examples in this category. One assigned new reparations to be paid to the Westerners, opened still further ports and navigable waterways to international commerce, and established new concessions to be administered by Europeans. The classical game of power that had appeared to fade away was now reconstituted as a means of organising the competition between the States of the Old Continent; China was not a *subject*, but the *object* of power. Thus Russia obtained through the Treaty of Aïgun (28 May 1858) the left bank of the Amur River and the piece of territory between the river and Korea. There, Russia would build Vladivostok, a name that means 'domination of the East': a consolation for the Czar, beaten by his peers in the Crimean war, two years earlier. And then there followed, as a mechanical effect of the forced opening of ports, the war of Cochinchina fought by the French (1860), the Sino-Japanese War (1894) and the Boxer Rebellion (1900). Later, but

[32] Comte d'Hérisson, *La Destruction du palais d'Été* (Paris, France Empire, 2012 (1860)) 177.

along the same lines, was the Japanese conquest, begun in 1931. Most particularly, there was the Nanjing Massacre (December 1937): 200,000 victims, according to the International Military Tribunal for the Far East; 300,000, according to Chinese sources; between 20,000 and 80,000 women and children were assaulted.[33] The Japanese military command 'suspended the protective measures' applicable to prisoners under international law, and murder contests were organised, with Japanese officers competing.

In Mao Zedong's day, he knew that he had to remain discreet regarding such atrocities, whose cruellest details we shall not review here; they are, for that matter, contested by certain revisionist Japanese historians.[34] Diplomatic reason and social behaviour do not always pull in the sanem direction, and this is especially true when the People's Republic of China is attempting to enter the classical game of power, to standardise relations with its neighbours, and forget inegalitarian diplomacy. It remains true that 100 years of humiliation leave a mark that becomes a constant parameter, made up of xenophobia, a defiant attitude towards the other, sovereign defence and identity affirmation.[35] There is also an element of the spirit of revolution, expressed by many secret societies, especially those of the Boxers. Equally, and this is an eternal paradox, there is an instinct towards reform, the import of models from the strongest sources, and new overtures towards the outside, in all probability the source of new inequalities.

William Gladstone, when a member of the House of Commons, voted against the first Opium War, and spoke of 'unjust war' and of 'the shame' to be brought upon the British flag, which could not 'fly proudly over Canton … except in order to protect an infamous traffic in contraband.'[36] On 25 November 1861, Victor Hugo wrote about the destruction of the Summer Palace:

> One day, two bandits walked into the Summer Palace. One sacked it, the other burned it. Victory can be a thief, apparently. The great devastation of the Summer Palace is something for which the two victors are jointly responsible. […] All the treasures of our cathedrals together would not equal that splendid and amazing museum of the East. […] Great achievement, a great treasure. One of the victors filled his pockets, and seeing this, the other filled his coffers; they came back to Europe arm in arm, laughing. Well, that is the story of the two bandits. We, Europeans, we are civilized, and to us, the Chinese are barbarians. Just look at how civilization has acted towards barbarism. Before all history, one of these two bandits is called France; the other is called England. […] The crimes of

[33] I Chang, *Le Viol de Nankin* (Paris, Payot, 1998) 157–158.
[34] T Yoshida, *The Making of the Rape of Nanking* (Oxford, Oxford University Press, 2006).
[35] ibid 11.
[36] chine-ancienne.e-monsite.com/pages/la-premiere-guerre-del-opium.html.

> the leaders are not the fault of those who are led. Governments sometimes are bandits, but the peoples, never […].[37]

***

Just war, encounter with the social, and *rise of the other* are the three main factors that upset power and cause it to deviate from its classical construction: three factors that produce diplomacies of humiliation.

[37] Letter to Captain Butler: www.chine-informations.com/guide/lettre-de-victor-hugo-sur-le-palais-ete-yuanmingyuan_1618.html.

3

Types of Humiliation and their Diplomacies

THIS HISTORICAL REVIEW demonstrates the unity and diversity of humiliation in international relations. There is unity in terms of the time period that marks the rise of this practice in the mid-19th century, and continuing up to the construction of the present globalisation; there is also a functional unity, which places humiliation as a diplomatic instrument that transcends individual choices and psychological or psycho-sociological parameters. The very diversity of factors involved is evidence of the effect of the increasing socialisation of international life, the emergence of actors who are not part of the European-North American oligarchy, and a widening gap between values, symbolised by renewed interest in the theme of a just war.

Constructing a Typology

These three factors appear to be three properties of the international system as it has been constructed, in the wake of the wars of revolution and empire. These wars already integrated the first factor, and the 19th century slowly gave birth to the second, especially through increasing contact with the Ottoman Empire and China; the third factor, an old resurgence of an ancient history, would experience a tremendous rise after decolonisation. We should note, all the same, that this process of construction did not integrate within itself previous situations, instances when humiliation was used on such and such an occasion. It was not yet a property of the international system, but a single act by a single actor, however important it might be. We also pay attention to effects of context,[1] which should never be forgotten. We distinguish between situations in which there is a structured context, marked by a strong construction (apparent or real) of international power, and situations in which the structure of power is uncertain or fluid. We will consider the hypothesis that the first kind involves international modes of acting in which practices of humiliation are embedded, so to speak (the Concert of Europe in the 19th century, bipolar system during the Cold War). With the second, on the contrary, influenced by the fragmentation of the international system, the game of humiliation is played outside of all structuring frameworks (ie the system of the 'between the wars' period, or the post-bipolar system).

[1] G Goertz, *Context of International Politics* (Cambridge, Cambridge University Press, 1994).

Table 1: Types of humiliation (and types of reactive diplomacy)

<table>
<tr><th colspan="3" rowspan="2"></th><th colspan="2">Targets of humiliation</th></tr>
<tr><th>Status</th><th>Type of integration in the international 'scene'</th></tr>
<tr><td rowspan="4">Explanatory variables in the production of humiliation</td><td rowspan="2">Socialisation of international life</td><td>Structured system</td><td>Type 1.
Lowering of status → weak revanchism (contained by the international system) Germany and Japan after 1945</td><td>Type 2.
Denial of equality → strong sovereigntism National movements.
Czechoslovakia 1968
Hungary 1956</td></tr>
<tr><td>Non-structured system</td><td>Type 1.
Lowering of status → strong revanchism
Germany 1918–1939
Russia after 1989</td><td></td></tr>
<tr><td rowspan="2">Emergence of actors from outside the club</td><td>Structured system</td><td>Type 2.
Denial of equality → strong sovereigntism
Clientelisation of States
Post-colonial
Françafrique</td><td>Type 3.
Relegation →
Confrontation
NAM, G77
Regime of NPT</td></tr>
<tr><td>Non-structured system</td><td>Type 2.
Denial of equality
China, Ottoman Empire in the 19th century
Type 3.
Relegation:
Ethiopia 1936
China from 1931 to 1937
Czechoslovakia 1938</td><td>Type 3.
Relegation →
Confrontation
Type 4.
Stigmatisation
Diplomacy of exclusion
Iran after 2005</td></tr>
</table>

(continued)

Table 1: ***(Continued)***

<table>
<tr><td colspan="3"></td><td colspan="2">Targets of humiliation</td></tr>
<tr><td colspan="3"></td><td>Status</td><td>Type of integration in the international 'scene'</td></tr>
<tr><td rowspan="2">Explanatory variables in the production of humiliation</td><td rowspan="2">Large gaps between the values of different States</td><td>Structured system</td><td>Type 2.
Denial of equality →
strong sovereigntism
Denunciation of non-Western regimes (Nasser's Egypt from Suez crisis to 1973)</td><td>Type 3.
Practice of tutelage</td></tr>
<tr><td>Non-structured system</td><td>Type 3.
Relegation →
protest
Type 4.
Stigmatization
→ Deviance
'Rogue states' or 'states of concern'
Islamophobia
→ Deviant diplomacy</td><td>Type 4.
Stigmatisation
Sanctions
Interventions
→ Deviant diplomacy, NIC</td></tr>
</table>

To these *explanatory variables*, there corresponds a set of *variables to be explained*, and these mark the *forms* that the effect of humiliation may take (see Table 1). These forms are distinguished by their *targets*: one may seek to humiliate the 'other' in terms of the other's *status*, or in terms of the other's variable right to *integration* in the international context. Finally we shall show how different kinds of diplomacy correspond to these different types of humiliation, diplomacies that are produced as responses from those who are victims of it, who become conscious of their situation and choose not to play into the hands of those who would humiliate them, who do not take refuge in submission or apathy. If diplomacy can be defined as the 'art of managing separateness',[2] then the phrase 'diplomacies of humiliation' can have two meanings. Either

(a) we are talking about the *use*, by the perpetrator, of techniques or discourses that dramatise the separation aspect in order to gain advantages and a dominant position. (Instead of bridging a gap, this practice

[2] P Sharp, *Diplomatic Theory of International Relations* (Cambridge, Cambridge University Press, 2009) 10.

widens it, and results in a series of undesirable effects that cast doubt on expected advantages.) Or

(b) we are talking about the *reaction* of the humiliated party, facing different types of humiliation, and this party may retreat into apathy or even resignation, but may on the other hand create a variety of different responses, many of which make things worse, but some of which develop into some kind of appeal to the 'international community'.

Type 1: Humiliation by Lowering of Status

Historically, humiliation by means of the lowering of status appears before all the other forms, as a simple arrangement linked to the evolution of war and to relations between states. This practice consists in imposing upon the defeated party a brutal reduction in its status in the ranks of powers, creating on that basis an emotional shock that has a great effect upon public opinion. The practice therefore aims to give the defeat a subjective reality, to the point where this reality is unbearable for those who must endure it. For those people, defeat means demotion, a lowering of the status that the people had claimed for their nation. It can be understood that such humiliation is closely bound up with the arrival of certain societies (and the public opinion that prevails among them) on the international scene, an entry that is correlated with a rise in national feeling. It might also be admitted that the practice affects status more than a claim to integration. Integration, generally, is only affected at the margins (such as when Germany was isolated by the League of Nations and then by the UN, when it was created). Generally, humiliation through lowering of status does not direct its attack against the principle of equality between competing or aggressive States.

René Girard had already shown this: relations between France and Germany, from this point of view, are archetypal. The defeat of Prussia at Jena (in 1806) constituted in objective terms a brutal challenge to the status of a State that had benefited from spectacular expansion during the 18th century. This figured heavily in the appearance of national feeling, in which pride in power, entry into the Enlightenment, and the formation of a rationalised State were mingled together. Defeat set in motion a mechanism that would become classic: a loss of status too great to be accepted, counterbalanced by a desire for revenge, mixed with hate, of denigration and of a secret fascination, leading to a desire to imitate the enemy.[3]

This stance thus leads to *revanchism*, based at the same time on a strong diplomatic mobilisation intended to rebalance relationships of power in a particular group's favour, and an intense political mobilisation for the purpose of constructing a collective memory that perpetuates and aggravates

[3] R Girard, *Achever Clausewitz* (Paris, Carnets Nord, 2007).

popular animosity towards the other. Thus the confrontation opposes the dominator, who mobilises material and symbolic goods in order to lower the status of the defeated party, and the defeated party, which thinks that it can only emerge from the game through unilateral actions of affirmation and symbolic displays about revenge, leading to real tension. After 1871, on the side of the winners, we find the official stamp on the birth certificate of the Reich in the Gallery of Mirrors, the annexation of Alsace-Lorraine, making possible the subsequent restoration of the Castle of Haut-Kœnigsbourg, decorated with the Imperial coat of arms and the installation of a Bismarckian system of containment applied to France. On the side of the losers, we see a vigorous Germanophobic mobilisation, the ferment of nationalism under the Third Republic, and the vindictive diplomacy of republicans, placing the security of France in danger because of its excesses, as the Schnaebelé Affair revealed in 1887. After 1918, the roles were reversed and the characteristics were made worse: we saw that Clemenceau, less of a realist than Bismarck, went much further in his effort to lower the status of the defeated parties during the negotiation of the Treaty of Versailles. It is apparent that tensions rose to extreme levels: there was the exaltation of the German race, the theory of Lebensraum, methodical expansion at the expense of Austria, Czechoslovakia and Poland, to say nothing of conspiracy theories, whose principal victims turned out to be the Jews. A deputy of the Zentrum, Konstantin Fehrenbach, had predicted this as early as 1919, in this warning: '*Memores estate, inimici ex ossibus ultor*' (Remember, oh enemies, that from mere bones an avenger may be born).[4]

We note that these two historical sequences occurred in an international context that was not very structured, as was the case from 1871 to 1914, during which time the Concert of Europe was collapsing. Its partial continuance played an important role in protecting France from a wrong turn that would have led to a policy of exclusion, which would have endangered the very integration of the nation into the international system. Evidence for this is found in France's presence at the Berlin conferences on the Balkans (1878) and on Africa (1885), where new advantages were gained at each conference. The same remark is valid for the between-the-wars period, during which Germany was reintegrated, through the continuation of Concert of Europe meetings (Locarno, 1925, where Germany prepared, with Gustav Stresemann, its entry into the League of Nations; Stresa, 1935; the pact of Four, 1936; Munich, 1938, etc).

By contrast, the structured nature of the post-1945 system contributed to the neutralisation of German or Japanese 'revanchism', aided in this by the policy of the Allies, who were anxious to draw a distinction between the

[4] HA Winkler, *L'Histoire de l'Allemagne* (Paris, Fayard, 2005) 338.

defeated country and the overthrown regime. In fact the idea of revanchism was used more by adversaries, especially Russia, which often used this position to discredit and stigmatise the German Federal Republic, which was then mainly occupied with reconstruction, carried out in the context of Germany's new European and Atlantic alliances.

This is not quite how things went in Japan, in a regional context that was, clearly, less structured: in accepting the office of Prime Minister in 1957, Nubusuke Kishi, a former collaborator with Hideki Tojo during the Second World War, who was condemned to prison by the International Tribunal, reinitiated a nationalist discourse that could be likened to timid revanchism. He set free a number of prisoners who had been imprisoned for deeds done during the war, produced several texts reintroducing new 'principles' and 'objectives' for Japan's national defence, and most of all decided to renegotiate the 1951 treaty, which in practical terms placed Japan under American tutelage. The new treaty he managed to obtain, which came into force on 19 June 1960, replaced the notion of tutelage by that of 'mutual assistance'. Some time earlier the Kishi-Eisenhower communiqué had introduced the idea of 'sovereign equality and mutual cooperation' between the two countries.[5] Anti-Chinese incidents occurred about this time, actually leading to an interruption in commercial relations with Beijing. His grandson, Shinzo Abe, led the Japanese government in 2006–07, and again after 2012. He quickly took up some nationalist and even revisionist themes: he reintroduced the teaching of 'patriotism' in schools and the salute to the flag, he resumed paying homage at the Yasukuni shrine, and he supported a revision of the 1947 constitution written by Americans in order to permit Japan to operate its military defence in complete freedom, and to give Japan the sovereign right to make war. At the same time, he multiplied the number of provocations aimed at the Chinese, who responded in kind.

Contained or not, this cycle of status-lowering and revenge was part of a potential medium for violence. It was denounced as such by John Maynard Keynes, observer of and actor in two end-of-war periods. Such events constitute, in contemporary history, a major factor in the reinvention of war. Japan in 1922 was already caught up in such a cycle when, at a conference in Washington, Great Britain and the United States limited the tonnage of the ships in the Japanese Navy to 3/5 of the tonnage of their own, in order to secure their already evident superiority. At a more modest level, the cycle appeared in a brutal manner, though in a context of high activity, in the attitude of Russia. Russia was pushed off its superpower pedestal in 1990, and its diplomacy ever since has been motivated by the desire to obtain 'sweet revenge' through blocking motions or making proposals, with the aim of recovering its former status. Russia wants to lessen the sting of

[5] G Delamotte, *La Politique de défense du Japon* (Paris, PUF, 2010) 44 ff.

the lowering of status that was clumsily and unnecessarily inflicted upon it, through the use of symbols, through containment, and through instances of exclusion. This is how we interpret the succession of blocking actions that allowed Russia to have influence during the conflict in Bosnia (1994), in the several conflicts in Kosovo (1999), and in Iraq (2003) and Syria (from 2011 on). And we should not forget its opening towards Iran, admitted to the Shanghai Cooperation Organisation, outside the apparent 'connivance' between Russia and Western powers in the 5 + 1 group.

Type 2: Humiliation through Denial of Equality

Exposure to what was outside the Westphalian world quickly led to another kind of humiliation. As we have already seen, the Westphalian system, confirmed at the Congress of Vienna in 1815, was first constructed and understood by the system's protagonists as a game of relations between equals; the princes were sometimes even related by blood, though they could be bitter enemies in particular circumstances. The discovery of the 'outside' other introduced a new dimension. The 'other' was first of all the bearer of a different ideology, even on European soil; beyond this, it was a matter of a culture that was other, a religion that was other, even a different 'race', as they said then; this other could no longer be reduced to the 'same' relation. This other was not their equal, and it was inconceivable that he should become an equal. The rule of Westphalia did not reach him. Belonging to 'barbarism', to 'bestiality', or a 'rabble' affected by 'imbecility' or 'savagery', this other could not claim any status on the same level, nor become an integral part of the system of which he could never be the joint manager.[6] Lord George Curzon, Viceroy of India, denounced the people he governed, noting that they 'lacked the sense of the truth'.[7]

This 'other', which entered international life by the back door, could only exist under tutelage, and had to be submitted as quickly as possible to conversion and correction, in other words being brought into line with the 'standards of civilisation'. Inferior to all at that level, he could not enjoy the same rights, but might suffer even greater punishments. The fact that the prohibition on the opium trade was judged in the West to be 'an attack on freedom' illustrates this: humiliation here is expressed in the refusal to grant any equality of rights.

The socialisation by means of international life obviously becomes the first reason that justifies the abolition of all sovereignty, de facto if not de jure. Metternich, at Laibach (modern day Ljubljana) in January 1821

[6] For some of the other epithets used by western intellectuals in the 19th century, *cf* D Losurdo, *Contre-histoire du libéralisme* (Paris, La Découverte, 2013) 253, 114, 280, 349, 281.

[7] ibid 118.

spoke in humiliating terms of the popular revolt that was going on at Naples; after having been called 'a calamity' at the conference of Troppau (1820), the insurgents were next described as 'vice', while Ferdinand I of the Two-Sicilies, a confirmed despot, was described in contrasting terms as 'virtue'.[8] He was requested to write a fictional letter calling for an intervention by the powers of the Concert of Europe, so that they could put down the insurgency.[9] The same thing happened the next year when, following the Congress of Verona, the France of Louis XVIII sent '100,000 sons of St. Louis' to fight a liberal Spain, characterised as a 'yellow fever'. The promoter of this effort, Chateaubriand, called it 'the great political event of my lifetime'. In the words of the King of France, it was a question of 'protecting' the kingdom of Spain from 'ruin', and of 'reconciling it with Europe'.[10] Much later, the USSR would give itself up to a similar game of humiliation in Budapest in 1956, and in Prague in 1968.

This level of ideological combat against new ideas fairly quickly developed into a broader stigmatisation of every kind of otherness. However, the episode of Naples, like that of Spain (immortalised by the capture of the Trocadero), constituted one of the first dents in the modern principle of sovereignty, and opened the way for many future conflicts and acts of defiance. This form of denial experienced a new wave of popularity, and even became commonplace, as Asia and Africa saw the emergence of new actors that were not politically but 'ethnically' external to the membership of the club. So it was not only popular movements that could be targeted, but whole peoples, and with them, empires, kingdoms and States. The principle of intervention became generally accepted, as a mechanical method for meting out whatever humiliation was decreed.

This second type of humiliation translates itself first by a reconstruction of the status of the intruder, who is taken as qualitatively inferior to a Westphalian state: capitulation, placement under tutelage, territorial concessions where soldiers or European merchants are given a foothold under no supervision but their own; then, later, in a postcolonial situation, the clientelisation of States, 'cooperation agreements', 'Françafrique', etc. In a structured international context, such a rearrangement of statuses is limited, so as to maintain a network of alliances working to maintain the security of the powerful and the 'protection' of the weak. Ultimately, as was often the case during the Cold War, formal sovereignty gave the illusion of placing Sukarno's Indonesia, the Guinea of Sekou Touré or the Ghana of Kwame Nkrumah in the Soviet camp, and the Zaire of Mobutu, the Iran of the Shah and the Morocco of Hassan II in the Western camp. Absorbed into bipolarity, these regimes became the stakes in a competition between superpowers,

[8] J-A Sédouy, *Le Concert européen* (Paris, Fayard, 2009) 117.
[9] ibid 118.
[10] J Perez, *Histoire de l'Espagne* (Paris, Fayard, 1996) 526.

such that their previous humiliations might be soothed through flattery and cajolery. After 1989, these precautions tended to disappear.

Faced with these practices of denial, little by little a sovereigntist diplomacy was created, first as a reaction, and later as a routine. The sovereignty of today's Chinese diplomacy has its origins in the practices of denial that the Middle Kingdom had to suffer up to 1949, or beyond. The hymn to sovereignty proclaimed at Bandung, which still motivates the 'non-aligned' nations, is of the same type. It has touched almost all of the emergent powers, with India and Brazil in the lead, as the reaction to a difficult liberation from that which collective memory constructs, from something like ancient demons.

This sovereigntist diplomacy is difficult for the Western powers to understand; they view it alternately as arrogance or as a refusal to share. It gives rise to many impasses in international negotiations, it can damage multilateralism, and it makes collective regulation formulas seem uncertain. It has been denounced time and again—in Beijing, during the Cairo conference on population (1994), by emergent powers at each of the negotiation meetings on the climate, and by most of the states of the South when accusations are levelled at them concerning a lack of human rights.

We can take these reactions as incidental, or as delayed reactions to sovereignty that was for a long time badly administered. But they seem to stand for something more: adhesion to a law that has been the condition of European development and which was at the heart of the Westphalian system—and the lack of it has left many new States unable to act, mired in dependency. We find here proof of the extreme fragility of diplomatic equilibria that are reached through practices of humiliation. We also find a trace of the defiance that exists between actors in the present international system, defiance that influences the system in a lasting way, and which inevitably leads to an over-interpretation of the acts of people on opposite sides.

Type 3: Humiliation by Relegation

The denial of equality itself opens up the way to its own radicalisation. Refusing to admit the other as 'like me', and proclaiming this loudly is part of acting methodically to exclude the other from world governance or regional governance, and thus to relegate or demote the other to the status of a passive citizen among the nations, in the international sphere.

In fact, this is a double relegation, corresponding to two logics that mutually reinforce each other: it is objective, to the extent that a level of development appears, thus a level of capacity and power, that is clearly inferior; it is subjective, when it leads the great powers to relegate and then keep in place certain nations that together could be said to form a 'second division'. The double status that is produced in this way can lead some of those who have been relegated to develop an original diplomacy which we shall examine here under the title of 'oppositional diplomacy'.

Inequality with regard to level of development is inevitably perceived as de facto relegation, and is thus a humiliation for those whose countries are less developed. It must be said that the international system that came out of decolonisation is indeed exceptional, completely unique in history, placing States in competition that are at very different levels, which had never happened before, and which could only give rise, automatically, to feelings of injustice and to disputes, more or less restrained. It is notable that this was the atmosphere at the Bandung conference in April 1955. The final resolution of the conference called for efforts to contain what was called a dynamic of distress, and issued an appeal seeking the full participation of wealthier and better developed States in the further development of the poorer States, even at the risk of endangering a sovereignty that had not been acquired so very long ago. In the same vein, the first project that followed the great movement toward decolonisation of the early 1960s was to obtain the creation in 1964, on behalf of new States, of the UNCTD (United Nations Conference on Trade and Development), and then in 1965 the UNDP (United Nations Development Program). This was followed by the experience of many humiliations, constituted by failed attempts to bring public development aid up to 1% of the GNP of rich countries, then attempts to reach 0.7%, after which the level of aid plateaued at 0.35% amid general indifference. The programmed failure of the 'Millennium Development Objectives' proclaimed by the UN did the rest.

But the most sensitive and the most visible element of this kind of humiliation is not concerned with relegation as a state of things, but as an act, that is, the act of a power that chooses to relegate the other to a situation that is inferior to the one he thought he might occupy. In non-structured systems, where the alliance of the weakest does not seem vitally necessary, where the observance of formal rules is not considered necessary, relegation can affect the very status of the victim, although in most cases relegation is related to a request for integration into the international game.

We see the effect, starting in the 19th century, when the Ottoman Empire was excluded from the Concert of Europe, and was only episodically invited to grand conferences—in whose agenda, nonetheless, the Porte had a direct interest, especially as concerned the Balkans. In the same way, as we have seen, the League of Nations and the UN have shown themselves to be very selective, under pressure from the victorious powers, when it came to admitting sovereign States, even those who had not been allied with the defeated parties. We find here a habitual diplomatic stance, excluding or marginalising countries from collective decisions, or from a sector of international life, pushing away those who do not do what the leaders want, or who are simply not members of the club, in its institutionalised or imaginary form.

Today, emergent powers regularly experience humiliation. This may occur in relation to their potential accession to the 'Holy of Holies', the circle of the permanent members of the Security Council, whatever may be the situation in terms of friendly gestures or rhetorical promises, or it may have to do with their participation in more informal decision-making processes. The long process of constitution of a G20, which at one time was going to be substituted for the G8, and which continues to be marginalised in diplomatic terms, is an example; and so are the closely monitored 'contact groups' that are operating. Brazil and Turkey were reproached by many in the Spring of 2010 because they engaged in a diplomatic initiative on the Iranian question.

The Treaty for Nuclear Non-Proliferation, signed in 1968, which closed the door of the club to those who wished for a bomb of their own, obeyed this same logic of relegation, today brought up to date in a way that is as humiliating as it is selective: India was 'pardoned' for its refusal to sign the treaty, and it eventually came to benefit from a nuclear cooperation agreement signed with the United States in 2006; Israel was helped to obtain a bomb and Pakistan benefited from benevolent indifference, whereas Iran saw mobilised against it the opposition of those who said as publicly as possible that Iran would never be allowed to be a member of that particular club.

A 'diplomacy of exclusion', more and more fashionable these days, though still contrary to the very vocation of all diplomacy, appears as the most extreme point of the logic of relegation. Thus, one places Hamas in quarantine, as soon as they win elections in the Palestinian territories (January 2006); Syria is excluded following Security Council Resolution 1559 (September 2004); Gaddafi in Libya was periodically excluded; sometimes it is Cuba, Belarus, Zimbabwe or Sudan; at one point the decision was made that Iran could not participate in negotiations over Syria; in July 2013 Hezbollah was placed on the long list of 'terrorist organisations'. Thus quite a collection of 'relegated' states and actors is formed, who are nonetheless most often at the centre of the conflicts that the international community is responsible for sorting out.

Some of these countries are undoubtedly guilty of serious crimes against international law or human rights; others less so. But the selection is humiliating because it does not apply evenly to all the states that break rules, but remains targeted on actors from the South, from the developing world, on actors from outside the 'closed circles'. In fact, over and above value judgments, legitimate as they may be, humiliation is constructed here in a sort of double break that has deeply marked contemporary international life: there is the importance acquired by the kind of *comparison* that leads each actor to judge his or her lot in life in relation to what his or her competitors experience, especially by what they may avoid; and there is the erasure of the dialectic of power, which previously judged everything as a court of last resort, and which now gives up its place, ceding it to a confrontation of values. There are many elements that aggravate the feeling of relegation and which sharpen the perception of inequality in the international system.

In a context in which the international system is only weakly structured, relegation can also affect the *status* of certain States, which—although formally accepted as sovereign and recognised as such– may find themselves devalued; they may even have their *de facto* existence questioned. This contemptuous abandonment will become even easier and cheaper for the 'international community' if the state in question does not belong to any network of binding alliances, and its disappearance or weakening would not represent any gain for the opposing camp.

The example of Ethiopia is archetypal. Italy's pretentions, to make itself master of a nation recognised as sovereign, were met between 1930 and 1936 by nothing but pro forma protestations.[11] The meetings of the League of Nations during the summer of 1935, before the Italian offensive, then in the autumn, during the offensive itself, had no effectiveness at all, because the powers that met considered that the survival of the threatened State was less important than the hypothetical benefits of a policy that managed Mussolini. This relegation of Ethiopia was confirmed by the Franco-British project, agreed between Pierre Laval and his opposite number in the Foreign Office, Samuel Hoare, who in November 1935 proposed to cede two-thirds of Ethiopia to Italy without even asking Ethiopia's opinion. We know that after the fall of Addis-Ababa (May 1936), the Negus was politely welcomed by the General Assembly of the League of Nations, despite some cries from the public calling him a 'Pickaninny'. After the welcome according to protocol, sanctions without great effect were adopted, to save face—sanctions that the British lifted after three months. Then they recognised Italian rights over the Ethiopian Empire, which ceased to exist less than two years later.

The status of the sovereignty of an African state was thus at an all-time low: this is really the basis of humiliation suffered, not only for those who are direct victims, but also for all who identified with the cause. We certainly know that the event was felt as such by Kwame Nkrumah, at that time a young student, who was shaken by his experience, and it was a determining event in the development of his political career.[12] In fact, Ethiopia was not worth much in the eyes of Europeans. Henri Massis once spoke of the country as 'a collection of ignorant tribes'.[13] Relegation was really based on this amalgam of disdain and strategic opportunity, of cultural and realistic considerations. The same 'international community' greeted news of the Japanese invasion of Manchuria in 1931 in the same way, and

[11] AJ Barker, *Rape of Ethiopia 1936* (New York, Ballantine Books, 1971).
[12] K Nkrumah, *Autobiographie* (Paris, Présence Africaine, 2009).
[13] J Frémeaux, *Les Empires coloniaux* (Paris, Éditions du CNRS, 2013) 454.

their invasion of mainland China in 1937 as well. Here Japan represented a civilisation that had become 'hyper-Western', its ultra-nationalism notwithstanding, nor its impending participation in the Second World War. The relegation of China, then very weak, appeared to belong to the same kind of diplomacy in which a laissez-faire policy was forced, but where humiliation had a delayed effect. The same could be said of the relegation of Czechoslovakia in 1938, although there the notion of 'small country' was more to the fore than that of a nation of savages. As we shall see, this case establishes precedents.

Humiliation by relegation gives rise, among the victims, to a *diplomacy of protest, of opposition* whose vigour and vitality have little by little reshaped the international system which was once completely insulated from it. Partly based on affectivity, partly on strategy, this policy consists in gaining positions and advantages in the international arena by contesting control of structures as well as protesting to the countries that have top billing. The classical game is more or less reversed: instead of practising competition with powers, the policy is to put this competition to the question, and to make that the basis of a foreign policy. This style of politics undoubtedly harks back, in spirit, to Bandung and the origin of the non-aligned movement: at that time, it was based on a challenge to the bipolar structure of the international order which was believed to be unfavourable to the Third World. Its targets have diversified, but it is also true that many, through this policy, have gained visibility and a measure of influence on the agenda, all at low cost. Wherever relegation is practiced, this policy constitutes an almost inevitable response, sometimes at great cost to the international system.

Type 4: Humiliation through Stigmatisation

Finally, we distinguish a type of humiliation by stigmatisation, which focuses on a defamatory denunciation of the other in terms of what differentiates the other from the privileged group. This type of humiliation obviously takes on meaning in a double context: in one, the other displays characteristics—perhaps political but especially cultural ones—that are very different from the corresponding traits among the dominant group, even opposed; in the second, the other simply exists at a much lower level of power. The first condition explains the type's relative modernity: previously it had only existed to symbolise States that were really excluded from the international system, like the Muslim empires during the period of the Crusades, who were stigmatised as 'infidels', with everything that the label implied.[14] The second condition presupposes the structural inferiority of

[14] *cf* the works of de Jean Flori, notably *La Guerre sainte. La formation de l'idéé de croisade dans l'Occident chrétien* (Paris, Aubier, 2001).

the stigmatised party: the denunciation of the powerful USSR as an 'Evil Empire' was practically forgotten in the development of the rivalry, and in the process of establishing a balance of powers. The latter notion implied that ethical denunciation could be practiced as part of 'realism', which tended to neutralise the denunciations, or to identify them with an exclusively ideological use.

We should thus not be surprised to find this type of humiliation in non-structured systems: in the others, it only appears as a marginal phenomenon. It is more insistent when associated with questions of integration, rather than questions of status. For all these reasons it did not really appear until after 1989. Islam would turn out to be its principal target. Islam did not give rise to any stigmatisation throughout the period of bipolarity. On the contrary, Jimmy Carter gladly wagered on the creation of a 'green belt' that could contain the USSR, and Ronald Reagan, champion of the second Cold War, was able to ally with Islamist forces to counter Moscow in Afghanistan and in Sudan. American diplomacy was able to embrace exceptionalism and a Saudi regime lacking democratic values at the same time, without any discomfort.[15]

At the end of bipolarity, the American hegemon was the first to combine asymmetric warfare with the denunciation of the values of the new enemy, who was no longer at its level of power. From this combination, America fashioned a return to the theme of the 'just war' and a use of stigmatisation that was as polemical as political, a mixture of opportunity, selectivity and flexibility as needed. This produced at first the concept of a *rogue state*. Created during Clinton's presidency, the phrase is said to have been coined by Clinton's national security adviser, Anthony Lake, who in 1994 referred to States 'that were not capable of dealing with the outside world'. This new category in international relations is distinguished from the classical notion of an enemy and from the grammar of power, and justifies itself through moral condemnation and opprobrium.[16]

These notions, of course, are hardly precise. Yes, the concept is structured: little by little, criteria appeared, including infringement of international law or of human rights and opposition to terrorism and to possession of weapons of mass destruction. The list of rogue States has stabilised to include Cuba, North Korea, Iran, Iraq (under Saddam Hussein) and Libya, although at one point Libya was taken off the list. Over the longer term, diplomats like Madeleine Albright preferred to speak, more primly, of states 'of concern', the idea of concern appearing to fit in better with the

[15] M Ayoob, *The Many Faces of Political Islam* (Ann Arbor, University of Michigan Press, 2007).

[16] W Blum, *Rogue State: A Guide to the World's Only Superpower* (London, Zed Books, 2006); R Litwak, *Rogue States and US Foreign Policy* (Washington, Wilson Center Press, 2000).

classical dogmas of realism. With American neoconservatives, we returned to the notion of an 'Axis of Evil' that was even more openly demonising, used by George W Bush in his State of the Union address of 29 January 2002. Later, in February 2005, Condoleezza Rice would speak in terms of the 'outposts of tyranny': now the conversation would include Cuba, North Korea, Iran, Burma, Zimbabwe and Belarus, but Syria—whose help the United States needed—was excluded from the list, much like Saudi Arabia, which has no democratic attributes at all.

This flexibility lessens over time, to the extent that the target changes, so that practices that targeted a regime begin to target a culture, thus aggravating the humiliating effect of a discourse of stigmatisation. After 9/11, Islam entered the sphere of foreign policy, especially when styled, in an intentionally imprecise way, as 'Islamism'. We would have to go all the way back to the Wars of Religion to find such a religious reference attached to a state policy, and even so the meaning is not the same. Protestants and Catholics battled as powers on the same level, based on a direct theological opposition. The designation of 'Islamism' in contemporary diplomatic practice is completely different. It is a play on the ambiguity of portmanteau words, and the object is to slander the opponent by associating him or her with pejorative categories that make further analysis unnecessary: 'Islamo-fascism', 'Criminal Salafism', 'Islamist terror'—so many epithets that allow one to take the other and (worse still) all those who look like him and place them in the status of potential enemies of peace, law, and democracy. These constructions make all negotiation illegitimate, and all but prohibit it.

The imprecision that remains, concerning the exact place of religion and civilisation associated with this type, is sufficiently well marked that it can create mistrust among some, humiliation for others; it can distil a bitterness that goes as far as hatred, more and more diffuse, more difficult to control. Thus, branding an enemy becomes worse than any strike: it suffices to orient behaviour and to provide guidelines for diplomacy; an excellent example is furnished by the speeches on the progress of the Arab Spring, characterised by an ultra-simplistic approach.

Stigmatisation through branding is applied to potential deviant elements, and in so doing you convince those who are stigmatised that an active diplomacy of deviance can be precisely the most effective response, because it carries visibility with it, and a potential for mobilisation. Thus there arises, as a response, a diplomacy of deviance, which we shall define as the art of gaining advantages within the international system by openly breaking its stated rules.

***

Thus four types of humiliation give rise to distinctive models of diplomacy, whose synthesis is presented in tabular form below (Table 2). We note that these reactive diplomacies are not inevitable, especially when it is a matter of very weak States that may prefer forms that are more passive, and forms of 'wise' clientelism. Their vigour and their rise are, however, not negligible events, since they appear to bring rewards, in particular circumstances and even structurally. We may observe that their forms vary, depending on whether they were produced by a great power (Russia), an emergent power (China, Brazil, India, South Africa) or smaller powers.

Table 2: Reactive Diplomacies

Types of humiliation	**Types of diplomacy**	**International Cooperation**
1. Lowered status	Revanchist — Strong (non-structured system) — Moderate	Instrumentalised cooperative game
2. Denial of equality	Sovereigntism — Offensive (great powers) — Militant (emergent) — Self-protection (small powers)	Limited connivance Conditional mistrust
3. Relegation	Contestation — Reformist (emergents) — Radical (small powers)	Conditional cooperation Use of tribunician instruments
4. Stigmatisation	Deviance — Symbolic — Active	Use of tribunician instruments Rejection of all cooperation

All these have an effect on international cooperation. In their extreme forms, revanchist diplomacies relegate this to nothing but an instrumental exercise. Sovereigntist diplomacies engender mistrust and spontaneous, pro-active defence, modulated by a prudent and limited game of collusion, as with Russia today,[17] or by reformist militantism expressed by emergent powers looking to obtain a more advantageous position in the international system. Oppositional and deviant diplomacies tend to promote tribunician stances, and to use multilateral meetings and conferences as the real forums.

This first glance has revealed how the transformations of the international system give more importance and more urgency to the question of humiliation. Humiliation, along with the parameters of the present international system, has become a dangerously central element. But is the connection

[17] B Badie, *The Diplomacy of Connivance* (Basingstoke, Palgrave, 2012).

here really mechanical? In analysing certain sequences, have we simply discovered the inevitable? Looking at the weight of strategic choices, certain constructions chosen and analyses articulated, it seems that the hypothesis is barely credible. In fact, the role of the actors seems to be the most important. From humiliations created, up to reactions recorded, all leading to the obvious disturbed state of the international game, the part played by individual choice is more than determinative.

Part Two

An International System Fed by Humiliation

TODAY, THE INTERNATIONAL system is suffering from humiliation and its associated pathologies. Humiliation runs through the system, causing various strategies to be adopted, and elicits reactions of all kinds that lead to a desperate deadlock. No one is claiming that humiliation is the only, or even the principal, factor in all international conflicts; as we have seen, humiliation takes so many different forms that we cannot speak of it as a singular phenomenon. It may be conscious or unconscious, but it is always expressed through organised political forms that could be reformed, rethought, and corrected. In this sense it is part of a real international public policy.

This meaning-laden condition of humiliation within the current system is the result of three factors that reflect the characteristics of our international system. Each will be discussed in a separate chapter. First, there is the matter of *constitutive inequality*. Our international order is the result of a badly-conducted decolonisation process. That failure remains a heavy weight upon the system, and affects more than two-thirds of contemporary States. The colonial past, taken in the sense of a submission to dependency, is the key to the original inequality between States that affects the present shape of globalisation. Alongside this is a *structural inequality* that gives only some States access to the international decision-making process, and thus access to resources; this inequality is all the more difficult to endure, because the situation it creates no longer corresponds to reality as regards power relationships, demographics, and economics. It no longer matches the cultural or political relationships between States, or even between political actors. Finally, the first two forms of inequality are potentiated, as it were, by a *functional inequality* that has to do with the very conditions of governmental functioning within the present system, which are oligarchical, outdated and exclusionary.

4

Constitutive Inequality: The Colonial Past

CONTEMPORARY ANALYSES HAVE, without doubt, largely ignored the need to account for colonisation, and its total effect on the organisation and functioning of the international system of today. Significantly, Hans Morgenthau, in his central work, only deals with colonisation in order to add a new twist to the story of rivalries and struggles for power between European States of a previous era, and in order to mention the 'colonial revolution' that was taking shape on the horizon, leading old dependencies to don in their turn the uniform of the Nation-State.[1] The idea gained currency in the post-war period: we were thought to be entering an era where everything between States could be negotiated. But things were not so simple. The effects of the colonial past are components present in the modern international game. But hanging over this game there is a 'Bandung syndrome', which returns us to the atmosphere and the final declaration of the great Afro-Asian conference held in Java, bringing together the first of the de-colonised, properly rejoined by China upon the initiative of Zhou Enlai, and by a few national liberation movements, such as the Algerian FLN, represented by Aït Ahmed.

Let us return to April 1955. The Indian leader, Nehru, the Egyptian Nasser, and the Indonesian Sukarno, host of the summit, were present, joined by Mohammed Ali Bogra of Pakistan and John Kotelawala from Sri Lanka. These, together, were the organisers of the conference. One can easily perceive the quest that unites them, so different individually: some progressives, some conservatives. Anti-communist and highly Westernised, Sir John Kotelawala had the ambition of 'making Asia's voice heard'.[2] 'Where are we today [we, the people of Asia and Africa]?', asked the Indonesian Prime Minister, Ali Sostroamidjojo who, significantly, had been the first representative of his country at the United Nations.[3]

[1] H Morgenthau, *Politics among Nations. The Struggle for Power and Peace* (New York, A Knopf, 1964 (1948)) 355 ff.

[2] *Asia, Africa: Bandung, Towards the First Century* (Djakarta, Département des Affaires étrangères, 2005) 40.

[3] ibid 40.

The countries participating were very diverse, judging by those present: apart from the five organising states, also participating were Vietnam, Sudan, Ethiopia, Iran, Turkey, Saudi Arabia, Ghana, and also China and Japan. Overall, 30 nations were invited, and only one failed to send a representative. There was one geographical common denominator: all the invitees were either African or Asian states. The true shared identity was a non-Western character that had led them all, in various degrees and in different forms, into situations of dependency and tutelage with regard to the powers that were then forcing everyone to accommodate them as they fought the Cold War. Japan, for example, was forced at one point to submit to the game of capitulations.

When we read the motions that were adopted, we can hardly be mistaken about what united these countries. Each of the ten points of the final declaration, directly or indirectly, points to the fact of colonialism.

1. respect for fundamental (human) rights;
2. sovereignty and territorial integrity;
3. the equality of races and nations;
4. against all intervention in internal affairs of other States;
5. respect of the right of every nation to defend itself;
6. against all collective defence arrangements that might serve the interests of great powers;
7. condemnation of the use of force against the territorial integrity or political independence of any country;
8. all conflicts must be reconciled through peaceful means;
9. development of cooperation;
10. respect for 'justice' and 'international obligations'.

In his closing speech at Bandung, Sukarno could not have been more explicit: 'We are united … by a common hatred for colonialism in all its forms. We are united by a common hatred of racism. We are united by a common determination to preserve and stabilise peace in the world'.[4]

Exceptions and Outrages

What, in fact, allowed Iran, China, Egypt and India to meet in this way on common ground? The answer is a reference to colonial practices, taking this in its largest and most structural sense: a novel system of domination. Some States had the suspicion that it was not completely abolished, continuing to restrain or even annihilate sovereignty, and imposing its rules through the effect of two properties, exceptionality and excess, which we

[4] ibid 52.

take here as fundamental and continuous properties of colonialism, through which the effect of humiliation is made possible.

The purpose here is not to issue a moral judgment, nor to prolong unreasonably the debate on the causes and effects of colonialism. The point is to understand how the consequences of this gap affect the current international situation. How could it be otherwise? A clear majority of States in the world have belonged, briefly or over a greater extent of time, to this category in all its diverse forms: colonial administration, mandate, protectorate or just a zone of what was once euphemistically called 'influence'. Without ever having been officially colonised, China, Persia, Turkey and Thailand, and even Japan for a time, through capitulations or through actual imposition of supervision, have created memories that could only leave them sensitive to the condemnations issued at Bandung, which underscored for them their own solidarity with the young States that had just gained formal independence.

In its essence, colonialism is not a regulated institutional form. It established a mode of domination over people founded on a perceived inequality. This characteristic must be placed in perspective, relative to an international order whose primary legitimacy, recalled in the United Nations Charter, is based on the sovereign equality of States. The memory of this inequality, and the risks of its being continued beyond the point when States gained independence, create the conditions for a humiliation that is—if anything—more endemic, given that those who were in power at the turn of the new century experienced the old system during their lifetimes.

We note that colonialism was all the more vigorous in its manifestations because it prospered in the context of the breakdown of the international system. From the second half of the 19th century, up to 1945, the near-absence of polarisation left colonial powers' hands free and placed them, de facto, in a place where they were protected from all stigmatisation coming from a competitor that did not exist. On the contrary, a spirit of connivance allowed many such powers to make their bargains under favourable conditions: all in all, the effect of competition, such as was manifested at Fachoda, was smaller than that of the connivance which was expressed at the congress of Berlin (1885), when the European powers divided up the Congo Basin, and in the pursuit of this initiative, all of Africa. Only defeat revealed bad faith: for instance, Germany was deprived of its colonies at Versailles in 1919 upon the pretext that it had badly treated its captive populations.

The game of connivance could only inflame the humiliation of those at the expense of whom it was exercised. Fundamentally, the game was constructed in a mechanical manner. Insofar as it was based on exceptionality, colonial domination normalised the denial of equality. When functioning in an excessive manner, it reproduced itself through a learning process that validated stigmatisation as a mode of government. At this price, the construction of a memory was equivalent to the invention of a culture that was sworn to endure; graver still, the establishing of the system called for its continuation, even after independence, by other means. The effect of the humiliation thus generated drew its strength as much from subjective sources as from objective ones.[5]

Colonial domination is fundamentally based on the idea of exception. Europe is distinguished in history for having invented a culture of law, particularly insofar as it was connected to the work of Romanists, but its colonial adventures were built as exceptions to the rule. We see here the origin of a lasting contradiction when today, often with good intentions, Western powers call for the immediate installation of a State based on the rule of law in a former colony, in a case where the existing leaders, whether sincerely or cynically, cultivate a memory of the colonial system, which in its heyday was lawless enough. Western systems like those in France or Great Britain are considered parliamentary, but the management of their colonies was outside the realm of the Parliament. Colonial order in France was not in the legislative domain, but was a matter, in essentials, for Presidential decree. For everything else, especially the government that functioned in daily life, order in colonies was maintained by colonial governors and administrators. In British colonies, a preference for assemblies appears to have conferred a degree of power on local Parliaments, but these continued to be controlled by the colonial authorities, who decided who was to be named to the assembly, so that their control would be maintained.[6]

This exceptionalism is continued in daily life through differences in the status of individuals, which concretise inequality between people. In the case of France the 'Code de l'indigénat' (code concerning indigenous persons) appears as a compendium of circumstances leading to the forced lowering of status. This Code was put in force in Algeria and in Cochin-China from 1881 onwards; later, it was applied in Senegal and, starting in 1904, it was extended over all of French West Africa. The Code was drawn up without regard to any general principles of law, and it provided for punishments for a whole range of practices that were not prohibited by the law. This all lay in the arbitrary power of colonial authorities, and everything was based on their perception of what was needed to maintain order. Thus beginning in 1881 we see lists of new crimes, which would soon be used to charge elite members of the indigenous population: 'disrespectful acts', 'meeting without permission', 'no permit to travel', and 'saying offensive things'. There was punitive confiscation of property, especially land, and this amounted to appropriation without any formalities; imprisonment was possible without

[5] We are in agreement here in part with the argument developed by the literature known as 'postcolonial'.

[6] J Frémeaux, *Les Empires coloniaux* (Paris, Éditions du CNRS, 2013) 106–109.

any judicial involvement. In all, 1,500 cases of these 'special' infractions led to charges in Congo-Brazzaville between 1908 and 1909.[7] Obviously, there was no provision for appeal.

In terms of personal status, the blending of metropolitan laws and custom-based laws was the responsibility of the colonial authorities, and this produced a complex code that did nothing to facilitate an understanding of the laws, nor to produce in the public the feeling of being governed as other people were, in conformity with the will of the public. But the main thing, on the political level, was that the distinction introduced between citizenship and nationality would exclude the local population from the management of any city's affairs. At best, this population was conceived of as a group of passive citizens who never obtained 'full French citizenship' by way of naturalisation. This way, only Algeria, Cochin-China, the Antilles, a few cities in Senegal and the Indian *comptoirs* (French settlements in India) would send a handful of deputies or senators to Paris. Under the Popular Front government the Blum–Viollette project opened a tiny window for about 20,000 Algerians, who would have been able to vote without giving up their personal status, but it was not even presented to the clerks of Parliament.[8] This demonstrates that ideologies and political choice had, in reality, very little effect on a system that remained at the fringes of the debate until the Second World War broke out.

We may complete these observations by broadening them to cover the areas of economics and society. The rules of real estate and property in colonies tended to be deeply marked by inequality that was all the more humiliating because those rules were often used for confiscations and expulsions, and they dramatically worsened the inequality of income between colonists and indigenous people. The turmoil occurring today in Zimbabwe cannot be understood unless we recall that when independence was declared, 4,000 white farmers were farming 11.5 million hectares (1 hectare = 2.47 acres) of land including the best land available, while 850,000 African farmers, farming in a traditional manner, shared 16 million hectares, including the poorest land available. Going back to the early 1980s, the question of agrarian reform was the cause of all debates, as well as all the blockages, all of which led to a hardening of the line followed by the colonial regime, whose populist and authoritarian excesses continued to be demonstrated.[9] Humiliation is not abolished by decree: there is even a moment when the memory of humiliation, still hanging on, can be used to implement strategies for the personalisation of power and the activation of a dictatorship.

[7] M Phyllis, *Leisure and Society in Colonial Brazzaville* (Cambridge, Cambridge University Press, 1995) 83–87.

[8] Frémeaux, *Les Empires coloniaux* 265–268 and 425.

[9] B Badie, 'Avenir incertain pour le Zimbabwe' (1988) 11 *Études* 437–448.

Its façade is emotional, but its substance quickly becomes the centrepiece in some of the most uncompromising reactive strategies.

The facts of the case in Zimbabwe were replicated almost everywhere else, especially in places where colonisation involved settlers. In Algeria, before independence, the best lands, like those around Mitidja, were shared between a little more than 5,000 European agriculturalists, and the rest was left for the support of 500,000 Algerian families. The first group controlled an average of 3,000 hectares per farm; the Algerian families ended up with an average of 4 hectares each.[10] In Kenya, in 1945, Europeans represented less than 0.5% of the population, but they controlled 20% of all arable land. As exceptional as it might seem, the case of Palestine is equally remarkable: just before the beginning of the war, 66,000 Jewish colonists had been able to build up a real estate portfolio equivalent to 20% of all cultivable land in Palestine. Today, looking just at the occupied West Bank, 42% of the land there has been confiscated from Palestinians. In the Jordan River valley, 37 Israeli settlements and 9000 colonists hold (with the help of the Israeli Army) 87% of all useable land. The Oslo agreement formalised this inequality, stating that 80% of water reserves must belong to Israel, and only 20% to the Palestinians, although a United Nations report found that 90% of the Bedouin community was living on a quarter of the recommended minimum supply of water, as established by the World Health Organisation (WHO).[11]

The denial of equality is thus found in everyday life under colonialism. Through daily humiliations, joined with physical suffering, a system of representations is built that prepares us to for a political order that mixes populism, xenophobia, authoritarianism, arbitrary decisions, corruption and impromptu actions of all kinds.

Excess is the natural counterpart to this, almost mechanically. The colonial order is an exception to begin with, and so the breaking of rules becomes the norm, and nothing can stop it. In this sense, this type of domination stabilises as normalised brutality, in which excess and outrage declare their partnership. Even the chance of encountering a virtuous colonial administrator is a risk attenuated, perhaps even abolished. Symbolic excess is a daily issue: small humiliations scattered around in the form of mockery, derisive and hurtful expressions of the kind that Aimé Cesairé once associated with the 'decivilisation' of the colonisers. The life of Gandhi was full of such challenges; he was thrown off a train between Durban and Pretoria by a white traveller who could not endure travelling with Gandhi in first class seats; his nudity was criticised, and he was called a 'half-naked fakir'.

[10] Frémeaux, *Les Empires coloniaux* 147–149.

[11] www.whoprofits.org.

The art of punishment derives directly from all this: for example, the decision taken by British military police in India in 1919, ordering the local population to travel on all fours down a street where a European missionary had been assassinated.[12] We could add examples of acts of discrimination of all kinds, in education, in leisure activities, and above all at work; the indigenous people did not receive the same guarantees as white workers, and they obviously were not allowed to sign the same contracts. The worker's identity book, abolished in mainland France, reappeared in Tonkin. Forced labour was a fact of life, even if it was only something that allowed local populations to work off the taxes the colonists demanded from them. And we should not forget the insults, the slurs, the jibes, and the many different places that were 'off limits to dogs and Chinese', or on another continent, 'no Blacks'.

Governing by excess means repression without limits. The periodic return of unheard-of violence, openly engaged in, in order to convince people to stop doing something, but obscure enough in terms of the exact relationships involved that the image of a State of laws is not too badly stained—this heightens the effect of humiliation while it prepares people for a postcolonial world that will not worry too much about having to show all persons the proper respect. Absolute repression equals a total negation of the being upon whom it falls. Its procedures are shocking and disturbing, because they place the system and its preservation far above any responsibility for the human person, above his or her rights, and above the simple recognition of a person as a person.

The Mau-Mau rebellion, which took place between 1952 and 1960, caused the deaths of 32 white people. The secret society, which emerged from Kikuyu populations in Kenya, made its members swear they would kill a white person each time a signal was sent out. It was repressed by the massacre of between 10,000 and 90,000 Kenyans. Some sources claim the number was as high as 300,000; 160,000 prisoners were taken. This was so completely excessive that the British government, in June 2013, a half-century later, paid out £20 million in compensation.

Cameroon is also distinguished by the same history of immoderation. On 20 September 1945, a strike began in a suburb of Douala. A demonstration became violent, although no colonist was killed. The demonstrators were shot at, shops were looted; a vendetta was declared by the colonists, the army was called out and military planes with machine guns were used. The official toll was 9 dead, but in all likelihood the actual number was about 100.[13]

[12] M Brecher, *Nehru* (London, Oxford University Press, 1959) 63.

[13] T Deltombe, M Domergue, J Tatsitsa, *Kamerun ! Une guerre cachée aux origines de la Françafrique (1948–1971)* (Paris, La Découverte, 2010) 43–45.

Was this the long-ago origin of the rebellion in Bamileke country, begun in 1955, which continued until shortly after independence? That rebellion was punished by 120,000 deaths, which amounted to half the people in the region affected, and the repression that occurred left behind the memory of a previously unheard-of level of barbarity, including the decapitation of some rebels, and exhibitions of the severed heads.

The particular conditions of repression in Madagascar deserve the same attention. The revolt that was the cause was already involved in the cycle of humiliation. The island was occupied by the English in 1942. They handed control over to representatives of Free France, who proceeded to order multiple reorganisations, and to apply a strict version of the 'status of the indigenous' rule, with doubled punishments. Local elites had seen the end of the Second World War, with all its tumults, as an occasion to seek reform. Madagascar might have chosen integration with egalitarian guarantees, or total independence, the wish of Joseph Raseta, a deputy of the constituent Assembly, who had been sentenced to have his travel rights suspended for three years for the crime of denouncing an 'evil law'. On 29 March 1947, a few hundred individuals attacked Europeans in several cities near the coast. 18,000 soldiers were sent to reinforce the colonial force. On 6 May, the commandant of the camp at Moramanga had 100 Malagasy activists shot in the wagons in which they were imprisoned. A series of punishments ensued. Some suspects were thrown out of aeroplanes, alive. The repression caused 89,000 victims out of a population of 700,000, even if the total is now thought to have been inflated in order to cause more fear. The date, 29 March, the day when the insurrection took place, is now a holiday celebrating independence.[14]

Algeria, in this regard, retains some of the most painful memories in any nation's history. The story begins with the great uprisings between the years 1871 and 1881, the time of the brotherhood of Ouled Sidi Sheikh, the Mokrani, the sheik El Haddad, leading to acts of 'pacification' which ended only when independence was declared. Before, strictly speaking, any real national movement, several insurrections took place in the 1930s, all related to expropriations of property. That of Margueritte, at the foot of Mont Zaccar, in April 1901, is iconic.[15] Led by Yacoub Mohamed Ben el Hadj, it was based on a denunciation of repeated thefts of land and a host of onerous obligations; for example, according to a witness of the period, the indigenous people were required to pay a fine of 20 francs each time

[14] www.herodote.net/29_mars_1947-evenement-19470329php; http://www.globalmagazine.info/article/382/94/Les-Insurges-de-Madagascar-en-1947.

[15] C Phéline, *L'Aube d'une révolution, Margueritte, 26 avril 1901* (Toulouse, Privat, 2012); miliana.comuv.com/insurrection_Margueritte.html.

a donkey wandered onto the land of a colonist. This particular rebellion led to the assassination of four Europeans, who had their throats cut on 26 April 1901. The arrival of rifle companies led to the death of 16 insurgents. The movement, which was limited to one village, led immediately to several punishments, including the arrest of 107 indigenous people, which was followed by the largest criminal court trial in legal history. It was held at Montpellier, and lasted two years. The defendants received prison terms and multiple fines were imposed; the members of the tribe behind the attacks had even more of their land seized. The trial was much talked about in mainland France, and because of its excesses, gave rise to a feeling of solidarity with the indigenous people. There were some acquittals, and some stolen land was restored to its rightful owners. However, Yacoub died mysteriously in prison a short time later.

Undoubtedly, Sétif remains the most important case of this kind of repression. On 8 May 1945, 10,000 demonstrators marched to demand the release of Messali Hadj, who had just been arrested: 102 people died, including 19 soldiers. Then the repressive actions reached their most excessive level. 10,000 soldiers were mobilised, along with the battle cruisers *Triomphant* and *Duguay Trouin*, which shelled the city from the harbour of Béjaïa; the operation continued until the insurgents surrendered on 22 May. The official death toll was 1,500 'Muslims' (and 14 French soldiers), but some historians have argued that it might have been on the order of 6,000, 10,000 or even 15,000, and Ben Bella claimed 65,000 died. Many other cases could be brought forward, including the Battle of Algiers in 1957, and the instances of torture associated with it, which are only too well known to the world.

We should mention the Libyan memory of Italian repression during the inter-war period, repression that caused the deaths of half the Bedouin population of Cyrenaica; and we could also mention the reprisals that took place in Ethiopia after the assassination attempt aimed at the Viceroy, Graziani, in February 1937, which caused at least 3,000 deaths. We could speak of the *puputan*, a mass ritual suicide practiced by the Balinese at the beginning of the 20th century at the time of the Dutch capture of the last bastion of the Insulinde party. In 1906 the last of those resisting threw themselves at the Dutch machine guns. Sukarno's grandfather was in that group, and Sukarno never forgot this. More recently, in the Christmas 2008 Israeli attack on Gaza, an operation called 'Cast Lead', about 1,500 Gazans died along with 11 Israeli soldiers.

Excess shows up in the disproportion of the death tolls, in the unbalanced means of combat employed by each side, and in general in the difference between the operation as executed and the operation as suffered through. Such excesses underline the disproportion involved; but the impotence that it leads to, at the same time, outlines the pathways of humiliation. Beyond all Pyrrhic victories, these defeats trigger a formidable and often very long sequence of events, in a search for a more meaningful status. This quest may well turn violent, or fall into barbarism or extreme ideologies. One of its characteristic features is its length; the other is the mediation exercised by the actors involved.

Pathways of Humiliation

The creators of States have all known journeys of humiliation, although some of them were close to the colonists and, like John Kotelawala, were defenders of the West, which after Bandung was defined as the Great Accused. Kotelawala was judged to be too closely tied to the independence movement of Ceylon, but he had been expelled at the age of 18 from the Royal College of Colombo, thus losing all hope of social advancement. He and those who agreed with him did not defend the old colonial powers, but intended to attack the Soviet camp for having practised domination themselves.

Thus the journey of humiliation comes to be seen as essential. It produced a political culture, a vision of the world and international relations. It shapes the politics—national and international—of the one who has endured it, but it also creates a model that can be associated with the hero, someone people can identify with, or just the governmental actor one becomes accustomed to, who in his daily activities and in the excesses of his own actions, creates a new conception of politics. In all cases, the pathways of humiliation are highly structured.

When we look at the lives of those who founded the postcolonial States, we find at the individual level the same symptoms that characterise the collective adventures we have been describing: relegation, denial of equality and stigmatisation. Those who want to place themselves in the front ranks of power once independence was won, initially experienced the end of the colonial system as a loss of status in comparison with their family position in traditional society. Torn between a desire for modernity (something often identified with a dominant West), which was seen as the source of new ideas that make life better, and the powerful memory of a bygone society in which one's family held a position of respect, these elite individuals experienced the change as a relegation, and one that gave a firm foundation to their political activism. Zhou Enlai was born to a Mandarin family of Jiangsu that was in financial straits. This forced Zhou to give up some of his plans for studying at university, and led him to enrol as an auditor in courses at the University of Waseda (Tokyo) and also to attend several conferences at Kyoto, before leaving for a period of wandering in Europe as part of a Work-Study programme. He worked briefly at the Renault factories in Billancourt. One of his future subordinates, Yang Shangkun, was the son of a wealthy *rentier*.[16] Hô Chi Minh came from a family of educated bureaucrats, and was the son of a Mandarin, sub-prefect at the Court of Hué: his brutal dismissal in 1911 deeply scarred the future Vietnamese president,[17] who thus embarked upon a long period of adventure abroad. Pham Van Dong, who succeeded him, was also the son of a high-level bureaucrat who was close to the imperial court of the Nguyen family. Pham too became the victim of political choices made by a Governor-General.

We know that Jawaharlal Nehru was born a member of the Brahmin caste, and that the affluence of his childhood contrasted with the number of years he was forced to spend in prison. Ahmed Sukarno, the father of Indonesian independence, was born into a family that belonged to the traditional aristocracy. His father, Raden Soekemi, a minor member of the Javanese nobility, was a respected professor, and his mother came from a family of Javanese Brahmins. His youth was spent in pursuit of a career as an architect, enlightened by Western science. Westernised and polyglot, he sought to free himself from a feudalism he considered mired in the past. Marxism appealed to him, but he was also influenced by Islam.[18] The equation has been formulated: find among the dominators the instruments and tools that will enable you to battle and overthrow them, combining modernity and a sort of restoration to the rank previously occupied.

This was also the kind of turn the journey of Hô Chi Minh took: the man who had signed articles with the pseudonym O Phap ('one who hates the French') boarded the *Amiral Latouche-Tréville* at Saigon and sailed to France. He disembarked at Marseilles, where it astonished him to hear people calling him 'Monsieur'. He discovered the Enlightenment, socialism, anarchism, and the Republican emblems; he benefited from the support of the Human Rights League (la Ligue des droits de l'homme) and ended up, in a most logical progression, as part of the 'Third International'. More than that, he tried to make the voice of Indochina heard at the conference at Versailles, tried to enrol as a student in the Colonial School, and wrote petitions to Albert Sarraut, the Colonial minister at the time (no answer was ever made). Other pathways were possible within his destiny. His form of humiliation involved the fact that his path forward was consistently blocked.[19]

Many future African leaders had the same painful experience of social relegation, experienced by children who came from the highest levels of

[16] Gao Wenqian, *Zhou Enlai. L'ombre de Mao* (Paris, Perrin, 2010) 39, 49, 59; L Bianco and Y Chevrier (eds), *Dictionnaire biographique du mouvement ouvrier international. La Chine* (Paris, Éditions ouvrières, Presses de Sciences Po, 1985) 705, 767 ff.

[17] P Brocheux, *Hô Chi Minh* (Paris, Presses de Sciences Po, 2000) 15–16.

[18] C Adams, *Sukarno. An Autobiography* (Indianapolis, Bobbs-Merrill Co, 1965).

[19] Brocheux, *Hô Chi Minh* 15–21.

traditional authority. Eduardo Mondlane, leader of Frelimo and the first of the Mozambican nationalist leaders, was the son of a tribal chief, had been well educated, and had a degree in anthropology. Julius Nyerere, the first president of Tanzania, was from a noble family. He was the son of a traditional chief, and was able to complete graduate study at the University of Makerere, in Kampala, and then in Edinburgh, Scotland before being prevented from pursuing the university career he desired.

In many cases, this is where the problem lies. These are ambitious personalities, often very gifted, attracted to science, modernity and even to the West. Our heroes experience relegation as a series of doors that close in front of them. Yasser Arafat, future leader of the Palestinian resistance, dreamed as a young man of studying science in Texas, but apparently the United States denied him a visa.[20] Agostinho Neto, nationalist leader in Angola, also wanted to go to America in 1962, but was refused a visa and then turned to Marxism. Both in South Africa and in England, Gandhi sought to pursue a professional career but was unable to do so.

The attraction of the West was often as strong as it was unrequited. The Palestinian Georges Habash, who would soon found the Popular Front for the Liberation of Palestine (PFLP) chose to attend the American University of Beirut (AUB) in order to finish medical school, as soon as his family had been expelled from Palestine. Attempting to put his Western education to use, he was able to open a clinic in a Palestinian refugee camp in Amman. Nyerere was preparing to continue his studies in Edinburgh, and to prepare himself for career as a schoolmaster, a choice he said he had made for himself before getting caught up in politics 'by accident'.[21] Before beginning to lead the nationalist movement in Gold Coast (Ghana), founding the CPP (Convention People Party) and becoming the first president of Ghana, socialist, Marxist-leaning and anti-Western Kwame Nkrumah went to university in Lincoln, Nebraska, USA, experiencing in his daily life the difficulties of being black in the greatest of Western powers.

Ahmed Sukarno chose to attend a Dutch school, and later the technical school in Bandung, the best education available to the local population. Mohammad Ali Jinnah, the founding father of Pakistan, finished his secondary education in a school run by a Christian mission in Karachi, and then studied law in London. At his first school, he agitated in favour of cricket as opposed to billiards. He quickly assimilated British customs. The future leader of the Muslim League had a taste for whisky, bacon and eggs, starched shirts, and silk ties and he had an impressive collection of

[20] S Aburish, *Arafat: From Defender to Dictator* (New York, Bloomsbury Publishing, 1998) 7–32.

[21] A Blumberg, *Great Leaders, Great Tyrants?* (Westport (Connecticut), Greenwood Publishing Group, 1995).

200 suits, always immaculate.[22] The desire for the West is never far from nationalism. Nehru attended Harrow School and then Trinity College, Cambridge, which brought him in contact with the Fabian Society, led him to become a militant supporter of progress and integration into a concert of nations, made him an admirer of Garibaldi—all before getting to know British prisons, where he had all the time he needed to study Marxism.[23] One of his future ministers, the very nationalistic Krishna Menon (1897–1974), studied at the London School of Economics, where he became the attentive and faithful disciple of Harold Laski. One of the 10 marshals of the People's Republic of China, before becoming the Minister of Foreign Affairs, was a poet in his off hours; Chen Yi, studied at the Polytechnic Institute of Grenoble, as did Nie Rongzhen, the father of the Chinese atomic bomb.[24] As for Zhou Enlai, it is said that after Waseda, he had a plan to attend the University of Edinburgh that came to nothing.

These are so many dreams of the West, shattered. In many cases, the difficulty of the immediate social conditions was the reason. In order to reach France, Hô Chi Minh had to work as a kitchen helper and cabin boy; he would also work later as a janitor, and then in Le Havre, as a gardener. Great ambitions can be quickly destroyed: stuck in a meaningless job working for the postal services, Sékou Touré was practically forced into syndicalism and began his political career by creating the 'Union générale des travailleurs d'Afrique noire' (UGTAN: the General Union of the Workers of Black Africa) before becoming president of Guinea. Similarly, Julius Nyerere got tired of teaching English and biology under poor working conditions, and decided to revive the Tanganyika African National Union in 1954.[25] In Dakar, where he attended the *École normale* William-Ponty, Modibo Keïta, father of the independence of Mali, was identified as 'anti-French' and reacted to this stigma by founding, along with Mamadou Konaté and Ouezzin Coulibaly, the Union of Teachers of West Africa ('Syndicat des instituteurs d'Afrique occidentale'). Faced with a ban preventing him from pursuing a real political career, he created (still with Konaté) an association of educated persons in Sudan.

When the 'union solution' is not possible, there is also a 'military solution' that serves as an alternative career path. The young Ahmed Ben Bella chafed at his failure to be promoted, which he attributed to anti-Muslim discrimination; he joined the army of the coloniser and reached the grade of warrant officer. He received the Croix de Guerre and the Médaille militaire

[22] S Wolpert, *Jinnah of Pakistan* (New York, Oxford University Press, 1984) 9 ff.
[23] F Moraes, *Jawaharlal Nehru* (Bombay, Jaico Publishing House, 1968).
[24] Bianco and Chevrier (eds), *Dictionnaire biographique du mouvement ouvrier international* 140 ff.
[25] Blumberg, *Great Leaders, Great Tyrants?* 221 ff.

for acts of bravery during an action at Monte Cassino. He refused to be promoted to officer rank after the acts of repression that struck Sétif, and he left the Army. He would not be alone in making this choice—far from it: Abane Ramdane, who had participated in the Italian campaign, also left the Army after the brutality in Sétif. Among future leaders of the FLN, we find Mostefa Ben Boulaïd, who had also been decorated for bravery in Italy, and Belkacem Krim, Master Corporal of the first Regiment of Algerian riflemen.

These pathways are to be compared with those of Hafez el-Assad and Moammar Gaddafi. The first was a member of the Alawite minority, and had little hope of social advancement. Assad's family had been fairly friendly with the French, something common among Middle Eastern minorities, but his desire to pursue medicine was hampered by a lack of money, and his father had to abandon the idea enrolling him at the medical school of the Saint-Joseph University of Beirut. Thus the military academy at Homs—and a military career—was the only upward pathway that remained. The future Libyan leader also ended up having this choice made for him indirectly; he went into the army not because he preferred it, but because he wanted, as he said, to fight the foreigner, the dominator: the United States, Great Britain, and Italy, influenced by memories of a colonisation that was particularly brutal.[26]

Thus the path of unions and the military were routes destined to manage and channel many individual and collective humiliations, and this had the effect of politicising them as much as possible, giving them an orientation that went far beyond their original function. Military institutions, in particular, were a means of gaining power, and a durable instrument for the formulation of foreign policy. In charge of the symbols of national reconquest, the military route was going to be the active ingredient in the integration of new States—a difficult and bumpy process—into the international system.

All in all, these pathways through humiliation were constructed around the discovery of a double obstacle: the dream of those who have been dominated is to attain equality and integration, and both of these were unattainable. The inability to obtain equal treatment is significant in the story of Samora Machel, who led Mozambique to independence. Machel came from a family of farmers who were forced to sell their products at a lower price than white farmers, deprived of a brother, who had been killed in an accident in a mine that lacked basic protection for workers. Machel worked in the hospital in Lourenço Marques, where he quickly discovered that he was being paid less than white nurses for the same work. This experience led to his first participation in a social movement, when he

[26] S Alianak, *Middle-Eastern Leaders and Islam, A Precarious Equilibrium* (Peter Lang, 2007).

discovered the Mozambique Liberation Front (Frelimo), which he joined. He rose to the leadership of Frelimo when Eduardo Mondlane was assassinated in February 1969.[27]

As for the second obstacle, we see an illustration of it in the unparalleled learning curve created by repression. Never before in History was a political class formed to such an extent in foreign prisons. This exceptional event is obviously related to forms of politics that have been minutely constructed in relation to humiliation. Many, many leaders of postcolonial States found themselves on an international stage as representatives of the powers who had once expelled or imprisoned them. Among those who were expelled we find Li Lisan (1899–1980), the leader of the Chinese Communist Party, one time Minister of Labour, deported from France for having participated in a demonstration at Lyon. This also happened to Cai Hesen (1890–1931). We find that the future marshal Zhu De was expelled from Göttingen (Germany) where he had been studying. The same thing happened to Deng Xiaoping, who lived for five years in France (1920–1926), in these cities: Marseilles, Le Creusot, Bayeux, Montargis, Châtillon-sur-Seine and Billancourt. He was dumped at the border immediately after having occupied the Chinese legation in Paris, rue de Babylone. The future Chinese minister of Foreign Affairs, Marshal Chen Yi, was a stevedore, and later a dishwasher in a Chinese restaurant in Paris in 1919, before working for Michelin in Clermont-Ferrand. He was expelled for having occupied the Franco-Chinese Institute in Lyon in 1921.[28]

Even if they had not been through this type of experience, a great number of leaders from the South could still speak to their European counterparts about their experience of imprisonment. Modibo Keïta, the first president of Mali, was held for a month at la Santé, from February to March 1947. Agostinho Neto, the first president of Angola, was arrested several times and eventually jailed for two years in Cape Verde, and later in Portugal. Kwame Nkrumah, the first president of Ghana, was arrested after a demonstration in Accra in February 1948, released, and then jailed again until the moment he was nominated to be prime minister. Ben Bella, the first president of Algeria, was arrested in 1951 and escaped in 1952. In October 1956 the aeroplane in which he was a passenger was intercepted and forced to land; he was returned to prison until the moment of independence. Jomo Kenyatta was jailed for seven years, then kept for two years under surveillance at his residence, before becoming the first president of Kenya. Pham Van Dong was held in prison for ten years, including seven

[27] I Christie, *Machel of Mozambique* (Harare, Zimbabwe Publishing House, 1988); B Munslow (ed), *Samora Machel: An African Revolutionary* (London and New Jersey (USA), Zed Books, 1985).

[28] Bianco and Chevrier (eds) *Dictionnaire biographique du mouvement ouvrier international.*

years of forced labour at Poulo Condor (1929–1936); Vo Nguyen Giap spent two years in French prisons, as did his wife, who died after having been tortured. Sukarno was arrested in December 1929 at Yogyakarta and spent two years in prison, oddly enough, at Bandung, before being arrested again and deported in August 1933 to Flores, and later to Sumatra. Nehru spent no less than ten years in prison between 1920 and 1945; even his daughter Indira and his son-in-law Feroze Gandhi suffered the same fate, having been imprisoned during the war.[29]

Powerful experiences, a personalisation of humiliation, the fabrication of myths and patterns that the whole population knew how to endow with meaning: these pathways through humiliation are indeed at the centre of a system that is being created for the long term. Between a desire for the West and the increasing rejection of the West, between a West that is welcoming and a West that expels and imprisons, between a West that is longed for and a West that rejects, between a West that stands for human rights and progress and a West that is characterised by regimes that tolerate illegality, the contradictions are many. And they are all the more difficult to resolve because the flight towards the Soviet camp had, up until 1989, the flavour of defiance, although this rapidly became a source of new frustrations and reinvented humiliations. All of this was difficult to overcome, because although colonial domination had passed, new forms of patronage appeared to stop progress in its tracks.

New forms of Patronage

Since the time shortly after the end of the Second World War when independence was acquired by most of the countries in Asia, something which did not happen until the 1960s for most of the countries in Africa, people have never stopped talking about the 'neocolonialism' of dependency, and now more recently, about 'post-colonialism'.[30] Such analyses are often denounced as 'simplistic', but it is difficult to deny that a softer version of colonialism succeeded the colonialism of long ago. Some will say that it is less obvious or less formalised, but as a reinvention of metropolitan domination, it only prolongs the humiliation that took place in past centuries. The forms are different, and the actors change places: but the force of 'Françafrique' lies in its ability to 'manage the client', that is, to confer upon the client a reasonable status that in ordinary situations makes him seem more deserving of respect, and in crisis situations, offers him the illusion of a kind of power. Let us call to mind, over and above the classical attributes of States whose supposed sovereignty was mostly for show,

[29] F Lecomte, *Nehru* (Paris, Payot, 1994) 251.
[30] A Appadurai, *Après le colonialisme* (Paris, Payot, 2005).

the state dinners held by General de Gaulle for his newly 'equal' African brothers in the early 1960s. As an exceptional case, we could consider the ability that someone like Omar Bongo demonstrated in obtaining the resignation of at least two ministers of the French Cooperation agency, who wanted to change things too openly, or to change too quickly the way things were done. We might also consider the case of someone like Idriss Déby, who was able to hide or perhaps to redeem his own enormous failures in terms of human rights and democracy in Chad, simply by offering the assistance of his troops at a decisive moment in the French intervention in Mali.

The effectiveness of the relationship between powers and clients, something that is abundantly written about in political science, is based on an exchange, and not principally on constraint. It presupposes a sharing—admittedly unequal and selective—of satisfactions.[31] The classical 'patron' offers protection in exchange for advantages of various kinds from the client. If we now move from ordinary individual patronage to State patronage, things change, although not in their essence. This type of relationship remains fundamentally inter-personal: Françafrique, like American protection (which was once offered in Latin America and is still offered today in many Middle Eastern countries or even Asian countries), works through local leaders who (it is thought) must be dealt with, elites in government, in business, or in the media, who receive material and possibly symbolic advantages, but most of all protection. This is the meaning, for example, of the 48 military interventions carried out by France in its former colonies in Africa; the very first one, in February 1964, restored to power the Gabonese leader Léon Mba, who had been overthrown by a 'soft' coup d'état that for a brief period had been accepted by the victim.[32] It must be said that this man was an ideal client, even if he veered off for a short time towards radical nationalism. He is said to have been the son of the barber of Pierre Savorgnan de Brazza; he was a good student at the seminary, and a very conscientious minor government employee while working for the customs agency. He was docile and disciplined, but tyrannical towards his subordinates. He was particularly well-liked by General de Gaulle after declaring, on an official visit to France, that 'every citizen of Gabon [has] two countries: Gabon and France'.[33]

Three remarks should be made on the subject of such practices. The first makes the relation of client and patron an inclusive one; the exchange comprises all the satisfactions that the patron thinks are worth trying to obtain. The patron does not confine himself to a single strategic, political or

[31] E Saïd, *Orientalism* (New York, Vintage, 1979).
[32] P Pesnot, *Les Dessous de la Françafrique* (Paris, Nouveau Monde, 2008).
[33] M N'Solé Biteghe, *Échec aux militaires au Gabon* (Paris, L'Harmattan, 2004).

military level. He also focuses on the economic dimension, thus increasing *de facto* the number of actors implicated on both sides. The oil company Elf appears to have participated in a decision-making process that led to military intervention in Libreville in 1964. Based on this fact, a second observation is made: what is essential to the patron-client relationship is the identification of a fairly large circle of 'beneficiaries' who exemplify client status, and whose survival is closely bound up with the reproduction of this mode of exchange—hence the rarity of acts of dissidence among African political elites, and the relative stability of the patron-client relationship.

And hence, in addition, the dramatisation of all deviant behaviour, whenever it may appear; examples may be provided by the case of someone like Laurent Gbagbo in Ivory Coast, at the very beginning of the 21st century, or by the case of Thomas Sankara, who seized power in Burkina Faso thanks to a 'revolution' in 1983, and who was assassinated in 1987 in circumstances that have never been explained. This pattern is exemplified to a lesser degree by Major Mathieu Kérékou who proclaimed on 30 November 1975 a 'Popular Republic of Bénin', complete with red flag and the Internationale playing, shortly before being returned to power in an election, in a far more docile mood. We may say in any case that this patronage tends to remove a thin layer of the leadership class and place it under protection from humiliation; and that this relationship tends to fuel a special kind of humiliation that is unclear, less political, less personal, and thus very likely more social; and in this way more dangerous, more difficult to neutralise, and more likely to be expressed through cultural attributes, especially religious ones.

This is where the third remark proves crucial. The relationship with the client becomes an actual mode of governance, whose stability over time is the best indicator of its strength. But the point is precisely this: like all relations of this kind, it is deeply inegalitarian: the client has a vital need of the patron, but the patron will accept the loss of a client as a slight setback. This inequality inevitably becomes, in times of crisis, destructive of sovereignty. The patron is the one who decides when protection will be extended, sometimes by asking for a 'request for assistance' from some authority in place, just as Metternich did, in dealing with King Ferdinand of Naples in his time. France became involved, in the winter of 2010–2011, in the installation of Alassane Ouattara, despite an equivocal election result in Ivory Coast. But France did not intervene to protect General Bozizé, who was overthrown by a military coup in the Central African Republic in 2013. France acted in Gabon but not at all in the Congo, and decided what to do on a case-by-case basis throughout the turbulent history of Chad.

This capacity for deciding what to do in exceptional situations brings us back to the most classic definitions of sovereignty. It leads mechanically to the most accepted kinds of rhetoric, but these may also logically contain humiliations that have been reinvented and perhaps made worse. Suddenly, the patron has become a sovereign decision-maker. We are thinking of a famous interview with French President François Hollande, already cited above, after the intervention in Mali: 'We want there to be elections in Mali at the end of July. And on this point, we cannot be shaken...' But is the electoral timetable of a sovereign State something that should be handled, or worse, controlled, by foreigners? The President renewed his proposal on 5 June 2013 when speaking to UNESCO: 'The elections will be held on the scheduled date, and at Kidal'. His own Minister for Foreign Affairs declared on 5 April at Bamako, 'We must have elections in July...' And the idea of a 'commission for dialogue and reconciliation' for Mali was announced from Paris—just like the Franco-European reform of the Malian Army, France's administration of military zones or the alliance of convenience with Tuareg groups on Malian soil.[34] The French Minister of Defence believed, for his part, that 'it is necessary to say things forcefully'. 'Forcefully': the voice of sovereignty.

Only a few months had elapsed when the same rhetoric was used in regard to the Central African Republic. On 7 December 2013, at a moment when a French intervention was beginning, intended to re-establish peace with this former French colony, François Hollande noted, when faced with the press, that 'we *cannot leave in place* a president who has not been able to accomplish anything, and who has not allowed anyone else to accomplish anything either'. We have passed imperceptibly from a discourse about protecting populations to an affirmation concerning the devolution of power that is decided on elsewhere. All these events were characterised by the President of Guinea, Alpha Condé, a former professor of political science, as 'a humiliation for Africa'.[35] A month later, on 10 January 2014, the president under discussion, Michel Djotodia, submitted his resignation to his counterparts at the CEEAC (Communauté économique des États de l'Afrique centrale) in a meeting at N'Djaména. Two dictators, the Chadian Idriss Déby and the Congolese Denis Sassou-N'Guesso, distinguished themselves in the process.

These words and actions are thus perceived and received as obvious forms of 'recolonisation', according to a phrase coined by Aminata Traoré in a book entitled *L'Afrique humiliée*.[36] This reinvented humiliation is brought up because of *continuity*: this form of action and intervention does not come from just anywhere, but comes from the long-ago coloniser—something

[34] M Galy (ed), *La Guerre au Mali* (Paris, La Découverte, 2013) 88.

[35] Interview with François Hollande on TV5 and RFI, 7 December 2013; concerning A Condé, *cf Le Devoir*, 6 December 2013. One might add a curious exchange between the French Minister of Defence and his colleagues on a plane on the way to Bangui: one of them said regarding the CAR president, 'We need to get him alone as much as possible', 20 heures de France 2, 13 December 2013.

[36] A Traoré, *L'Afrique humiliée* (Paris, Fayard, 2013).

the new emergent powers do not fail to whisper in the ears of Africans. This form of humiliation is also federative and aggregating, mingling in the bitter and sometimes summary military intervention and the management of immigrants, persons who have been badly treated, suppressed or expelled. It exists on *many levels*, aiming at the national power that is in place, and at external powers. It is above all social, denouncing policies held (by colonial governments) to be impractical, corrupt, even criminal. In this sense, it becomes a symbol of civil society, a possible locus of ferment for xenophobia and social violence. It is capable of affecting the most vulnerable people, the jobless, the young, and the categories of the forgotten.

This is to say that constitutive inequality resists change. Moreover, it reproduces itself and makes use of the memories it generates in order to invent, sometimes in a forced manner, renewed visions of a phenomenon that evokes the fateful character of domination. The humiliation of yesterday was perhaps too powerful not to produce, at least in part, the humiliation of today. But at any rate it is deeply rooted enough in the international system to rise from its own ashes in order to re-orient and reshape the system of today. Its effects are facilitated by the present structure of the international order, and its cortege of marginal States, states that are on the periphery, excluded or simply living on the outskirts of world governance.

5

Structural Inequality: To be Outside the Elite

COLONIAL HISTORY PERSISTS in the configuration of the contemporary international system, whose structure creates new inequalities that often are combined with those inherited from the past. When the modern international system was emerging, especially during the period of the Congress of Vienna (1815), this matter did not seem particularly important. The participants were in their element, among equals, and there were not very many participants, at that. Certainly ambiguities existed: the kingdoms of Portugal and Denmark lacked importance and played only a marginal role in the Concert of Europe, but those inequalities were not as glaring as the ones that today separate the United States from Sierra Leone. Furthermore, contact was maintained through dynastic alliances and through a subtle game of balance that excluded no one.

Two major ruptures created an enduring structure that was strongly anti-egalitarian, causing frustration and diplomatic humiliation: first, the installation, in 1945, of a multilateralism based on a strange compromise; second, the emergence of bipolarity, which gave power more authority than it should ever have. Both, even the second, remain at the heart of our current international system, with all its ambiguities.

The compromise of 1945 that founded the United Nations is well known, but seldom do we identify all its consequences. The man responsible for this compromise was Franklin Roosevelt, who wanted a 'united nations' that was controlled by the winners, or even by one winner. Fearing that Congress would play the same trick on him they had played on Woodrow Wilson in 1919, he came up with an idea: the collective deliberation of all nations would have to depend on the agreement of the five great Powers who considered themselves the winners in 1945. This was the beginning of what is known as the Perm 5, the five permanent members of the UN Security Council, each of whom is able to veto UN actions. From then on there were two categories of State: those who remained masters of the collective game, and those who were supposed to submit to them. Two years later, the official beginning of the Cold War placed at centre stage a rivalry between the United States and the Soviet Union, such that collective deliberation was replaced by a virtual, and then a real, condominium, giving military power alone the last word. At that time there were two superpowers … and everyone else.

This hierarchy is as tenacious as it is structuring. The effect of the veto obviously survived the fall of the Berlin Wall; the idea of a military condominium is far from having disappeared, even if Russia in the 21st century is no longer what it was during the half-century after World War II. This stratified structure, which gave rise to a culture of international grading, not only resulted in inequality among States. It also engendered complex kinds of bitter behaviour among those who aspired to make something of themselves, or simply to continue existing. These humiliations, more or less contained within a defined space, are encountered among the 'middle powers', who dream of a world that will eventually become multipolar, among the 'emerging powers', who think that they have already reached the status of a great power, and among the small States, who, far from bettering their status, simply want to survive.

The Broken Dream of the 'Middle Powers'

When the Berlin Wall fell, the middle powers thought their moment had arrived. Their category, indeed, had existed for 40 years already, having been created in order to allow them to claim a status placing them between the very large and the very small. The phrase probably came from the Canadians, perhaps from Lyon Mackenzie King (1874–1950), their prime minister who, before the war, had not abandoned the idea of coming to some understanding with the Axis powers, and who after 1945 had some misgivings about closing his country up in a military alliance. It was primarily popularised by his successor, Louis Saint-Laurent, head of the government from 1948 to 1957, a man who was diplomatically active, especially during the Suez crisis. His intention was to make his country's voice heard, beyond the automatic game of power.

What can such countries do? They are too small to impose their will alone; too big to sit quietly. Middle powers can continue to exist through the riches of multilateral diplomacy, utilising their know-how, their image, and the unprecedented ways they find to make themselves heard. Mediation and humanitarian diplomacy are ideal forms through which this goal may be attained.[1] Canada constructed this novel status through a remarkable level of diplomatic activism, an example that Scandinavian countries would later follow. By means of contingents of soldiers placed at the disposition of the United Nations, and their promotion of human rights, they accomplished what they set out to do. France also tried to follow this pattern,

[1] C Pratt, *Middle Power Internationalism* (Montréal, McGill-Queen's University Press, 1990). The author speaks of a '*humane internationalism*'.

particularly after 1989, along with other countries claiming middle power status, such as Japan and Brazil. Peace, development and other international social questions became 'diplomatic niches'[2] that allowed a middle power to shine. Economic, cultural or geographic resources accumulated by these countries were supposed to make possible the construction of a 'multipolar' world, a real attempt to strike back against the minimisation imposed on everyone during the period of US-Soviet condominium. The word sounded good when Jacques Chirac said it, and also when it was spoken by Inácio Lula da Silva, and quite a few others.

What was the real situation at the time? Certainly, the end of bipolarity dramatically liberated foreign policies and enhanced their autonomy. We saw this in 2003, when the United States invaded Iraq, and was severely criticised by many allies in a manner that would have been unthinkable before 1989. Brazil, Argentina, Mexico, Canada, Turkey, Germany, and France did not moderate the expression of their views to suit the United States. Evidently, the world had changed.

We can easily understand the coherence of this new strategy, in a new context, within a complex international system, ie one composed of many actors, a system that is only weakly structured, in which lines of division may be blurred at times. It is significant that the middle power strategy had already been tried out by Canada in 1956 during the Suez crisis, the first exception to the head-on clashes of the two superpowers. Lacking sufficient military resources to achieve their aim by using force, middle powers suddenly discover that they have enough resources and can get their way through working for peace, through mediation, through solving conflicts, and in general attempting to wield influence. At this level the activism countries like Finland, under Martti Ahtisaari,[3] or Norway, taking part in negotiations throughout the long Sudanese war,[4] the collection of Scandinavian countries, plus the Canada of Jean Chrétien and Lloyd Axworthy on the question of human security, is particularly instructive.[5] Great hopes were born in the hearts of middle powers when the Wall fell.

But is this game still playable? Does it produce the satisfactions that were expected from it? Is it not, when all is said and done, a source of frustration, even failure, and thus of future humiliations? Are we far enough away from the classical game of power, for a different syntax to be successfully introduced and accepted? The tragedy of middle powers is that they think they are in a multipolar world, but it really is not multipolar; and they seem

[2] A Cooper (ed), *Niche Diplomacy* (New York, Macmillan, 1997).

[3] M Dieckhoff, *L'Individu dans les relations internationales: le cas du médiateur Martti Ahtisaari* (Paris, L'Harmattan, 2012).

[4] M Gabrielsen, *The Internationalization of the Sudanese Conflict*, PhD dissertation (IEP de Paris, 2010).

[5] M Kaldor, *Human Security* (London, Polity Press, 2007); S Tadjbakhsh and A Chenoy, *Human Security: Concepts and Implications* (New York, Routledge, 2007).

doomed to repeat some of the gestures that made sense in the old bipolar world, which no longer exists.

Multipolarity as such would presuppose that apart from the one great superpower, America, there should be a certain number of other powers of lesser stature who have enough in the way of resources to play a card or two of their own, and to establish around themselves a zone of stable and credible influence. The wager is somewhat risky in an only weakly-structured world, in which national resources are dwindling, where the temptation to go one's own way gets stronger and stronger, where the weight of societies in the international game tends to win out, reducing by so much the relevance of choices and durable strategic lines worked out by the States. The failure of Chirac's diplomacy after 2003 may appear paradoxical, but it is no less significant: he was able to stand up and criticise the American giant, refusing to be associated with the invasion of Iraq (which quickly became a debacle), but so far from being able to reap a dividend for his diplomatic victory, he was forced to recant almost immediately.[6] He patched things up with his American counterpart at the G8 summit in Evian in June 2003, and initiated a policy of cooperation with the United States in the Middle East. The alliance in Afghanistan was reinforced, and France co-authored with the USA the famous Resolution 1559 concerning Lebanon and Syria (August 2004). In addition, Ariel Sharon received a particularly warm welcome in Paris in July 2005. Thus neoconservative attitudes gained ground within the French diplomatic world: the rate of change was even faster when Nicolas Sarkozy was elected. He rushed to support George W Bush, despite Bush being politically weakened, and then in 2008 decided that France would rejoin the integrated command structure of NATO. The France of Chirac, Sarkozy and Hollande, of neo-Gaullism, liberalism and social democracy, appears as a middle-sized power in the post-bipolar world, all in all less autonomous than she was during the most rigid days of bipolarity.

The paradox is only apparent, of course, since the French syndrome extends far beyond France and individual political choices. Two series of factors must be examined here. First, the scarcity of resources which caused the precariousness of these 'diplomatic niches', a phenomenon linked to the destruction of an international system in which each country preferred to play its own cards. Until 2004, the year of enlargement of the Union, France might claim with some justification to have managed the foreign policy of the European Union, sitting across from Germany, which could not perform the task, and Britain, which had lost interest, and finally across from the average and small powers who were not up to the task. The end of bipolarity and the further enlargement of the Union through the

[6] D Lagrange, *La France face aux États-Unis pendant la crise irakienne* thesis (IEP de Paris).

accession of Eastern European countries gradually made this management impossible, and this marked the awakening of the weak EU States, who now absolutely refused to be told, diplomatically, what to do. France could not balance its decreasing power in Europe by displaying multilateralist zeal, because it was being held back by American neoconservatives. It could not take advantage of its lingering influence in Africa, which at that time found itself in a crisis of post-bipolarity, as witness the unforeseen consequences of the Ivorian crisis, from the coup d'Etat of 1999 up until the presidential election of 2010. At that time France re-engaged with the problem, on a more precarious basis than ever, during the period that saw French troops put Léon Mba back in power.[7]

It is remarkable that the disintegration of the structure of the international system in the aftermath of 1989, by reducing the need for solidarity and protection, undermined the middle powers at the very moment when they were hoping to gain more autonomy. This is why multipolarity never really emerged, and why it gave way to a system that was simply 'apolar'. Deprived of decisive resources, and still mired in a culture dominated by the ascendancy of superpowers, the middle powers saw their strategic hopes dashed.

Not only did the middle powers, the former allies, have to 'get back in line' like France, but they also had to accept their relative marginalisation. Great Britain, for example, can only muse upon the downgrading of its 'privileged ally' status, which in Iraq did not permit it to have any weight in important decisions. And in March 2003 the Azores conference displayed a Spain under Aznar and a Portugal under Barroso that had outsourced their decision-making process to the United States, even more than previously.[8]

Is this a case of 'humiliation' being inflicted, this time upon middle powers who had cherished certain illusions for a time, but whose hopes were quickly deceived? The relative relegation of the European continent—which for the first time in modern period was not the world's battlefield—deprived the main European powers of geopolitical resources that in previous eras they had been able to bargain with. At the same time, public opinion in these countries more than ever affirmed their neutrality, their pacifism, and even their anti-Americanism. In a nutshell, Europe is no longer something that interests the United States, and the United States is able to make this known.

So it went, when Barack Obama favoured Asia to the detriment of Europe. There was the ostentatious ignorance directed at Europeans during

[7] B Badie, 'French power-seeking and overachievement' in T Volgy et al, *Major Powers and the Quest for Status in International Politics* (New York, Palgrave, 2011) 97–114.

[8] WR Thompson, 'The United States as global leader, global power and status-consistent power' in Volgy et al, *Major Powers and the Quest for Status in International Politics* 27 ff.

the Copenhagen climate change summit in December 2009, the complete circumvention of the Old Continent in the nuclear disarmament projects discussed during the visit of the American president to Berlin in June 2013, and the relaxed reactions of Washington authorities following the revelation of a vast programme for the interception of communications on the European continent carried out by American intelligence services. Europe is a divided continent that no longer can claim the Cold War as an excuse, which cannot put forward a single speaker who might explain its policy, and which in fact is no more than a group of commercial partners.

On the other hand, the projection of Europeans outside their own territory remains problematic. The Franco-British initiative with regard to Libya in 2011 could be seen as a desire to be perceived as effective on the international scene. But their initiative could only succeed with the active support of the United States; and that is exactly how things stood in Kosovo 12 years earlier. A dependency that is no longer balanced by a need for protection, an international activism that is limited to humanitarian action, as with the Scandinavian States, or brief military interventions which fall within an unwritten division of labour, as was the case with France in Mali: this is akin to humiliation.

Certainly this humiliation has little in common, in terms of intensity or quality, with that which we described in colonial or postcolonial contexts. However at the level of international relations it does share three aspects that appear to be quite essential. First, this humiliation belongs to an identified type: it is an example of relegation. Humiliation that is suffered by middle powers, especially those in Europe, is similar not only to a loss of status, but also to the effect of frustration relating to the rank they had hoped to attain. During the exit from the Cold War the middle powers were hoping for renewed autonomy, but instead they suffered from the strategic decentring of Europe, which was no longer the most important focus for questions about world security.

Second, this humiliation becomes a property of the system, and not an emotional relationship. American diplomacy, more than ever, wants to circumvent its partner or partners, who are thus de facto marginalised in the context of the issue of globalisation, and whose participation in global negotiations is a source of more complexity, unless they are willing to accept the role of yes-men. We find ourselves faced with an inverted version of the Monroe doctrine: Europe must remain contained upon its continent, and it does not seem necessary to involve it in negotiations. As early as the 19th century, Washington was declining invitations to participate in the Concert of Europe.

Third and finally, this humiliation—tempered by the illusion of existence—is at the same time accepted by European powers in the name of an abandoned vision of the international order, based on an overvaluation of military power, particularly that of the United States, a certain inability to understand globalisation and the new role of societies, and an obvious difficulty with taking new, emerging powers into account. It is Europe that likes to speak about the American superpower, ironically at the moment when the country's impotence is revealed.

Emergent Powers and the Bonds of Past Humiliations

Emergent powers reflect yet another configuration, in addition to the ones mentioned above. Rather than 'relegation', these countries would speak readily of the 'denial of equality', perhaps even 'stigmatisation'. Instead of having its source in the discovery of modernity, humiliation here is more about a memory of the past and a desire to overcome it.

The very notion of 'emergence' and the debates that surround it are our starting point. Emergence, as an idea, does not have the best reputation among those who are called emergent, who from São Paulo to Istanbul, consider it a little offensive. It must be admitted that there is a considerable paradox involved in labelling China, the oldest political system in history, or Russia, the former superpower, or Turkey, with its long imperial history, as emergent. Part of the problem is probably related to the fact that this category was hastily created in order to describe the trajectories that disturbed the Western monopoly over burgeoning globalisation: the slight air of condescension, ready to forgive teenage tantrums or even spoiled children, is irritating when you feel it is aimed at you.

The arguments put forward by those who consider themselves offended are all the more convincing, because economists today agree that the category is rather artificial. For China, Brazil or South Africa, the trajectories are so different that defining these as a unified category seems less and less convincing. On the other hand, as is often the case, even though the expression was hastily coined, it has passed into the language and has influenced perceptions (those of others) and identifications (by the countries who are labelled). Thus the idea of 'emergence' in this sense is still widely used, and is even more credible in the area of diplomacy than in economics.

The group of emergent powers feel allied to one another, based on the fact that they have all been excluded in some way from the diplomacy of a club that is essentially Western, and so they have grown used to working together, making coalitions, and standing together at times in a common front. At first, there was an analytical category created by observers (especially Goldman Sachs), that of the BRICS countries (Brazil, Russia, India, China, South Africa), which became politically significant, and ended up being the reason for annual summits. The IBSA (India, Brazil, South Africa) countries pursue cooperation on a transcontinental level. When commonalities seem scarce, the temptation arises to define the group no longer in terms of what it is, but in terms of what it is not: hence this mixture, made up of mistrust of the West, defiance of entrenched oligarchies, and frequent use of references to a colonial past. It has not been tested in the same way in all places, but it carries with it an impetus towards federation. This also leads to the strategic use of the memory of humiliations received in a more or less distant past, which becomes the social motivation for States who cannot find much common ground in terms of geography, economics, culture or politics.

History constructed in this way, or even reconstructed, is not short of references: India and China were at Bandung, while their diplomacies, always opposed to one another since 1945, could only find common ground with regard to a celebration of the principle of sovereignty, and various reminders of what they had had to suffer due to violations of that principle, mostly at the hands of Western powers. South Africa undoubtedly has a history filled with martyrdom, which can be laid at the door of the same powers. Brazil has a painful colonial history, more distant in time, which intertwines it with the history of Africa, since both share in the difficulty of post-colonial self-affirmation, where the brutality of military regimes was often associated with pressure from the United States. Russia, quite different, is nonetheless caught up in efforts to gain recognition that are not so different from those of other nations. It was an imperial power, though not a colonial one; it had been a superpower, but was defeated by today's superpower; humiliated, more than anything, and excluded from the international game that began after 1989. Their style is angular, but their strategic line is consistent: Moscow rather cynically portrays itself as the unconditional defender of sovereignty. In order to be credible, the group is obliged to portray itself as perpetually suffering humiliation. At the same time, the approach is incessantly reactivated, especially to the extent that a Western directorate pretends to take over the management of the world. The overvaluation of humiliation is a way of being, a way of surviving, and a way of defining oneself in opposition to a power that is perpetually trying to marginalise you. The result is an original kind of diplomacy.

Sometimes, collective entities are like individuals. The diplomatic positioning of 'emergent states' evokes some of the well-known analyses of American sociologist Samuel Stouffer. Studying the soldiers of the U.S. Army, Stouffer noted that frustrations over failure to be promoted were stronger, the more educated the soldier was.[9] The reasoning here is similar: the power that certain States have recently acquired sharpens their desire to participate actively in world governance. It makes the rebuffs they receive and the difficulties they experience in trying to force their way into the club all the more unbearable. This experience, which seems to be repeated at

[9] SA Stouffer et al, *The American Soldier* (New York, J Wiley, 1949).

each stage of international negotiations, has also affected Russia since the end of bipolar condominium, and to this extent is like humiliation, if only because the construction of the West as a 'reference group' (Stouffer's phrase) is humiliating, since you identify with it without being able to match its power of domination.

Thus sovereigntism becomes an affirmation that is a reaction to humiliations past and present, and a means of limiting the oligarchic pressure that continues to exclude. Anti-Westernism—more or less hidden—is a way for an emergent power to rebuild itself in front of the 'reference group', which tends—during crisis situations—to present itself as a Board of Directors for the world. The commitment to opposition of the emergents is strong in this kind of context, and this strength is often quite surprising to Western diplomats. The fact remains that the pairs *denial of equality—sovereigntism* and *relegation—contestation* function perfectly in terms of the model we have been describing.

The denial of equality plays a constant and structuring role in the diplomatic production of the emerging powers. This is first expressed through a constant mistrust, in which there are alternating phases of hostility and moments of reduced tension, featuring forced and illusory agreements. Before emergence was an international issue, U.S.-Brazil relations were held hostage by this oscillation. Recognised by Washington in 1824, the Brazilian Empire refused for a long time to grant the US navigation privileges on the Amazon, which the Americans repeatedly requested, and which Bolivia promptly granted to them. Brazil did not relent in this regard until 1853. In addition, the Brazilian government publicly rejected US mediation in the conflict between Brazil and Paraguay between 1865 and 1870. Much later, Brazil was dragging its feet before entering the war against Hitler's Germany, and made public its dissatisfaction at having been relegated during the peace conference in Paris (July–October 1946), and again at the peace conference in San Francisco in 1951. In a similar manner, Brazil protested and then left the League of Nations because it was not given a permanent seat on that organisation's Council. A military assistance treaty was finally ratified after great difficulties in 1953, despite the fact that President João Goulart continued to defend Cuba against Washington.[10]

The same can be said of China. Among other signals, which are quite numerous, we will mention only an observation from François Godement: at a large military parade held in October 2009, to celebrate the 60th anniversary of the People's Republic, each soldier was ordered to march 169 steps, one for each year separating China from the humiliating Opium War that

[10] C Paiva-Leite, 'Constantes et variantes de la politique étrangère brésilienne' (1969) 34(1) *Politique étrangère* 33–55.

brought the Middle Kingdom into conflict with Europe.[11] In a country of symbols, the meaning was clear. This memory of denial of equality is indeed constitutive, ready to surge to the front, if the old powers should ever try to contest the three principles that Beijing excludes from any discussion, in order to underline its absolute sovereignty: its territorial integrity, even including Tibet and Xinjiang; the absolute control of the existing regime; and China's right to development, whatever the ecological or commercial repercussions. In the name of inequality suffered in the past, China asserts an absolute right to perfect its sovereignty.

Another image, just as instructive: Turkey reacted vigorously, perhaps even more than that, to the admonishments of the European Parliament following repressive actions in Taksim Square against demonstrators who were critical of the government in June 2013. 'Who do you think you are?', eloquently demanded prime minister Recep Tayyip Erdogan of the European parliamentarians. 'With what audacity dare you make such a decision?' His minister for Foreign Affairs, Ahmet Davutoglu, in a significant manner, placed the question of Turkey's status at the centre of his response: 'Turkey is a first-class democracy and needs lessons from no one. This resolution, when it is sent to us, will be rejected immediately'. Egemen Bagis, minister for European Affairs, felt obliged to stipulate to Catherine Ashton that 'Turkey [is] *the strongest country*, and the most reform-minded country in Europe'.[12]

It is not just a matter of phenomena or of particular expressions. Behind these images, it is interesting to see the 'emergent' nations constructing an image of themselves that engages their diplomacy and allows them to be understood. India and China never miss an opportunity to portray themselves as developing countries, something that causes them to regard the principle of international constraint as unjust. How can the same regulations that are supposed to be binding on States that are already developed, be used to regulate States that have not yet finished their process of development? How can we accept this situation, in which the earlier-developed States entered modernity without any international policeman putting them under surveillance and punishing their excesses, while the States in a later group have to slow down their development for the benefit of richer countries? The old Hobbesian argument wins out: sovereignty extinguishes any idea of an external constraint. India repeats this position during negotiations about climate change: the effort to produce growth in a nation is legitimate. Globalisation can also serve the cause of development.[13]

[11] F Godement, *Que veut la Chine?* (Paris, Odile Jacob, 2012) 256.

[12] *Le Monde*, 15 June 2013, p 4. Emphasis mine.

[13] J-L Racine, 'L'Inde: émergence ou renaissance?' (2010) 12 *Agir* 44; S Ganguly and MJ Pardesi, 'Explaining sixty years of India's foreign policy' (2009) 8(1) *Indian Review* 4–19.

This thesis is very similar to that of China, whose unfinished development connects it to humiliations of the past. The 'Chinese dream' is to emerge from this inferiority by following the path of modernity that is appropriate for the third millennium. In their words, they want to follow the path of globalisation 'by accelerating exchanges and cooperation with the rest of the world'. The recipe is simple and explicit: replace old strategic schemes that were based on a 'zero-sum game' with policies based on a win-win scenario. In China, globalisation is not something to be frightened of, but is a source of hope, and the Middle Kingdom is probably the country most willing to place confidence in that hope. At this point, sovereignty is no longer Hobbesian: the Chinese intend to remain masters of their own destiny, at the same time as knowing that the outside world is more a source of riches than of threats.[14]

Insisting on the importance of a nation's self-perception, Ahmet Davutoglu, a professor of international relations before he went into politics, constructed a vision of his own country by setting in opposition States of the centre and States of the periphery. Turkey has emerged from the second category, and must now construct its diplomacy in order to become part of the first: emergence is indeed a remedy for humiliation. To a denial of equality, the response must be the creation of a new meaning produced by the 'historic and strategic profundity' of this country, which has suffered greatly at the hands of others.[15]

Emergent diplomacy, therefore, has a shared meaning, that of a restoration that erases past humiliations by means of a strongly affirmed sovereignty, but a sovereignty that is constructed *within globalisation* in accordance with initiatives that continue to surprise Western powers. Well entrenched in their conservatism and facing globalisation with trepidation, the Western powers are missing an opportunity that the emergent powers quickly seized thanks to their experience and their vision. This subtle articulation in fact follows several pathways.

The Chinese way is that of *self-managed globalisation*, which in fact is very pragmatic. They take what allows them to win and they leave the rest. China needs raw materials, especially coal and oil, and so the nation wants to expand existing markets, and to prospect for future ones. These are the things China is looking for in Africa, Central Asia, Southeast Asia and even Latin America. In fact, Chinese leaders, especially after

[14] Yang Jiechi, 'Innovations in diplomatic theory, practice', *China Daily*, 17 August 2013, p 5 (after the 18th Congress of the CCP and the definition of the line to be taken by Xi Jinping); *cf* also *People's Daily*, 5 September 2013.

[15] M Yesiltas and A Balci, *A Dictionary of Turkish Foreign Policy in the AKP Era: A Conceptual Map* (Ankara, Sam Papers, Centre for Strategic Research, ministère des Affaires étrangères, 2013) 7–8; J Jabbour, 'Le monde selon Ankara', *Telos*, November 2011.

Deng Xiaoping, have all understood that globalisation could in a way consolidate sovereignty. Also, sovereignty is oriented towards globalisation, just as strongly as the old Confucian wisdom rejected universalism and messianism: for China, globalisation is not an attempt to convert others to its practice, but an effort to protect its own development. China only expresses itself on the international scene with regard to something it perceives as a threat to its regime or to its territorial integrity. China does not act except in the interest of its own development. Otherwise, prudence and even passivity are its watchwords. With regard to Afghanistan, the conflict between Israel and Palestine, conflicts in Africa, coups d'état, instances of repression, outbreaks of authoritarianism, etc. China is prudently passive. The humiliation of the past can, as it happens, lead to a sort of passivity of revenge.

In contrast, Brazilian diplomacy promotes a type of *extrovert sovereignty*, particularly active and enterprising since the Worker's Party came to power, in the administration of President Lula da Silva, and under the direction of minister for Foreign Affairs, Celso Amorim. If sovereignty equals nationalism, as a general principle, it also claims to contain and defeat past slights that are deeply resented. So, Brazilian diplomacy is certainly pursued in the name of a national interest, but it is also intended to put forward a vision of the world, projecting a presence and offering a solidarity that was once denied to Brazil: hence the energy invested in multilateral engagement at the United Nations, or in matters concerning the World Trade Organization; hence the activism in international negotiations, the alacrity in forming coalitions, especially when dominant nations can be wrong-footed, and the high degree of interest in the BRICS and IBAS groupings; hence the many visits made by Lula to Africa and to the Middle East. In a manner that could be described as diametrically opposed to the Chinese *démarche*, Brazil is actively and visibly involved in the management of the major conflicts occurring around the world, intervening, for the most part, on behalf of the weaker side. And this is the source of Brazil's biting criticism of the interventionism practiced by the Western powers.

Between these two poles, other models of emergent diplomacy are now coming into view. Particularly notable is the originality of the Turkish model, which might be characterised, borrowing the words of Davutoglu himself, as a 'rhythmic sovereignty'. Beginning with a concept of 'strategic depth', Davutoglu puts forward the notion that the history and the geopolitical situation of Turkey give it a significance that has nothing to do with a bridge over the Bosphorus, or the gateway that it would represent between the West and the East. The old Ottoman Empire can find in the depths of its own history the resources necessary for its own restoration in the Middle East, in the Balkans, upon the Caucasus, in Central Asia, all of which Turkey does not fear to describe as 'the geographical centre of the world'.[16] Thus Turkey's foreign policy must be active and proactive, mobile, and visible across an environment mapped by concentric circles that take in enough territory so that at the limit, they form an arrangement that is equivalent to globalisation, which has points of contact with all important global issues. Ahmet Davutoglu takes pride in being able, through these policies, to help Turkey escape from the static and outmoded diplomatic syntax of the Cold War, and to make its way by the light of the dynamic and mobile vision that makes 'rhythmic' an apt description of its diplomacy.[17] This ability to adopt multiple positions, associated with a flexibility that breaks with yesterday's alignments, undoubtedly makes us think of a model that is freeing itself from Schmittian rigidity, that moves in rhythm with globalisation whilst at the same time safeguarding and restoring a sovereignty that has felt the pain of deep wounds for a long time. This instability—this heightened reactivity—of Turkey under the AKP Party in relation to Israel, Iran, Syria, Europe, the United States or Russia, becomes a pattern, but it is still an act of liberation with regard to a past that Ankara would like to be finished with.

These sovereignties seem to know how to promote their brands, something that bears exploring. Brazil has had success presenting itself as the champion of diplomatic ideals, by focusing on 'peace diplomacy', on 'prevention' or prohibition of the use of force, thus reaping a dividend by pointing to the low level of its own military expenditures.[18] Brazil, India and South Africa have denounced as anachronistic the composition of the Security Council, and they have attempted to put on trial a Western interventionism that has failed almost everywhere. The IBSA (India, Brazil, South Africa) group, constituted in 2003, invented a new kind of transcontinental cooperation, based on an association of former pariah States.[19]

These diplomacies, which know how to appropriate globalisation otherwise than by perpetuating old methods left over from the Cold War, undoubtedly have their modernity in their favour. What chance do they have for stability? Certainly, they change and transform as a result of success. Excluded from the international game, these new powers find in the rapidity of their ascent the necessary conditions for their socialisation in terms of institutions that ignored or marginalised them up until that

[16] Yesiltas and Balci, *A Dictionary of Turkish Foreign Policy in the AKP Era* 8.

[17] ibid 12.

[18] A Patriota, 'En Syrie comme ailleurs, la protection des civils passe par la diplomatie', *Le Monde*, 27 March 2013, p 17.

[19] A Costa Vaz, *Intermediate States. Regional Leadership and Security: IBSA* (Brasilia, UNB Press, 2006).

moment. This has been studied by Alastair Johnston in connection with China, with the emphasis on contact with the United Nations as a system.[20] This situation may have even more to do with socialisation in terms of the rules of power and domination. China is in a particular situation as a member of the Perm 5; Brazil has to reckon with its neighbours, great and small. South Africa has to shape its diplomacy with regard to other African States who already speak of its 'white diplomacy'; such a comment shows that in the growth of South Africa's power, there is a risk that 'the illegitimacy of South African power' may be reborn, precisely from the humiliation associated with apartheid.[21]

What can we say about the tensions that are born because of this active and instrumentalised globalisation? What about the one million Chinese nationals in Africa, who are inevitably beginning to experience friction with the local population in Zimbabwe or Mozambique, in Algeria or Ethiopia? What about the Chinese mining companies with lax workers rights, whose supervisors shot and wounded 10 Zambian miners in 2011? What about the Chinese mine operator who in August 2012 was killed by his own workers, who were on strike?[22] Perhaps there is a sort of threshold, beyond which the restoration of a wounded dignity can only generate new humiliations.

Small Countries' Narrow Range of Action

This is what the international system is made of: the order that resulted from decolonisation also favoured the proliferation of very small States, which have had a very difficult time finding their place in the new concert of nations. The simple act of listing them is a particularly stinging kind of humiliation, containing an element of derision. What student knows anything about the island of Nauru, or even where it is located, with its 10,000 inhabitants and its status as an independent Pacific State since 1968?[23] Who knows anything about Palau, situated between Asia and Oceania, or about its 16,000 citizens? Or about Tuvalu, made up of nine coral atolls, which may one day be only a footnote to History as the first State to disappear for ecological reasons, ie being submerged under the rising ocean, and seeing its 9,700 inhabitants forced into exile? Some island nations are familiar because they appear in the catalogues of travel agencies; for example, there is Antigua and Barbuda (274 km^2 and 83,000 inhabitants), or the Maldives, 184 km^2 if you add together the land masses of 2,000 islands. Others survive

[20] AI Johnston, *Social States: China in International Institutions 1980–2000* (Princeton, Princeton University Press, 2008).

[21] S Perrot, 'Les nouveaux interventionnismes militaires africains' (2005) 98 *Politique africaine* 129.

[22] *Le Monde*, 24–25 March 2013, p 3.

[23] Concerning Nauru, *cf* L Folliet, *Nauru, l'île dévastée* (Paris, La Découverte, 2009).

because they have made themselves into tax havens, or because they do a brisk business in flags of convenience. A small number, like a certain principality embedded in the south of France, are familiar thanks to the tabloid press.

The supreme humiliation is that many of these States have seats at the United Nations, next to China and its 1.344 billion people, although they do not even have the money to send a delegation to the headquarters in New York (much less maintain one). Palau, the Marshall Islands and Micronesia have outsourced the definition and execution of their foreign policy to the United States; the personnel attached to their delegations at the United Nations are distinguishable in the Glass House by their English, spoken with a Texan accent.

The entry of most small States into modernity has been painful. At one time, they were elements of the decomposition of European empires, and they lived through the 20th century as so many prizes disputed by the great powers. First this happened in the Balkans, and then in Central Europe:[24] after periods of precarious existence came a period of marked neglect. They disappeared, they were revived, sometimes they banded together, and sometimes they aligned with or submitted to the biggest and strongest. Sometimes they were deserted by their guides and protectors, when those worthies had something better to do. Let us imagine the condition of the memory of a Czech who lived during the period 1938–1968, considering all the changes in the political control of his home; or the memory of a Serb, whose country was officially created by a Russo-Turkish treaty in 1829, then recognised as an independent State by a European congress, in Berlin in 1878; which then was redrawn in 1913, federated in 1918, became independent again in 1992, shorn of its Kosovo province in 1999. And then there are the States that appear, disappear and reappear, eternal pawns in a relationship between powers: the Baltic states, or Montenegro. There are States that switch patrons: Micronesia was supposed to belong to Spain, then to Germany, then to Japan, and finally to the United States. There are States that emerge only to whet the appetite of neighbouring States, the case of Cyprus. Some States alternate between potential and real existence, like Bosnia and Moldova. The invention and the generalisation of the principle of sovereignty not only fail to protect such nations from humiliation—they may even cause humiliation.

In order to survive, a small State has, at times, to be a 'cunning state', utilising its own resources in the game (like Qatar), or its strategic position (Djibouti), or its transnational, that is, meta-statist or even meta-sovereign virtues (Dubai, Singapore). There are buffer states, deviant states and even

[24] T Mathisen, *The Functions of Small States in the Strategies of the Great Powers* (Oslo, Universitetsforlag, 1971).

Mafia states, dealing with great powers in order to gain their protection, and offering themselves as vassals (Bahrain). Some suffer the worst of humiliations: they passively accept a perpetually incomplete status. At best, these may be 'weak states' who officially recognise their own weakness, and hand their sovereign functions over to stronger States (Yemen in relation to Saudi Arabia, or Lebanon in relation to Syria, until 2005). There are also *collapsed states* that have folded up under pressure from militias, bandits, religious communities or warlords.[25]

Of course, they can join forces, promote their cause, play the game of multilateralism, and even compete with the great powers.[26] Without question, there are someadvantages to being small. The proper proof of such an assertion should be found in real initiatives towards unity and collective action. In the spring of 1994, in Barbados, two years after the summit in Rio, there was a 'world conference of sustainable development in small States'. 111 countries participated. The main argument was quite clear: small States are less polluting than larger ones, yet they are the ones who suffer the most from climate change. They are also the most dependent in terms of energy supplies, especially oil. The Environment Minister for Mauritius, Deva Virahsawmy, pushed this line of reasoning to its logical conclusion when he complained that 'whenever it is a question of allocating money, it is Gross National Product that is taken into consideration, which is unjust' (8 March 2013). Far from being a reason why a nation might deserve support, weakness itself is a reason for marginalisation and for the paucity of aid. Power is not a good standard to hold the weak to. This is at the very heart of of humiliation.

In fact, these collective demonstrations remained tribunician. The Association of Small Insular States (AOSIS) includes 43 States and observers, of whom 37 are members of the United Nations, thus representing about one-fifth of the total number. Having no secretary and no budget, their periodic meetings are intended to 'call on the world to pay more attention to (their) vulnerability to climate change', and especially to the rise in the level of the oceans. Their effort to be heard, in the context of the General Assembly of the United Nations, came after the discourses of the august princes of the bipolar international system, when most people in the delegations were not even present. They spoke only to diplomats of modest rank. They were politely listened to, but their audience was partially distracted and, all things considered, their presentation amounted to a series of pious wishes without any follow-up assured at all. The Prime Minister of Barbados

[25] W Reno, *Warlords and African States* (Boulder (Colorado), Lynne Rienner Publishers, 1999); R Rotberg, *State Failure and State Weakness in a Time of Terror* (New York, Brookings, 2003).

[26] A Fox, 'The power of small states' in C Ingrebritsen (ed), *Small States in International Relations* (Washington, University of Washington Press, 2006).

expressed himself in this manner in September 2011, in order to make people understand that the survival of these States hung in the balance, and that their populations were not only threatened by more powerful hurricanes, but by the world's unrestricted use of fossil fuels and by improper handling of wastes. This idea was taken up by the Prime Minister of Grenada, Tillman Thomas, who called for a perceptible reduction in greenhouse gases, and for massive aid for island States. Ralph Gonsalves, Prime Minister of Saint-Vincent and the Grenadines, denounced the 'intransigence of the principal polluters, who refuse to support the struggle against climate change, which is itself linked to their wasteful policies'.[27]

One might take into account other versions of suffering inflicted by power and the humiliations undergone by small island nations. Take, for example, an old disagreement between France and the Republic of Comoros, concerning a visa policy that causes very painful separations for families, when some of them live in Mayotte, and others live on islands in the same archipelago that have declared independence. In a curious example of diplomatic pedagogy, the president of Comoros, Abdallah Sambi, was refused a French visa when he wanted to travel to Réunion. The incident occurred on 18 March 2011.[28] Certainly, the situation has been improved since then, but through this startling anecdote, a sort of caricature of humiliation, we can measure how easy it is for such a faulty policy to end up causing even worse behaviour.

We are faced here with a two-fold kind of inconsistency that serves as a basis for our international system. As soon as sovereignty is put forward as a constitutive principle of that system, any collective entity can claim it, as long as the will of a majority is behind the claim. The size of the entity cannot come into the picture, at least not at the level of principles, except to make desperate those whose insular isolation or enclave status condemn them to be dominated forever, or to some sort of federation they do not desire, with partners they do not want. For these reasons sovereign equality simply does not manifest itself, and the formal concessions made to the rule of law or to other great principles lead directly to a humiliation that is produced almost mechanically. But we must add, this occurs in a situation that is more and more dominated by the idea of a common good, so that the smaller the State is, ie the more meagre its resources and the more dependent it is on collective efforts, the more intense its needs and aspirations are. At the same time, the marginal contribution of the small State in the service of the common good is too weak (sometimes microscopic) for

[27] S Besson, 'Les petits États insulaires tirent la sonnette d'alarme à l'ONU', www.actualites-news-environnement.com/27143-petits-Etats-insulaires-ONU.html.

[28] Adjmaël, 'Plus de visa pour les Comoriens désirant se rendre en France', nomansland.mondoblog.org/2011/03/30/plus-de-visaspour-les-comoriens-desirant-se-rendre-en-france/.

its voice to be taken into account or even heard at the negotiating table. There, where expectations are great because they are expressed in terms of survival, the actual contribution to global governance is zero. It is as if the small countries were obliged to exist as States, following which they must forever consider, rhetorically and passively, the question of their own existence. From this true denial of equality comes a sovereigntism that can be no more than a façade. To a relegation that is strong enough to send an entity tumbling down to the lowest rungs on the ladder, there is no response other than verbal challenges, and these countries do not have the resources to make even that effective. Only the re-enactment of the scene of humiliation suffered can serve as a response, and it is a weak one at that.

6

Functional Inequality: Being Excluded from Governance

THE INTERNATIONAL SYSTEM has its own rules of procedure, even if they are fragile, imprecise, incomplete or ambiguous. But what happens if these rules are simply imposed, not worked out by the entire community, accepted by some without ever having been really chosen, leading to a form of governance that leaves many people out? The international game weaves together powers of the past and the globalisation of today, the appearance of inclusion and the obstinate reality of exclusion; the memory of the Congress of Vienna, of the time when oligarchies were at their zenith, contrasting with a planetary scope that appears to set aside all absolute leadership. This forced distinction, made by some of the larger powers, raises humiliation to the level of a diplomatic ritual, at the risk of blocking regulative mechanisms that were put in place with great difficulty. 'Minilateralism', oligarchic pressure and diplomatic paternalism are the three most common symptoms of this blockage.

Minilateralism

Shrinking the perimeter of multilateralism has often been an obsession of the great powers, in accordance with the argument, which has support today, that too many leaders inevitably leads to bad choices, and may even make consensus impossible. Multilateralism is set up to be the visible form, but minilateralism is associated with action. The desired shrinkage comes in a number of packages: nations can promote a club of oligarchs within international institutions, such as the famous Perm 5 of the UN Security Council; create an informal circle of powerful nations to whom all essential choices would be referred, as with the G8 or G20; set up, in response to any new international issue, a 'contact group' that would take responsibility for the crisis in question, excluding others from negotiations; surround any targeted State with a collection of guards, euphemistically referred to as 'friends' of the nation affected, to improve monitoring. In all cases, those who are left outside these arrangements are exposed to the kind of gradations we are familiar with: denial of equality, as soon as these nations' right to participate in deliberations is reduced or eliminated; relegation, when they lose a position once acquired in relation to an issue; stigmatisation when their request to participate is vetoed.

Realists understand this situation. Stephen Walt likes to remind us about the unavoidable role of leadership, and insists that important questions can only find solutions if there is cooperation between great powers.[1] This thesis may be tenable, but only with two reservations that deserve to be highlighted. First, such a simple view of governance reduces governance to a minimum: regulation is accomplished through games of connivance and pragmatic forms of *bricolage*, but between the most powerful countries, these ties are fragile. When disagreements become too great, as is the case with regard to climate change, the situation grinds to a halt; when a basic agreement is possible, it is often obtained at some cost to the common good, or at the least some cost to the weakest States. Second, this argument has a weak basis. Just because it happens often, does not necessarily contradict the effect of reason; it is commonly used as an easy pretext for denouncing blockages. How many international conventions have been negotiated by all and approved by the General Assembly of the UN, and have resulted in a record number of ratifications? For example, the convention of 1965 against racial discrimination was ratified by 182 countries; the convention of 1979 against gender discrimination was ratified by 187, the convention of 1959 on children's rights by 190. And this does not count the innumerable conventions on international transport, communications, or health, which were all carried by large margins. Certainly, one can observe that in these negotiations every State does not carry the same weight, and that multilateralism is therefore only a façade. In the argument, one might point to the centralising role of the Secretariat or the Intergovernmental Negotiation Committee, which reduces the number of choices available. It is also appropriate to remark upon the extraordinary slowness of some procedures: the convention of 1982 on the Law of the Sea took 20 years to negotiate. And among the small number of those countries who have not signed up to this Treaty, we do not find the odd small sniper attempting to disrupt the game, but the American superpower itself.

By this reasoning, we are not assigning much importance to the dynamic of negotiation, or to the subtle coalition-forming games, which rarely leave the small states on the touchline. The G77, which comprises many more than 77 States, including the poorest, is rarely passive when it is a matter of orienting, amending, discussing, perhaps also blocking, but not to any greater extent than the great powers might try. The real multilateral game is truly inclusive: it is not without results, but these results irritate, embarrass and offend great powers, leading them to react.

And so the counter-offensive of the minilateralists is formidable. Realist mechanics draws them towards a kind of diplomatic practice that erects

[1] S Walt, 'On Minilateralism', *Foreignpolicy.com*, 23 June 2009.

denial of equality as a credo, and then later as a weapon of avoidance. We read in the writings of Moisés Naím that the smallest possible number of States should have seats at the negotiating table, because this will ensure the maximum likelihood of solutions.[2] In other words, the more we exclude local actors and those who are directly concerned, the more chance we have of resolving the crisis. Walt adds that 'the strong do what they will and the weak must endure it'.[3] It would be difficult to be more explicit or to ignore more clearly the increasing capacity of small States to have influence in a game that depends as much on interdependence as on proximity. This is also to mistake weakness for passivity, to wilfully ignore the readiness to react when faced with humiliation. We here rejoin a thesis from the political scientist Lloyd Gruber, who in his distrust of international cooperation notes that powerful States often force weaker States to accept institutional arrangements that appear unfavourable to them, upon the pretext that such forced acceptance is preferable to total exclusion.[4] This is a very reactionary view, a product of the 19th century, from a time when the battlefield belonged to the strongest; a view that is inappropriate in a world where the largest number of conflicts and sources of instability come from impoverished areas, consisting of weak States on whom globalisation confers a new capacity in the game.

What we mean is that minilateralism does not merely humiliate through exclusion: it also condemns itself to ineffectiveness. A formula put forward by a Western diplomat, denouncing the enlargement of the G8 in favour of a very prudent G20 has been widely circulated: when the circle is enlarged, the discussions will take place in a 'train station'. The difficulty of changing the world is too easily put down as a matter of too many cooks spoiling the broth. Change does not become consequential until it is a subject of the real agreement of all those who are concerned.

Minilateralism is thus more of a survival than an invention, more of a protection than an instrument of modernisation. All one need do is take a look at the history of the G6, born in 1975, upon the initiative of French President Valéry Giscard d'Estaing. It is significant that this grouping arose in a context of unparalleled weakness for the American superpower, hit by three crises: a fall in the value of the dollar, the Watergate scandal, and the entry of North Vietnamese and Viet Cong troops into Saigon.[5] It was, therefore, about compensating for that weakness, or profiting from it, to restore cooperation between allies, to return to the mores that allowed the

[2] ibid.

[3] ibid.

[4] L Gruber, *Ruling the World: Power Politics and the Rise of Supranational Institutions* (Princeton, Princeton University Press, 2000).

[5] B Badie, *The Diplomacy of Connivance* (Basingstoke, Palgrave, 2012); P Hajnal, *The G8 System and the G20* (Burlington, Aldershot, Ashgate, 2007).

founding, in the 19th century, through the Concert of Europe, of the first modern forms of diplomacy, a sort of governance before the term was coined. The initiative was not overwhelming because it remained limited, in those days of bipolarity, to only the Western camp. It was not intended to make any particular decision, and no one excluded was shocked, except Canada, which was definitively included the following year to form the G7. The others were still far off. No one was speaking about emergent states, since bipolarity prevented the success of any candidacy from the East, and the Westerners who had not been included in the club were not attempting to become candidates. Spain, in particular, fell back upon an agonised version of Francoism. The humiliation of others was not yet on the agenda.

The parameters were quickly modified. Caught up in their ultra-liberalism, Margaret Thatcher and Ronald Reagan disdained questions about economic regulation, and reoriented the G7 towards political questions such as the question of Afghanistan (Venice, 1980), of Euromissiles (Williamsburg, 1983), terrorism (Tokyo, 1986), Eastern Europe (Paris, 1989), the breakup of the Soviet Union (London, 1991), Russia (Naples, 1994), Kosovo (Cologne, 1999), Iraq (Évian, 2003), the Middle East (Sea Island, 2004), the Arab Spring (Deauville, 2011), Syria (Lough Erne, 2013). Everything would change: dialogue on economic matters became rarer, but from that point on, the club members spoke about the world, of things that were everyone's business; and short of deciding, in the best case people got along, in the worst one played the game of discreet connivance. Russia was admitted in small steps: there was not much more to do, to turn an intra-Western consultation into a directorate for the world.

Thus humiliation begins to take shape in the background, through a process of subtraction that also passed over 185 sovereign members of the United Nations. The effect of this exclusion was stronger because the club that was in the process of forming itself constructed an identity that would exercise influence over time. Coming from the West in the 1970s, it developed naturally into a governance of the West and a governance by the West. We remember the way the G7 in London (July 1991), humiliated Mikhaïl Gorbatchev, who had come to ask for help from the club in obtaining aid from the international community, and who was received in a very arrogant manner.[6]

This transmutation of the G7 into the Western core of the world, barely balanced by the admission of Russia and the formation of the G8 in 1998, soon found its rhetorical stride. The Deauville summit in May 2011, which focused on the Arab Spring, hastened, by this very fact, an identification set in motion 20 years earlier by the collapse of the Soviet Union. The French

[6] *cf* above, and R Dumas, with B Badie and G Minassian, *La Diplomatie sur le vif* (Paris, Presses de Sciences Po, 2013) 42–43.

president, Nicolas Sarkozy, host of the Deauville G8 meeting, spoke of the meeting as 'an informal consultation of the democratic *family*'. Barack Obama, stopping in London on the way to Deauville, characterised the West as the 'cradle of modernity' and even of globalisation. He rejected the notion of a 'decline of the West', and observed that the technological revolution had been born in Silicon Valley: '... China, India, Brazil [experienced] rapid growth... and [moved] towards market-based principles adopted by the United States and Great Britain. [...] From Newton to Darwin, Edison and Einstein; from Alan Turing to Steve Jobs, we have led the world in our engagement with science and cutting edge research. [...] We have built a world in which new nations can emerge, and individuals can prosper'.[7]

This nobility of origin had to define itself very quickly in comparison with a nobility of the robe, a product, precisely, of the effects of the globalisation that Barack Obama praised. This was a difficult transition that was first accomplished informally: up until 2008, the organisers were gracious enough to invite a few leaders from emergent powers to the table and to the feast of the G8. François Mitterrand, at the Summit of the Arch (La Défense, Paris, 1989), invited 15 such heads of state or government to take part only in the celebrations; this status of 'aspiring G8 member' actually led them to meet on their own, constituting a G15.[8] This procedure was repeated later at Tokyo, but in accordance with a different geometry. Not until the meeting at Évian in 2003 would the idea of an 'enlarged dialogue' emerge, which would include China, Brazil, India, South Africa, Mexico, Nigeria, Algeria, and Senegal. On occasion, the King of Morocco was invited (but did not attend); invitations were also extended to the Crown Prince of Saudi Arabia, the prime minister of Malaysia (then-current president of the nonaligned movement), the Egyptian president, and in Savoy, a close neighbour, Switzerland.[9] Each of the succeeding summits had its own configuration, something that was left to the discretion of the host country, even if the main emergent nations (the BRICS, who had just constituted themselves as a group) were present each time. Three concentric circles were drawn: the circle of the G8, the circle of the invitees who could not be avoided, but who were only 'coming to have a cup of coffee', and the circle of the special guests whose presence was an illustration of the benevolent protection of the host country. This 'third circle' included the King of Morocco and the president of Senegal, chosen by Jacques Chirac, Hamid Karzai (Afghanistan), Ali Abdallah Saleh (Yemen), the King of Jordan or the Ugandan president Yoweri Museveni, invited by George W. Bush,

[7] *Le Monde*, 27 May 2011, p 1 and p 4.
[8] Hajnal, *The G8 System and the G20*.
[9] ibid 48.

the prime minister of Thailand, invited by his Japanese opposite number (Okinawa, 2000), and Hosni Mubarak, chosen by almost everybody.

The second circle led to the creation of the G20 in November 2008, at the moment when the old powers recognised that they were entering a major economic crisis, and would need to reinforce their cooperation with the emerging powers. However, this transformation could not be accomplished except through another selection process. The 11 States that were co-opted by the G8 (there were only 19 Member States of the G20) were taken from the finance ministers' G20 meeting, which had been held because of a different crisis, the one from which Asia had been suffering since 1997. The criteria for selection included economic wealth and a certain political conformity. Obviously this latter criterion was not required from the powers whose absence would have been unthinkable, such as the BRICS members. But it applied to the category below that, which included Saudi Arabia, Australia, and South Korea. This triage, intended to nominate members of the circle of world governance, combined in itself all the elements of the denial of equality: exclusion of the poor, of the actors in the principal world conflicts, of states that were known for raising protests (the absence of Algeria is significant) and deviant states. As it turned out, the effort to open things up was just an effort; the G8 quickly became more important than the G20.

Oligarchic Pressure

Thus we observe an effect of the system that, in the manner of an iron law, tends to push any mode of governance towards its most selective variant. The neologism, globalisation, was coined to describe a pressing need for inclusion. Globalisation implied not only a larger association of States, particularly those engaged in local and regional issues, but also supposed the inclusion of non-state actors and actors from economic, social and cultural fields.[10] How things actually developed quickly went in a different direction, and exclusion was made into a standard principle for the regulation of tensions and conflicts.

The proliferation of 'contact groups' was the first sign. We can understand its close links with the end of bipolarity; here we find once again the hopes that middle powers had, of entering (or re-entering) the game. However, the formula led to failures and repeated blockages that are easy to understand: a small number of powers were given responsibility for

[10] Commission on Global Governance, *Our Global Neighbourhood* (Oxford, Oxford University Press, 1994); YH Ferguson, RW Mansbach, *A World of Polities: Essays on Global Politics* (London, Routledge, 2008); RB Hall, TJ Biersteker (eds), *The Emergence of Private Authority in Global Governance* (Cambridge, Cambridge University Press, 2002).

handling each crisis, but were themselves ruled by their own interests, interests that were sharpened by their turn towards oligarchy. This arrangement never had much of a chance of functioning properly.

The contact group model was first used in the Yugoslav crisis, when such a group was created in April 1994, including the United States, Russia, France, Great Britain and Germany. The paradox was already apparent. The solution to an internal conflict was supposed to be found during a deliberation from which the main protagonists would be absent, and which would be conducted by the countries that were patrons of the protagonists. The schema is exactly opposite of that which is recommended in real mediation; it led directly to a solution actually being imposed by the strongest country, as happened during the Dayton process.

The Iranian case reveals a mechanism that is even more subtle. In August 2003, Germany, France and Great Britain joined in an initiative, in the name of the European Union, to propose a framework for negotiations on the question of Iran's nuclear program. The empirical process, thus begun, little by little came to be the formalisation of a 'troika', which concluded upon the elaboration, in October 2003, of a 'Tehran declaration', proposing the application of an additional protocol to the Nuclear Non-Proliferation Treaty. This step at the same time gave political and diplomatic existence to a group made up of three middle powers, outside any institutional framework. The hardening of the line taken by Iran, which was associated with the election of Mahmoud Ahmadinejad, paradoxically led to the continuance of this group, which was then associated with the P5. Thus was born the G5 + 1, made up of the members of the Perm 5 plus Germany. The Islamic Republic contributed in an odd manner to this consolidation by making the G5 + 1 its quasi-official partner, and by addressing itself spontaneously to that grouping, especially in September 2009, when new propositions were put forward, and also on 3 January 2010 when Iran wanted to announce to the world its sovereign decision to proceed with uranium enrichment.

The oppositional and even deviant game played by Iran (an Iran that was wounded by being thwarted in areas that it believed were matters of strict sovereignty) contributed to making official a procedure established outside multilateral institutions. In reality, the pressure exerted by the oligarchs gave rise to an international game that was validated by the very countries who were opposed to each other. The contact group on Iran was the result of a European initiative, but had been formed by a gradual process of fusion with the group of permanent members of the Security Council. The addition of Russia and China made consensus difficult, at the same time as legitimising the body in terms of international legality. The extra-institutional genesis of the group reinforced the Iranians' conviction that they had been placed under supervision. The combination of these two logics produced deadlock in the process, and humiliation, and the tensions and escalations that go along with such things.

This selective reflex is found in connection with all crises, in different forms. Close to the same thing, the 'groups of friends' that arose proved to be less deliberative, less formal and more open than 'contact groups', often accompanying a decision-making process at a lower level, legitimising it, and perhaps insuring its 'parliamentary framework'. Their composition corresponds to a complex combination of invitations, co-optations and declarations of intentions. Their organisation is quite generally left to the initiative of those who are considered the most powerful, but can also result in a proactive diplomacy, as happened with Tunisia during the Syrian crisis. But it is still necessary, if such diplomacies are to succeed, for them to be supported by several great powers, almost always Western. In all, there is a circumvention—more or less declared—of multilateralism, and a reorganisation of the oligarchic game. The boundary between contact groups and groups of friends is, of course, porous, and return tickets are by no means rare.

The Libyan case deserves close examination. On 29 March 2011, 12 days after the Security Council adopted resolution 1973, instituting a no-fly zone over Libya, a 'conference' was held in London. It was significant that most Arab states, except for Qatar and the United Arab Emirates, were represented only by ambassadors; Egypt and Algeria had declined their invitations, just as the secretary-general of the Arab League and the African Union had done. In the absence of Russia, China and the emergent powers, the geometry of the meeting was reduced to the Western perimeter constituted by the main European powers and the United States. It is true that in the meantime, it had been decided that NATO would handle the operation. The chief officers of NATO were at the meeting. In less than two weeks, a rare thing, an international consensus, recorded at a meeting of the (Western) Security Council, was transformed into a Western high table that gained just enough consciousness of its own identity to form a contact group, in accordance with a familiar method. That group would monitor the crisis through successive meetings at Doha, Rome, Abu Dhabi, twice in Istanbul, where the National Transitional Council was recognised as 'the legitimate governing authority in Libya' (July 2011), and where a road map was drawn up in order to 'build a new Libya' (August 2011). Another meeting was held in Paris on 1 September 2011, in order to substitute for the contact group a new formation that would be known as the 'Friends of Libya', which later met in New York (20 September 2011).

With this change, the architecture expanded somewhat and the role of the group became more consultative than deliberative. In Paris, there were 23 States who were members, and a certain number of observers. The full members all belonged to the Western sphere: we find the great majority of NATO members, Japan and certain members of the Arab League who are notoriously pro-Western (Bahrain, Jordan, Kuwait, Morocco, Qatar, the UAE), and also Lebanon, in relation to a very specific situation. In fact the 'friends of Libya' do not include any African States, except Morocco. On the other hand, Australia is there, and Canada and Bulgaria. China and Russia were invited to join as minor members of the 'concert'; the former sent observers, and the latter did not.

Later, of course, the arrangements changed again, coming to include several African States (Chad, Gabon, Mali, Niger). But these changes only confirmed the trend: the group of friends was actually embedded in the Western sphere, and did not include any other sensibilities, coming from emergent powers or from the Chinese or Russian sphere, or from Southern regimes that have made no secret of their criticisms with regard to the West. This marginalisation of diplomacies that refuse to merge their programmes with that of the West was the main ambiguity that emerged from the Libyan crisis. It was the origin of the acts of defiance that marked the main stages of the Syrian crisis, which had already appeared. It showed that by a succession of displacements, almost insensibly, a multilateral and consensual matter could become unilateral and non-consensual. This almost systematic derailing is a tale of the ambiguities of post-bipolarity and shows that these ambiguities quickly engender functional inequalities and acts of appropriation that the other powers, Russia, emergent powers, and Southern nations who mistrust the West, receive as humiliations.

As the Syrian crisis worsened, a similar process was just starting to emerge. Nevertheless, things began differently. This time, it was Tunisia—shortly after it acquired a new government that united progressives and Islamists—that took the initiative to call for a 'international conference of the friends of the Syrian people' in Gammarth. The date was 24 February 2012: the Syrian civil war had been going on for almost a year and the Western powers were either on the back foot or playing a waiting game. The conference was, at his point, very inclusive: was somewhat limited at Gammarth, because Russia and China declined the invitation, but the later attendance was very impressive. In Paris, in July 2012, 121 States attended; in December 2012, 114 met in Marrakech (December 2012). This then fell to only 11 countries at the conferences in Amman (May 2013), and Doha (June 2013). As the crisis became an international issue, the number of countries involved shrank and became more homogenised according to a layout similar to that of the Friends of Libya. Tunisia retired, and the 11 comprised: Germany; Saudi Arabia; Egypt (in the final days of the regime of Mohamed Morsi, who was very hostile to the Baathist regime); the United Arab Emirates; the United States; France; Italy; Jordan; Qatar; Great Britain; and Turkey.

This rehash could not be thought of otherwise than as the reanimation of a quasi-alliance attempting to play the role of a Directorate, making reference to a friendship that is addressed to 'the Syrian people' in an effort to present separation from the official regime: in this regard the 'friends of Libya' and the 'friends of Syria' were alike. Obviously there was a certain range of reactions, outside the circle of the eleven, from prudent indifference to the feeling that—in a troubling and humiliating way—the Syrian dossier had been confiscated by a small group, a group strikingly similar to the one that had taken charge of the Libyan dossier.

It should be noted that this architecture had been in competition with other formulas. Kofi Annan, in his role as mediator in relation to Syria, at the urging of the United Nations, spoke in June 2012 about the idea of a contact group that would embody a joining of multilateralism and regionalism, by associating the five permanent members of the security council, Turkey, Saudi Arabia, Qatar and Iran. The proposition had the double merit of being inclusive and wagering on the benefit of an effective involvement by local actors: this might have avoided the dangers of functional inequality. But this initiative was not immediately accepted, and even drew a negative comment from US Secretary of State, Hillary Clinton, who said that the project would be 'difficult' to bring about. This feeling of diplomatic unease when there is a question about bringing the 'other' as outsider into the circle, sheds light on the impoverishment of the very concept of diplomacy, when it focuses only on managing homogeneity and ignores the question of 'separateness'.[11]

Not long after, Iran in turn proposed the creation of a regional contact group concentrating on Syria: the initiative was taken up by the Egyptian president, Mohamed Morsi, at a conference of the Nonaligned Movement that was held, deliberately, in Tehran on 30 and 31 August 2012. The idea was to offer a new geometry for this formula by only bringing in local actors, in this instance Saudi Arabia, Egypt, Iran, and Turkey. This was innovation and it came with a grand concept: the process of finding solutions for conflicts was a matter for those who lived in the neighbourhood, whose commitment to a solution could hardly be doubted, whatever might be said in coded diplomatic language. This sudden appearance of a 'truth in conflicts' criterion, in the sense in which one might speak of a 'truth in pricing', was favourable to the establishment of a new balance in the classic international game, to the benefit of both new and regional powers. The oligarchic process would be broken, and the feeling that powers belonging to another history and probably another geography were intruding again, was avoided. At any rate the initiative, accepted more or less sincerely by the interested parties, achieved no practical effect and was effectively dissolved when a military coup d'état occurred in July 2013 in Cairo, resulting in the removal from office of President Morsi.

Putting different diplomatic formulas in competition with each other, deviating from the demands of multilateralism, the almost mechanical

[11] P Sharp, *Diplomatic Theory of International Relations* (Cambridge, Cambridge University Press, 2009).

distancing of regional systems and local actors, the logics of patronage that are allowed to regulate the constitution of these mediating agencies, the recurrence of games of exclusion applied to actors considered deviant, all these are so many parameters that not only maintain but in fact aggravate functional inequality as it affects the international system. The repetition of these games, their visibility and their importance cause frustration and humiliation of the parties that are not so important, cause the states to reorient their diplomacies towards intentionally conflictual forms. Thus the question of status determines things so completely that it is more important than the nature of the conflict. International crises are crystallised, more and more frequently, by crises of credibility on both sides. Multilateralism must try to resist this; it has become the main victim.

One might speak of the anomic effect of the logic of the club, which dilutes norms, especially in relation to multilateral institutions, and which creates a situation in which there is an absence of rules governing interactions between the various actors in the international system. This programmed return to a state of semi-nature orients the associated social behaviour, to the extent that the solidarity of the deciders is shown more and more explicitly. In the Western sphere those who lead know each other and love to cultivate the coquetry that goes with a public friendship, but are all nonetheless exposed to universal mechanisms of socialisation.

The role played by university-related institutions is quite striking. Take for example the Massachusetts Institute of Technology, in Boston (MIT). Lucas Papadémos, a former Greek prime minister, once practically 'named' by the European Union in the middle of an economic crisis to succeed Georges Papandreou, who was being pushed out by the EU, went to school there. He took a course with Franco Modigliani, and had as fellow student Ben Bernanke, a former president of the Federal Reserve Bank. Bernanke's dissertation was directed by Stanley Fischer, a future governor of the Bank of Israel, who also played a large role in the design of the dissertation of Mario Draghi, president of the European Central Bank. Bernanke shared an office with Mervyn King, future governor of the Bank of England, and was later the professor of José de Gregorio, a former governor of the Central Bank of Chile. The successor to Ben Bernanke, Janet Yellen, did not go to MIT, but her husband, Nobel Prize winner in economics George Akerlof, defended his dissertation there. Everybody took a course with Paul Samuelson, who sat on the jury of Stanley Fischer's dissertation. Samuelson's nephew was Larry Summers, later a chief economist at the World Bank, and American Treasury Secretary, and also the professor of Charles Bean, a deputy governor of the Bank of England.[12] Draghi, Papadémos and Monti (who was also named the head of the Italian government because of

[12] *Bloomberg Businessweek*, 23–29 January 2012, p 15.

pressure from the European Union) had also all worked for Goldman Sachs investment bank.[13]

We should accept such 'trees' of power relationships with caution. The fact that people know each other or go to the same school does not mean they were all programmed to act in the same way, or to reject anyone not so programmed. But this caution is a double-edged sword. Such connections should not be ignored or excluded as marks of a 'distinction' that not only separates those that have it from those that do not, but inevitably raises the question in the minds of the latter, about whether they have any international status left.

A Certain Diplomatic Paternalism

In order to complete the table, we must take account of what we are doing, how we are doing it, and how we are presenting it. The status of an actor is devalued or revalued in the manner in which we address him. Excluding, punishing, bullying, making demands, these are characteristic manifestations that first become ordinary, and then are made the formal instruments of official diplomacy, in the name of a presumed superiority.

Exclusion has become a common characteristic of the international game, although it was formerly based on the notion of States recognising each other, whatever might be the nature of their regimes. For the State that benefited from this recognition, full status opened up as an actor on the international scene. Only bilateral relations were suspended, as in a formal break in diplomatic relations. Today that dramatic gesture is rare, while exclusion from the international scene is demanded by tighter and tighter jerks on the lead. Behind these initiatives there is a will to punish and to pressure. Thus Iran, a frequent target, was the object of an entire series of exclusionary demands: exclusion from negotiations over Syria (before the election of Hassan Rohani), from the system of interbank exchanges SWIFT (February 2012), from access to UNODC aid (UN programme against drugs and crime, August 2012), from the UN Human Rights Council, from the IMF (2012) and even from the World Cup (2006). Suddenly, Syria since 2005, the Iraq of Saddam Hussein, Cuba, Libya (off and on under Gaddafi), the Sudan of al-Bashir, Zimbabwe, Belarus, North Korea and many others, like Hamas and Hezbollah, fell under the same sort of prohibition.

Sanctions may sometimes be deserved. On the other hand, exclusion may well have perverse and unforeseen effects. In order to be convincing, the sanctions should not open up other pathways that would tend to bring profit to the one that signs up to the sanctions. That, however, is what

[13] 'Goldman Sachs, le trait d'union entre Mario Draghi, Mario Monti et Lucas Papadémos', lemonde.fr, 14 November 2011.

happens, in accordance with the way the international system currently runs. This situation did not appear prior to the colonial wars, if we except the condescending marginalisation that Europe visited upon neighbouring empires. The normalisation of exclusion stems mainly from the feeling of inequality that became active during the colonial wars, when the traditional powers said that there could be no question of negotiating with liberation fronts; they ended up doing exactly that every time. The phenomenon grew during the 1980s, when Western democracies had to confront non-state organisations acting as entrepreneurs of violence, described as terrorists. It was said that they could not be negotiated with, but again this principle was often abandoned, especially when hostages were involved. Finally, as the ambiguous concept of a rogue State was formed, a rhetoric of the same nature was generously applied to those who were thereby stigmatised.

The danger of such a posture is that negotiations may be blocked or disrupted, because the excluded parties are pushed even more strongly towards strategies that involve creating a nuisance. Dissociating Iran from the Iraqi conflict, from 2003, led only to a worsening of the conflict, except for the times when secret negotiations with Tehran were arranged. Obviously, exclusion interrupts the effect of socialisation upon the protesting party, which might occur through his participation in the functioning of international institutions. The country that is excluded ends up being thrown into a parallel international system that is structured around the accomplishment of many different kinds of deviant actions, rhetorical, normative, practical and even ethical, for example, the shocking use of negationist theories. Exclusion weakens the identification of the excluded party with the international system per se, which only aggravates a situation already rife with conflicts. Ignoring the opponent appears at the same time as a severe variant of the act of humiliation, as something that one does not inflict upon one's equal. During the Cold War, one excluded oneself from certain phases of the game, but one did not exclude the *other*.

The idea of punishment is in a similar vein, although it is obviously a more serious matter, since its moral weight is great. This kind of initiative is also intimately bound up with the denial of equality: in order to punish, one must direct the punishment at a reprehensible attitude, and at the same time consider oneself superior to the one who is incriminated. This hierarchy of authorities, in domestic law, confers its effectiveness upon the State and legal institutions. In international law, this is a prerogative of the International Criminal Court or the UN Security Council.

In an international context that is only weakly institutionalised, we speak more often of 'sanctions' than of 'punishment', especially with regard to a time when the International Criminal Court did not yet exist. Sanctions were thought of as a kind of pressure. At the end of bipolarity, the great powers became bolder and began to speak of 'punishment' in order to influence smaller States that had made nuisances of themselves at the margins of the Cold War. South Africa, during apartheid, was only sanctioned, but Operation Eldorado Canyon, authorised in 1986 by Ronald Reagan and carried out against Moammar Gaddafi, became a punishment in this sense—although this action also qualified as an act of reprisal for the attack that had killed a number of American soldiers in a discotheque in Berlin. The operation was nonetheless condemned by the UN General Assembly. In August 1998, President Clinton ordered Operation Infinite Reach to punish Afghanistan and Sudan, carrying out reprisals for attacks against American embassies in East Africa.

With the Syrian crisis of September 2013, a new step has been taken: the United States and France claimed to be 'punishing' the Syrian regime that was accused of having used chemical weapons against its own people, but by dissociating this punishment from regime change. Contrary to previous cases, the victims were not citizens of the states that were claiming the right to punish: we move away from retaliation and into the realm of pure—and increasingly explicit—administration of morality. Such language only becomes possible when it is assumed in the name of a hierarchical inequality that is precisely measured: that which separates the punisher from the punished, and thus highlights the difference in status.

This can also be expressed through different kinds of bullying or insults that no one would allow oneself to do except to someone weaker. An episode from the early summer of 2013 will serve as an example. At that moment, Edward Snowden—who had just revealed many things about the interception of communications American intelligence services were overseeing, especially in Europe—had just fled to Russia, and Washington was seeking his extradition, troubled by seeing one of its citizens seek refuge abroad. The president of Bolivia was at that very moment on a visit to Moscow, about to leave for home. France, Spain, Portugal and Italy suspected the Bolivian president, Evo Morales, of having Snowden with him, and for this reason forced his airplane to sit on the tarmac in Vienna for 14 hours by refusing it permission to fly through their airspace. The Spanish ambassador, on the pretext of having a cup of coffee with the delayed president, was dispatched to inspect the inside of the aircraft. President Morales' own account of this incident does not lie: speaking about the incident as an example of 'special punishment', he compared his adventure to the events that 'led to the oppression of the Indians' during the Spanish Conquest. He spoke about 'colonialism' and claims that he was a 'humble' person against the great powers.[14]

***

In fact, these three inequalities—constitutive, structural and functional—manage today to make a system and to reinforce one another. This effect

[14] 'Moi, président de la Bolivie, séquestré en Europe', *Le Monde diplomatique*, August 2013, 713, p 1 and 10–11.

is greater than it might otherwise have been because we have left a structured international system, and have entered a system known as 'post-bipolar', whose principles are not clear, and whose norms are not very solid. At the same time, inequality is perceived by the most powerful as a rational means of diminishing the transaction costs that inevitably entails more highly developed international cooperation. This vision is very probably wrong, and the opposite of a reality that makes exclusion more and more costly for everyone. But this trend, which is strong in post-bipolar Western diplomacy, constituting a real pathology of the dominator, is reinforced still further by belief in a windfall effect: the politics of inequality constitutes a means for improving one's own status at the expense of the other. Even more, reducing the status of most others becomes a diplomatic game, more and more frequently seen, and only those States who are in league are spared from it, the members of the club, the oligarchs. Through this process the system replicates itself and humiliation becomes something quite close to a mechanical result.

In fact, in an effort to preserve itself and continue its existence, this unstable and fragile system tends to produce another system outside itself, which is constituted around all the reactive ambitions nourished by those who have been victims of humiliation.

Part Three

The Dangerous Repercussions that Follow Humiliation: Towards an Anti-System?

HUMILIATION WOULD ONLY be potential, perhaps even an invention of the observer, if it was not confirmed in explicit behaviours that prove it has been received as humiliation. Our task, therefore, is to establish those models of behaviour, whose features are traced out by the operation of the mechanisms we have described. Our project is to consider these reactions at different levels, which must themselves be described and classified. It is also to show the connection that unites these various levels and makes a system out of them, even an anti-system, which is part of the opposition to the 'official' international scene.

This anti-system is part of modernity; it is part and parcel of globalisation. It is first deployed at the level of societies, where it quickly becomes the chief mode by which international humiliation is orchestrated. The second level is the level of diplomacies, oppositional or even deviant, which have the advantage of forming and developing at the junctions of the societies and political systems that are involved. The third level is that of 'conflict', which characterises current situations better than an account of wars between States, as in past eras, and which also operates in a liminal zone between societies and political systems. The system logic that is derived from a combination of these three levels is probably more proactive today than the classical political science model of a confrontation between powers.

7

The Mediating Role of Societies

WE HAVE ALREADY seen that 'socialisation by means of international life' hastened and normalised practices of humiliation. In this regard the societies concerned were widely affected by 'revanchism', which pushed their populations to mobilise, galvanised populism and the more diverse forms of nationalism. In turn, the denial of equality, relegation and stigmatisation affected these societies, and provided good material for political entrepreneurs who knew how to take advantage of such things, either in order to relegitimise their own power, or in order to contest more effectively the legitimacy of those in authority. But this social sensitivity to humiliation does more. It reverses the classical order of factors, by letting societies, more and more, be the initiators of action, overcoming the prudence or inertia of States, inserting themselves directly into the international game without going through a political system. We are seeing an increasing internationalisation of social dynamics, movements and social aspirations. International action will increasingly take concrete effect through the mediating power of societies.

This new tectonic of societies creates forms—already known or just appearing—of protest against international humiliation. This is part of a very strong trend, and the Arab Spring serves as a good model for it.

The International Mobilisation of Societies

We cannot today analyse the international system if we limit ourselves to competition between States in the sense of Raymond Aron. Societies have entered the game, sometimes in a dominant fashion, even if many do not wish to see this. The new arrangement has a great deal to do with contemporary modes of communication that allow us to see the 'other', the antagonist, easily and directly, such that a whole range of trans-national exchanges are immediately activated. But it is evident that this weight of societies, thrown into the balance, will have a greater effect because the existing political institutions are weak, fragile, and barely legitimate. It is precisely in such contexts of wavering institutionalisation that humiliation is most commonly received, and hence the remarkable importance of mediations that are carried out in this manner.

Two examples, which happened at the same time, yet which remain distinct, testify to this: China and the Arab world. In both cases, responses to humiliation surged up from the depths of those societies. Over and over, for centuries now, the Middle Kingdom has had to deal with powerful movements of social opposition that have arisen in order to attack weakening dynasties, or at least unsuccessful ones; social explosions were orchestrated by secret societies that were noteworthy for being able to organise the peasantry. In the 19th century, the Qing dynasty, weakened, was no exception. Beginning in 1851, the Taiping led social revolts that mixed together egalitarian politics and modernism, borrowing from the West and especially from Christianity. At that moment the effects of Western penetration were barely perceptible. But the second wave of social explosions was oriented in a completely different direction—towards xenophobia and anti-Westernism, and violently directed towards any Europeans on Chinese soil. The Big Swords Society—whose militants were termed 'Boxers'—was fuelled, at the turn of the 20th century, by an endogenous source related to Chinese magical traditions. Missionaries were no longer imitated: they were hunted down and killed. Significantly, a proto-nationalist and anti-European rhetoric was mingled with anti-modernist feelings. The elites in the Imperial Chinese system were bypassed and then nearly neglected: the anti-establishment position took hold, producing aggressive, even fundamentalist criticisms of the international sphere. At the same time, the political leadership counted for nothing in the face of their slogan ('destroy everything European'): the movement and its rationality were of a social nature. Recruitment started at the bottom of the ladder, first addressing the poor peasants already threatened, then little by little gaining the confidence of the inhabitants of towns, small-scale artisans and tradespeople.

Most of these characteristics were present in the Arab world. Their appearance happened somewhat later, because Western pressure took time to reach them; the end of the 19th century and the succeeding decades were affected. But in the West, as in the Arab world, the response did not come primarily from weakened political authorities, who were even more anxious to accommodate Western princes, like the Ottoman sultans after Selim III (1789). The movement arose from society, placed in context by the thinking of the Nahda, which was then relayed by a small intelligentsia, at the same time fundamentalist and modernist. This spoke to an urban population a little lost because of their 'depeasantisation', and made uneasy by the wave of Westernisation they had just experienced. In this radicalised atmosphere, in 1928, the Muslim Brotherhood was born, just as the level of concessions to Westerners reached its peak of visibility, and the Nile Delta became a zone for social change and an openness that was not controlled by the West. Bearing witness to this is the personality of its founder, Hassan el-Banna, the son of a clockmaker from Ismaïlia who was also the imam at a nearby mosque. He was trained as a teacher, but also worked as a muezzin. He was offered a scholarship to finish school in Europe, but he refused and stayed in Egypt. From that point, he sought to combine social Islam with a denunciation of Western influence.

The crisis of social integration that is being gradually revealed, and which will not stop growing, is more serious for regions of the world that are affected by severe socioeconomic disadvantages, painful shortages, and an accelerated pace of change, all of which throws rural populations into gigantic, faceless urban spaces; and these people subsequently find in xenophobia and anti-Western ideology a handy means of expressing their humiliation, their fears, and their despair. This phenomenon was noted and described very early on by political science, from the first moments of decolonisation.[1] Important research has emphasised that the poorest victims were no longer in the habit of adopting resigned attitudes in the face of rural poverty, which had formerly been the case. The anger of the poor had become urban, 'up close': it is shaped by contact with a perceived 'worldliness', and quickly associated with Western powers, who are themselves considered to be agents of colonial domination, the inventors of globalisation, and its main symbols, all at once.[2]

In many places in the South, a strong proactive capacity manifests itself in societies that are imperfectly integrated in two ways. First, inside the States concerned, where the gap tends to be yawning between a Westernised elite, financially comfortable, at least as regards the upper levels (often corrupt), and a largely unemployed mass, whose situation is worsening in terms of food, sanitation, and schooling. This is also the case on the international level, where social contrasts can daily be seen to aggravate the North-South divide. This potential for mobilisation appears to have a force behind it that could be called tectonic—leading to shocks that may be difficult to manage, since these social movements have gone outside the classical political framework. These movements rarely have an established political leadership, or structured organisations in the manner of classic political parties; and they tend not to have well-defined programmes. In the authoritarian context in which they find themselves, they remain under the radar politically, and operate through more or less clandestine networks. These may be religious, community-based, or related to an ethical position. They are most often configured as charities and care-givers, which makes them suited to address the challenge of incomplete social integration.

This lack of points of contact with the official political scene makes these social spaces less controllable, although the movements that occupy these spaces are often more legitimate than the sitting powers, which are

[1] K Deutsch, *Nationalism and Social Communication* (New York-London, Chapman and Hall, 1953); D Lerner, *The Passing of Traditional Society* (Glencoe, Free Press, 1958).

[2] M Keck and K Sikkink, *Activists Beyond Borders* (Ithaca, Cornell University Press, 1998).

authoritarian and only weakly representative, in every sense of the word. Hence the nature of the autonomous attitude that characterises such spaces was sustained over the long term by symbolic marks of rejection and humiliation coming from the outside: cartoons that feature a supposed image of the Prophet and burnings of Korans, some real, some carried out by institutions and some simply based on rumours. There have been multiple cases of disputes over veils or headscarves, or at a different level of intensity, racist taunts, and the discontent of immigrant populations in the West. Everything is likely to make someone angry in Karachi, Kano or Djakarta. These non-organised social actors become key actors on the international scene, but they cannot be reached by any structure of negotiation.

Obviously these non-State and non-organised actors are now being courted: more by political structures within States than by diplomats, who seem not to know how to take them, who fear them and often mistrust them without daring to say so openly. Within national political systems, the governing class, according to its diplomatic orientation, might seek to seduce these new actors, or to repress them. The first option supposes that populist or nationalist formulas are going to be used, formulas that point directly to international humiliations, in order to dramatise them, and to heighten tensions in connection with them, making them a source of legitimation and counter-mobilisation. Foreign policies that derive directly from such movements become explicitly anti-Western, but this formula would not have been used if the leader had not previously become embroiled in this anti-Western position. In this case we encounter people like Mossadegh in Iran, Nasser in Egypt, Sukarno in Indonesia, Lumumba, Nkrumah. We also find a very few 'conversions', such as those that regularly affect the leaders of Pakistan, who have acquiesced to foreign power following a rather pro-American line, and later changing, in a context of drone attacks and a stream of refugees coming from Afghanistan, putting out a rhetoric that is hostile to the United States, and which otherwise is becoming more populist. Zulfikar Ali Bhutto in the past, his daughter Benazir, and later Pervez Musharraf or Ali Zardari are indeed prototypes of a Westernised and/or militarised oligarchy, one which is prompt to adapt to its own purposes, when necessary, a rhetoric of humiliation suffered, in order to survive politically.

When the prince has a pro-Western diplomatic orientation, the game is much more difficult. Humiliation must be concealed, denied or denounced on an ad hoc basis, for example the very timid trembling of Hosni Mubarak when he was questioned by Western colleagues who were pushing him to adopt reforms. In the opposite kind of case, repression, carried on in the name of a 'war on terror', may be the only means of containing social pressure; and reclaiming, by reference to the nobility of the fight, some support from the great powers, who are quick to show their confidence in such regimes, and to confer on them the desirable status of a 'moderate'.

The actual nature of such a phenomenon can be established in several ways. The expression of public opinion—more visible than it used to be, and more reliably sampled—is already the beginning of proof, and this should not be ignored. Anti-Americanism makes constant progress, especially in sensitive areas of the current international situation. Even more, we can see that this system of attitudes is more akin to something implanted in society, than something constructed by political actors, as if once more society shows the way, and does so with all the more effect, seeing that the local political class had abdicated. That which Hadjar Aouardji calls 'social anti-Americanism' is first of all a dynamic that comes from societies trying to manage their own crises, frustrations and blockages.[3]

Surveys conducted by the Pew Center in 2007, at the end of the Bush era, show a particularly low approval rating for the United States in countries that had governments that were closely allied to Washington: 15% in Pakistan, 20% in Jordan, 21% in Egypt, 15% in Morocco. In Turkey, a member of NATO, approval was only 9%, the same as Lebanon, whose State is traditionally close to the West, leaving aside Palestine (13%).[4] In 2013, at a moment when neo-conservatism had receded and when Barack Obama was about to begin a second term, the approval rating was still only 16% in Egypt, 14% in Jordan, 16% in Palestine, 11% in Pakistan. On the other hand, when Turkey was headed towards a foreign policy that was more independent and more critical, the approval rate rose from 9 to 21%. Tunisia, which had broken with the pro-Western regime of Ben Ali, actually saw the US approval rating rise to 42%.[5]

Obama as a person was attractive, but only around the edges, without neutralising the effect of context or the historical profundity of the same. When Obama was elected, the approval rating of the US rose a little in Egypt (21% in 2007, 27% in 2009), but by 2013 it had fallen back to 16%. Similarly, 42% of Egyptians approved of Obama just after his appearance at the conference in Cairo, but by 2013 this number had fallen to 26%.

In fact, the more central a society is within the international game, the stronger the anti-American expression is. Thus, anti-Americanism has tended to decline in Latin America, and remains weak in the Philippines and in Senegal. Equally, when a society exposed to tensions is led by a person who is said to be close to the Americans, the same indicator hits new heights, at the very moment when the rise of a nationalistic left in South America moderates the degree to which public opinion is hostile to the big neighbour to the North. These are so many elements confirming

[3] H Aouardji, 'L'Antiaméricanisme social: le cas de l'Égypte, de la Jordanie et de l'Arabie Saoudite', PhD thesis (IEP de Paris, 2010).

[4] Pew Center, Global Attitudes Project, July 2007.

[5] Pew Center, 18 July 2013.

the activism of societies in crisis, the very ones that are not supported by a political class in opposition, and which become the drivers of international mobilisation, ready and willing to express themes connected to humiliation.

Measuring public opinion is only a technical means of obtaining an indication about the state of a society. The result can be quite credible, though it has limitations. Other manifestations, on the other hand, are more direct and explicit. Social movements have the benefit of expressing, more and more visibly, the symbiosis between the claims that belong to all national social or 'domestic' games, and an expression that intends to be more and more international. These arrangements are undoubtedly activated by the feeling of humiliation suffered by the other, the foreigner, whether close or remote. This feeling has an effect much more structuring than an abstract analysis. The designation of the act of humiliation replaces even ideological discourses or political dissertations, and gets straight to the point. One need only think of the marches through the streets of Athens during general strikes, marches denouncing budgetary austerity or other economic decisions made by the government. German Chancellor Angela Merkel's effigy was paraded in Nazi regalia, posed between two swastikas. When she visited the Greek capital in October 2012, she was greeted with 'Sieg heil' salutes. The marchers denounced the 'Fourth Reich', sent a Harlequin figure in Greek dress to chase Merkel out of town, and made other references to the Nazi occupation of Greece and 400 years under the Ottoman occupation.[6]

It is equally significant that the United States and the West in general were criticised by both sides in Cairo in July 2013; they were cried down in the pro-Morsi marches, but also in the pro-Sisi marches. Both sides denounced meddling by foreigners in Egypt's internal matters. Each side took a stance in favour of stigmatising all principals, consultants or models from abroad.[7] It was as if the essential energy that generated the event that had produced a coup d'état had been drawn from a re-enactment of the humiliations suffered by both groups in terms of the international scene.

Every social movement, at some point, is built around the denunciation of a form of domination that is judged unjust, and which has come to symbolise humiliation. In the context of globalisation, its international variant takes over and asserts itself at the expense of local influences, which are often relegated to the condition of mere instruments of a foreign power. In this (often oversimplified) dynamic, it is the social that orchestrates—even produces—the international, directing mobilisation outward, internationalising internal issues to an extreme point, hindering, limiting or trying to direct the foreign policy of local leaders. In short, the social dynamic

[6] *Lemonde.fr*, 10 October 2012.
[7] *Courrier international*, 4 July 2013.

generates energy that is difficult to control, denouncing diplomacies of humiliation, often quite real, sometimes exaggerated, occasionally invented in the name of an old conspiracy theory. Thus there is an awakening—or a re-evaluation—of nationalisms that in past eras were rarely built upon the basis of social discontent. This new symbiosis clearly directed the ideological forms that have just been constructed.

Neo-Nationalism and Fundamentalism

It was also from society, and for a while only from its elites, that these first doctrinal statements came, gradually rising up against a humiliation imposed from a foreign source. The princes in power do not play the leading roles, even if, on occasion, a prince appears who is receptive to new ideas coming from the intelligentsia. For every Mehmet Ali in Egypt, for every Chulalongkorn in Siam, how many more were like Mahmud II, the Ottoman sultan torn between passivity and collaboration with dominant powers, who were capable, after all, of rewarding his docility by saving his throne?

In reality, the game had two main parts, which in some ways are still related today. The first stage was not confrontational, but subtly made connections between anger at seeing one's group unfairly belittled, and the desire to imitate those who had seized a dominant position. The second stage was more tense, focused almost exclusively on aspects of identity, leading unhesitatingly towards the strongest forms of radicalism, and more interested in identity reconstruction than in any form of progress. From one point of view, the failure of imitation, and imitation that was too strong were both experienced as a new humiliation, leading to people retreating further into the shells of their identity.[8]

The original formula may be the source of all the ambiguities; it proclaims forcefully, though perhaps naively, that you can imitate the one who hates you, and thus gain his approval. This idea is more of a posture than a doctrine. No one theorised it. It survived because of support from members of the intelligentsia, who quickly made of it not only a programme for survival, but the instrument of an elevation and an internationalisation that could give them an advantage over traditional elites in a difficult position, or even over the prince himself, if by chance he was not watching everything going on around him. But strategies live a long time: this one can be found today among the members of a Westernised elite group from the South who know perfectly well how to instrumentalise the quasi-State they have control over, and how to manipulate it.

[8] On this point, *cf* B Badie, *The Imported State* (Stanford University Press, 2000).

The career of Wei Yuan (1794–1857) shows what the reality of the phenomenon was like in the 19th century, in China under the Qing. Wei Yuan was a well-known and highly educated intellectual, a refugee in Jiangsu, but also a servant of the Empire; he was the secretary for several high dignitaries, including Lin Zexu, the man who had destroyed the opium cargoes delivered by the British. Wei Yuan was one of the first to rise up against the humiliations China had suffered. The Opium War was particularly repellent; he wrote a book denouncing the disaster. Perfectly loyal to the Imperial court, he was not a revolutionary but a reformer. He openly identified with the 'neo-Confucian' current of thought, calling for empirical adaptations to the doctrine, and fighting against the fundamentalism of the adepts of a literal interpretation of ancient writings, against the ones who defended the Han Learning, who favoured a return to the past of two thousand years earlier.[9]

But his relation to the exterior is the most revealing part of his position. His refrain was to proclaim the necessity of imitating the West in order to accept the challenge embodied in the West. It was appropriate to use 'barbarian science' in the struggle against the barbarians. He was an advocate for an effective navy, and wrote another book explaining why Western knowledge was indispensable in the acquisition of renewed naval power, power that could keep invaders away from Chinese shores. In 1844, he published the *Illustrated Treatise on Sea Powers*. It was not far to the doctrine of Yiyizhiyi, in which he recommended 'use of barbarian methods in order to hold back the barbarians'.

We are still far from the time of the Boxers, from the appeals to magic or to tradition, from the exaltation of the culture of the countryside, and the symbolism of poverty. We are dealing with a discourse of power for which there is no nationality or culture—power that is destined only to serve the one who knows how to use it. It is not power that creates the humiliation, but the inability to take advantage of that power. This first wave of reaction is thus naturally involved in an apology for the State and political know-how. It represents a sensibility that is not close to leaving the arena, despite the defeats it has suffered. It is a factor in China today, as it is in all bureaucratic authoritarianisms of the South, from Mustafa Kemal to General Sisi, mixing nationalism, authority and tactical accommodations with a West that may be imitated, although the ones doing the imitating will know how to criticise the same West severely when it is necessary.

Wei had demonstrated mastery of the technique: in order to counter the British at the moment of the humiliating Opium War, he thought it would have been necessary to make use of France and the United States in order to dominate the modern art of diplomacy, as it was designed, specifically, in

[9] O Schell and J Delory, *Wealth and Power* (New York, Random House, 2013) ch 2.

the West. What is necessary is a rich and powerful State—the only kind that can negotiate treaties, acquire and manage revenue, provide weapons and organise armies—who, among those who rule China today, would reject such an analysis?

This complex mixture of fascination and repulsion, of a desire to imitate and a need to oppose, of fear of power and a taste for power, has doubtless provided fertile ground for many deviant positions and even some perversions. Of all the bad things caused by humiliation, the worst is probably that it opens the door to an ambiguous and often fatal fusion, between authorities seeing things in black and white, and an identity still unsure of itself. The entry of the Muslim world into modernity confirms this. The first reformers, the Egyptian Rifa'a al-Tahtawi (1801–1889), the Tunisians Ibn Abi Dhiaf (1802–1874) and Khayr ad-Din (1810–1889) often accompanied their sovereigns. Tahtawi served Mehmet Ali, while Abi Dhiaf and Khayr ad-Din served Ahmed Bey. For al-Tahtawi, the West was not the enemy, but the *ahl al-tamaddun* (people of civilisation). Here, we do not speak of 'barbarians', at least not yet: on the contrary, it is necessary to go to Europe in order to learn, and then to halt its decline. The decline, for someone like Khayr ad-Din, is caused by a defect in institutional capacity, which is the first thing that must be repaired. We have not even begun to evoke authority; even Montesquieu or the Orleanist Charter are acceptable in order to liberalise power.

This stance is nonetheless extreme, inasmuch as in this middle part of the 19th century, the West was not obviously all it would become. Power was only an image, not yet a plague. Over time, in the wake of Western conquest, radical forms slowly arose. Through Djemâl ad-Dîn al-Afghâni (for Persia and the Ottoman Empire) and through Mohamed Abduh and Rashid Rida (for Egypt and the Levant, respectively), the Arab Renaissance, the Nahda, would rebalance the equation to some degree.

Humiliation has passed that way and left its mark: it is no longer sufficient to learn from Europe; it is necessary to resist the Western coloniser and reunify a Muslim world that is broken into pieces. This is where the idea arose, that gained support, of the restoration of a caliphate—an idea that would impact Western civilisation to a great degree. Undoubtedly, a call to reason remains, as well as confidence in science, progress and modernity, which all value, seeing this as the road to the Reformation. Imitation of the West was always present, and al-Afghâni himself had talks with Christian intellectuals and was close to the Freemasonry movement; Abduh took refuge in Europe after having been expelled from Egypt (a penalty for his having supported the failed coup attempt by the nationalist Urabi Pacha). Between a West that must be fought because it is aggressive towards you, and the West you must imitate because it dominates you, the proper mediation is obvious: only Islam, the bearer of a different identity, can accomplish the necessary rebalancing. The *tawhid* (unity, especially of the community of believers) and the *ijtihâd* (an effort to innovate and thus adapt to modernity) now become important categories.

However, nothing can be taken for granted. If Islam comes into political debates and in so doing appears as 'Islamism' (political use of Islam), its mediation is only meaningful insofar as it is a mediator of the modernisation of the Muslim world. Imitation will no longer be carried out mechanically; Muslims will invent their own version of modernity, and in so doing delegitimise occupation and domination. Legal modernity will no longer imply the mere importation of European codes, but will spring anew from Muslim law, adapted to modern needs. Abduh thus makes concessions to 'modern' practices such as charging interest on loans, and in respect of social topics, he allows that in certain cases, a Muslim can eat non-halal meat. He will even speak about his misgivings with regard to polygamy.

This is a matter, therefore, of recognition, not yet of tension. It is a question now of channelling and controlling imitation, not battling it. All the same, one is defining oneself in the face of a model that is not just seductive, but dominant, oppressive, and arrogant. Introducing humiliation in this way, the response is a statement of two identities: that of the renaissance of a civilisation that will always keep its own personality, and that of a world where the desire for unity is sharpened by the state of the world as divided, broken up, and partially controlled by occupiers.

This identity under construction is not yet centred on confrontation, but is not far from it. The return to sources is not without its cost; the more radical its pursuit, the more it leads to an affirmation of the irreducibility of the self to the other; the more hybridisation is excluded, the more the other is suspected and opposed. Rashid Rida (who died in 1935), the most recent of the three leaders mentioned above, was therefore more radical, close to the Hanbali, the school of legal thought that refused all concession to the outside world, giving support to Wahhabism. Al-Afghâni rejected passive imitation; Rida went further. He did not travel to Europe, but stayed in the Muslim world, categorically rejecting whatever might be imposed from outside. Muslim modernity must affirm itself in the process of purifying itself. The idea of a Golden Age had escaped into the world and could not be recaptured, at a moment when almost the entire Muslim world was under Western administration.

In the meantime, humiliation split in two. There is external pressure, and to this there is joined an arbitrary combination of powers that suppress on the inside and subdue on the outside. The Egyptian monarchy is judged severely; this severity gave this Islamic form of dispute a more directly political orientation, which led to the birth of the Muslim Brotherhood movement. Thus the powers that are in place are, from this point, attacked where they are weakest, in respect of their more or less explicit lay status, which is connected to the imitation of a Western model, all the easier to target because it generates a legitimate space for confrontation that is difficult to minimise. At the same time, this trivialisation of religious discourse creates a double dynamic: it absorbs social discontent in the name of an Islam that is becoming more and more social; and it takes on an international orientation, by exposing and denouncing the solidarity between local powers and Western powers, in the name of an Islam that is more and more based on identity, and more and more exclusive.

The Brotherhood was well and truly a result of the ills of Egyptian society, and out of the atmosphere that characterises the world of the Nile Delta, which is most powerfully present in Ismailia, where the young Hassan el-Banna, as he himself says, befriended workers of the Suez Company who were denouncing foreign pressure and the humiliations associated with it. In order to live, be permitted to exist, and be recognised, in order to recruit nearly 200,000 militants in the first 15 years after its creation, the Brotherhood had to turn itself into a benevolent association. Everything the movement risked (and often lost) in strictly political terms, sometimes faced with repression, it regained and redoubled through the development of activities that involved social services, medical services, and defence of the elderly. The Brotherhood was complemented a few years later by an Association of Muslim Women (Association des femmes musulmanes) created by Zeinab al-Ghazali, also born of Egyptian religious society. The two groups could only gain influence by playing on the subtle meeting point between social Islam and a nationalism that defines itself above all on its distance from the West. It was no surprise that the Brotherhood should first seek to expand into the arab world in the direction of Palestine, the place where 'otherness' and humiliation were most closely linked. Nor was it a surprise that such an association should become the object of suspicion on the part of governments, from the Egyptian monarchy right up to the new military power and its nationalist, pan-Arabist and socialist character, a product of the coup d'état of 1952. Two models were in evidence at that time, competing responses to present and past humiliations: it was quite logical that they should attempt to outbid each other, since each one was attempting to mobilise the same population. If Nasser took the position of a progressive pan-Arabist, the Brotherhood could only respond with a religious appeal, and a dynamic that led Saïd Qutb to preach jihad against an impious State, logically less legitimate than the protests he promoted.[10]

Salafism is partly a result of this rise to extremes, partly a result of the political failure of the Brotherhood, and above all, a result of the globalisation that projects the societies of the Arab world into a universe where compromising, domination and humiliation go beyond the local or national sphere. Hence the return to the 'pious ancestors', carried out so the purification of Islam will continue to be emphasised, even if it must

[10] G Kepel, *Le Prophète et Pharaon* (Paris, La Découverte, 1984) 40 ff.

be reinvented in order to recapture its original purity.[11] By this very fact, Salafism at first leads to a return of society to itself, through the effort towards social re-Islamisation, in which the imam or preacher is valued more than the political leader. An example: Nâsir ad-Dîn al-Albâni (1914–1999). A native of Shkodër (Albania), his family emigrated to Damascus as a protest against Western influence. Al-Albani received a religious education; like the father of al-Banna, he became a watchmaker. For him, preaching was at the same time a concentration on oneself and a return to oneself, and a focus for his mistrust of classical politics, which was a good way to distinguish himself from a West that sought domination: fundamentalism is thus a counter-offensive that can only succeed by positioning itself at the boundary of intransigent conservatism, or perhaps at its centre. This Muslim integrity becomes a response, if not revenge, faced with a Westernisation that is judged to be humiliating. The battles over headscarves, education, women's rights, and even the ritual slaughter of animals are all part of a response that is a mobilising force, as we know. The more this battle is triggered by the Western side, the better it functions as a mode of political recruitment, or even as legitimate action, as a response to humiliation.

The question of politics almost becomes superfluous: between the quietism of some parties, the militant attitude and preference for conversion of others and the jihadism of an ultra-radicalised minority, sociological and doctrinal points in common largely carry the day, opening the way to all kinds of reclassifications. However, by cutting itself off from *ijtihād* and all effort towards innovation, Salafism forces an impossible choice on the societies of the Arab world: modernise by Westernising, or accept the challenge of Western domination by returning to the Golden Age. This *impasse*, which appears as a new humiliation, contributes to the devaluation of politics, and to the shaping of new reactive behaviours that are springing up from the deepest feelings of people in society.

The Insoluble Contradictions of the Arab Spring

This Arab revolution with a Westernised nickname is an astonishing paradox (the name is an attempt to compare the Arab Spring with the 'Spring of European Peoples' that occurred in 1848). It marks a tremendous break in Arab history, built upon uprisings that have required great courage. Tens of thousands of insurgents have lost their lives, an overpowering tectonic effect the like of which is rarely seen, although its political consequences remain largely uncertain.

It cannot be doubted that this movement is social, in the sense that we have established—deeply social. So much so that this is probably the

[11] B Rougier, *Qu'est-ce que le salafisme?* (Paris, PUF, 2008).

first post-Leninist revolution which, in contrast to all the uprisings that have punctuated the 20th century, has neither political leaders, nor avant-gardist parties that could organise the people, nor fixed doctrines capable of framing the revolutions and labelling them. Its timeline shows that it is a 'bottom-up' social explosion, in accordance with the *soixante-huitarde* model that may have found a new lease of life.

This social eruption has a central thread often called *karama* (dignity), the modern or even postmodern response to humiliation.[12] Its founding narrative teaches us much about the way in which a mixture of the real and the imaginary deliberately built the image of the humiliated at the heart of an autonomous social movement like no other. We know that this story begins on 10 December 2010, when Mohamed Bouazizi set himself on fire. The man would immediately become the symbol of a historic movement that quickly expanded beyond the borders of Tunisia. Streets and avenues have been named after him, even in Paris; stamps have been issued bearing his likeness, monuments built in his memory, a hospital named after him, video music clips created in his honour, prizes awarded to him posthumously. From all corners he has been declared, if not an actor, at least a symbol.

It is here that the part of imagination—referred to above—comes into profile and must be welcomed as a subliminal message of society. This message clearly turns on received humiliation, which was also the humiliation of a whole life. We know that Mohamed Bouazizi came from modest origins, and that his father, who died when he was still very young, was an agricultural worker. Young Mohamed was the main supporter of his family, and so he left school and signed up as a member of an association of unemployed persons. He lived on his earnings from small temporary jobs, and on the money he earned from a mobile shop, that he wanted to modernise and improve but lacked the means to do so. He lived his life by the pace of fines, confiscations and bullying in general. The day he decided to complain at the police station, he was mocked, snubbed, and humiliated again, following which he decided to set himself on fire in front of the government building.

The popular imagination has both embroidered upon and radicalised this story in order to present it as an episode in the legendary history of humiliation. Our hero is said to have been an unemployed graduate, but in fact he had been forced to finish his studies at an early age. There is talk of bribery or corruption that he is supposed to have resisted, although such pressures have not been proven beyond all doubt. One of the most important details is that he is supposed to have been slapped by a policeman, although this

[12] B Korany and R El Mahdi (eds), *Arab Spring in Egypt* (Cairo, AUC Press, 2013) ch 1.

also remains unproven, and the identity of the alleged guilty party has never been established. Even the police auxiliary who was arrested was released because there was no proof.

It does not make any difference: these narratives show that the representation of facts closely associates social movements and humiliation. The same vocabulary was used a few weeks later in Tahrir Square in Cairo, and then in Bahrain, Yemen, Libya and Syria. Dignity and humiliation appear to generate political unity: focal points for people to rally around, reuniting without distinction the unemployed, disaffected youth, the little people, the down-and-outs, the inhabitants of shacks in slums, a middle class frustrated in its desire for social advancement, minorities of all kinds. Humiliation is all the more striking when the magic of globalisation points out the difference at every level: the level of daily life, of economic insecurity, or insecurity with regard to food and sanitation; the level of national political life, including its deviations into authoritarianism, its arbitrariness, cynicism and corruption; the level of regional life, with its unending conflicts that are never won, but are prolonged in a general atmosphere of indifference, mixed with western sympathies for Israel and its policy of occupation; the level of the world, more and more visible and present, where Arab regimes have only an instrumental value, to deliver oil, to slow down the flux of migrants, and to watch over the security of the Western Mediterranean, and the security of the Hebrew State in particular.

The Arab world has been the only region not to benefit from the end of bipolarity, and the only one, indeed, to suffer from it. Latin America was able to free itself from dictators and 'live its own life'; Southeast Asia has progressed under globalisation by constructing high-performance economies and by getting rid of authoritarian regimes. A number of these regions have been able to develop connections to a new set of international partnerships. But the result has not been the same for the Arab world, which has become the sick man of the world, stigmatised, suspected of bad things at every turn, and able to be offered no more than a seat at the G20, ironically given to Saudi Arabia, something not calculated to gratify the demonstrators who marched in Tunis or Cairo.

This mixture of humiliations undergone, so intimately dependent on each other, continues to be expressed through social means, at a time when the political sphere is despairingly speechless. Beyond a confrontation between regimes that are distinct through relations of subordination or through exaggerated exchanges with the West, and beyond Islamic fundamentalisms reunited in their contemplation of a Golden Age, revolutionary discourse has had great difficulty in positioning itself. The second phase of the Arab Spring, intended for the accession of new powers, turned out to be a symphony of disappointment, a new humiliation that was made worse by the fact that the international environment, stunned and hesitant for a moment, recovered the initiative by seeking its own advantages, in the form of interventions exceeding the original UN mandate, as in Libya, or in the form of more or less secret support from one camp to another, as in Syria.

At this level, the blockage is more like an paradox: how can we convert a social, metapolitical movement, into an actor in elections, capable of bringing about change? The response was despairing, in Tunisia or in Egypt, wherever it was not simply prohibited by a system of active repression, as in Bahrain and Syria. The original equation reappears: a social movement can only win politically by becoming a political actor, bearing with it new political personalities and a programme of government. The French Revolution was social at the beginning, and accomplished this much, by drawing on a new political vision from the stock of ideas that had been produced during the period of the Enlightenment, working through clubs, literary salons and the new urban sociability, in the places where a new political elite was produced.

Having Islamist protest closed up in an exclusively defensive stance made the game particularly difficult. That which was possible in Asia and Latin America, even in Turkey, is closely linked to a new ruling class, for whom past humiliation leads to future affirmation, in a role as the re-founder of a society in the context of globalisation.

Through the Arab Spring we can see all the complexity that is derived from the recurrence of humiliation and the systemic construction that is the result. This is so true that we must say we are truly dealing with a vicious circle. Passing into the everyday life of the international game, this construction creates needs and situations that are contradictory, leading those who are affected to cultivate, at the same time, both imitation and rejection; the desire for modernity and the political use of tradition; the worry of entering—on an equal footing—a world that marginalises you, and the temptation to closing oneself off again; torn between the desire to move beyond humiliation through the conquest of new rights, and the irrepressible desire to oppose a past that is likened to a Golden Age; the need to construct a State, and its immediate absorption by corruption and authoritarianism.

The problem is that we cannot easily distinguish between these contradictions, except when we are borne along by the most favourable of international contexts, like certain emergent powers, who nonetheless seem unable to free themselves completely from old demons. These powerful contradictions are expressed in many episodes—real or fictional—of the collective life of the southern countries, and beyond. One has but to refer to the masterpiece of the great Indonesian novelist Pramoedya Ananta Toer (1925–2006). He was a man of the left, sympathetic to China and even to the USSR, where he travelled; he was a 'moderniser', the product of a family of teachers, a man who valued progress, a militant of the Budi Otomo movement, combining nationalist values with a search for education for indigenous peoples. Repressed by Sukarno and even more so by Suharto, who sent him to the prison camp of Buru, while imprisoned he wrote *The Buru Quartet*, creating a hero, Minke, who was a militant against colonial humiliation, but who fought with the weapons of Western thought; he was policed and repressed by a fellow Indonesian, and he encountered the degrading corruption of those he trusted:[13] a supreme humiliation that can be seen in the daily torment of societies of this type; a striking example of contradictions so sharp that they cause people to retreat into despair.

[13] Pramoedya Ananta Toer, *The Buru Quartet* (London, Penguin, 1975).

8

Are there Anti-System Diplomacies?

COULD THE STATES concerned retake the initiative by implementing foreign policies that would constitute new bids, attempting to meet some of the above-mentioned social expectations—or at least to show that they are trying? Recent research has shown that it is necessary to seek out, among the social changes affecting the various States, the primary source for foreign policies that are retained for too long, naïvely, solely as the result of some grand faceless strategy.[1] This observation holds even more strongly when social equilibria are the most uncertain, where there is no long-established tradition in foreign policy, where governments' need for legitimation is particularly high. Under these conditions, two paths are visible: either a very strong patronage of regimes in the South leads them to give up to the idea of an independent foreign policy; or an independent foreign policy becomes the pivotal point of the game played by the leaders, a means of finding new alliances and mobilising one's own people. In the second case, two types of diplomacy may arise: one based on opposition, the other on deviance. Both forms are described more and more often today as 'anti-system'.

Such an orientation had limited scope during the Cold War and bipolarity. The dual aspect of the system led to all kinds of ambiguity. Newly-decolonised States had, in reality, no choice but to remain diplomatically faithful to their former overseers. The only other option was to criticise them, which in the case of Guinea, Angola, and the Ghana of Nkrumah led to a migration towards the Soviet sphere. Then that sphere disappeared, leaving the second option in no man's land, and suddenly old orientations that were officially neutralist, those associated with 'non-alignment', were framed as anti-system, as militant, oppositional, 'bomb-throwers'. They were even pointed to as deviant with regard to the 'international community' considered as de facto equivalent to the Western powers alone. The reevaluation of this kind of diplomacy brings it more into line with humiliations that have been felt or displayed in the past: it tends to manage them, or even to exacerbate their visibility in order to make use of them. The political critique of humiliation has never been so strategic.

[1] C Hill, *The Changing Politics of Foreign Policy* (New York, Palgrave, 2003) pts 2 and 3, in which the author distinguishes between changes in the international context and those affecting societies themselves.

Oppositional Diplomacies

We define oppositional diplomacy as any type of diplomacy that devotes a significant portion of its activity to opposing all or part of the international system, from the perspective of deriving benefits from the action, inside a country and in the international arena. This category obviously does not extend to the criticisms traditionally aimed at a competitor, to the extent that such critisicms basically concern a competition between powers. Oppositional diplomacy is aimed at the international system as a whole, that is, as an arrangement of roles and institutions. In this sense, as we have noted, oppositional diplomacy was marginal during the Cold War: recognised since Bandung and carried forward principally by States that are former colonies, the first oppositional diplomacy appeared as reactive politics, reacting to humiliation; but lost an important part of its relevance in the bipolar game.

Bandung, the non-aligned movement that sprang up in its wake, and the Group of 77 were nonetheless at the root of this oppositional diplomacy, which would obviously gain strength after 1989. It was formed, even invented, in a world that was not accustomed to its actions, and it is directly linked to the use and the mobilisation of past humiliations more than to the activation of an ideology. We are far from what Soviet diplomacy might have been at the beginning of the 'between-the-wars' period, denouncing the international order in the name of a rigorously-constructed ideology. At best it was a matter of mobilising in response to and instrumentalising the humiliation of others for purposes that were intended to be more revolutionary than oppositional, as was the case in 1920 when the Congress of the Peoples of the East was organised at Baku. If we find there the ancestor of the first oppositional diplomacy, it was undoubtedly a diplomacy of power which was thus aimed at regenerating itself: 2,850 delegates attended, having been invited by Zinoviev, and they proclaimed their intention to extend the Bolshevik revolution to all the East, to condemn imperialism without possibility of appeal, and to join forces with 'proletarians in all oppressed countries around the world'.

The connection that developed between opposition and power was a kind of augury. Although its aspirations were guided by a bipolar logic and by the idea of condominium, the USSR never renounced these attitudes. However, when it continued to try to put them into practice, it steadily lost credibility. Moscow did not give up singing from that hymn sheet, especially during the period of colonial wars, supporting liberation movements but putting them at a distance when the interests of international co-management required it. Brezhnev went through with his trip to Washington in 1972, at the very moment when the United States was setting naval mines in the Gulf of Tonkin. The USSR was able to maintain its sang-froid, when the time came, with regard to nationalist movements in the

Maghreb that it had previously described as 'puppets of American imperialism', in order to help along the purposes of its grand diplomacy.[2] In fact, the USSR maintained this tribunician symbolism to the end (something Beijing was at pains to imitate) without anyone really being fooled. We would have to wait for the exit from bipolarity, so that oppositional diplomacy would take on its full meaning, but this time upon the initiative of countries of the South, much smaller powers, who were more credible because they were smaller.

This stance had been in preparation in the South since the 1960s. After the wave of decolonisation, there was inevitably a competition to see which of the States of the Third World would become the spokesperson of the poorest and most oppressed. Bandung had already accorded this role, in fact, to India's Nehru, Indonesia's Sukarno and Egypt's Nasser, without taking into account the somewhat distinctive case of China. In 1961, 25 non-aligned countries met in Belgrade at the invitation of Marshal Tito, who also rejoined the troika. The orchestrated opposition was twofold: opposition to the division of the world into two blocs, and opposition to all forms of colonialism. The break was complete. The international order was no longer composed, as it had been for centuries, of alliances and coalitions: but also included a denunciation of the entire game, which was not wanted, and which had—until that point—been quasi-consensual.

Undoubtedly these periodic meetings—called in the press the 'non-aligned summits'—acted as catalysts, socialising the participants towards the normalisation of the struggle associated with being in opposition. Interestingly, this spirit of intransigence was quickly amplified through an effect of imitation that could be seen from leader to leader, as if a sort of bidding war for leadership turned into a contest to see who could best express humiliation received, or argue the legitimacy of claims. At Belgrade, during the first summit, and despite efforts made by Tito to bring about a synthesis, there was no escape from the almost perfectly head-on opposition between Nehru, who wanted to make peace the emblem of the new world, and Sekou Touré and Sukarno who called on others to rise up against imperialism with a Western face. Nehru won, but it was necessary to accept, in the final resolution, incendiary declarations of support for national liberation movements, and a radical denunciation of any agreement with great powers.

From this point on, the bases of militant opposition were firmly set. In Cairo, at the second summit in October 1964, the non-aligned attendees numbered 47. To the theme of anti-imperialism was added another solemn cause for mobilisation, the theme of opposition to foreign interference in

[2] YH Zoubir, 'The United States, the Soviet Union and Decolonization of the Maghreb' (1995) 31(1) *Middle Eastern Studies* 58.

sovereign affairs. In Lusaka at the third conference in September 1970, before 54 attendees, a call for 'radical change' in the very structure of the international community was issued. But it was, above all, at Algiers in September 1973 that the course of oppositional diplomacy was sealed, under the urging of the host, Houari Boumediene, in the presence of delegations from 75 countries, to which were added some observers (such as Brazil) and three European invitees who passed for neutral: Austria, Finland and Sweden.

The play was performed in three founding acts. Fidel Castro spoke first and issued an indictment against 'American imperialism', a discourse that drew some of its force from the sting of painful economic sanctions. He took advantage of the opportunity to denounce the presence of Brazil, then under the yoke of a military junta supported by the great neighbour to the North. Muammar Gaddafi answered him in expansive terms: the young dictator was celebrating his own 31st birthday, drunk on a Pan-Arabism that would unite Libya with Egypt and Sudan. He also rejected both superpowers. This was acceptable for Boumediene, who was already juggling a break in diplomatic relations with the United States, a probable evacuation of the French bases of Reggane, Colomb-Béchar and Mers el-Kébir, and an impressive number of nationalisations; when he rose to speak, he had just signed a decree prohibiting Algerians from emigrating to France, as a protest against multiple racist incidents directed against Algerian citizens. It is not surprising that this contest to denounce humiliation opened up real arguments for oppositional diplomacy.

Such a diplomacy might easily be constructed as the result of a synthesis between Castro's discourse and Gaddafi's. A reconciliation between nationalists and Marxists came about by the deepening and stabilisation of a critical diplomatic discourse. The Algerian host might congratulate himself for a rapidly-expanding détente, but he might also highlight the risks. He could present himself, though, as the natural leader of those who could be the main victims of future collusion between the powerful and the wealthy. It was appropriate to validate, over the rich countries' objections, a 'right to development', an active cooperation between the countries of the South, and a defensive mobilisation to protect resources in Third World countries. Oppositional diplomacy emerged from mere rhetoric, and entered into the real: a month later, in Kuwait, a long process was set in motion that led OPEC to reduce production and pushed up the price of oil dramatically. Two humiliations were well and truly present: the defeats suffered at the hands of Israel and its Western allies, hardly assuaged by the war of October 1973, and the picture of an Algeria emerging, stumbling, from decades of domination and abuse.

No one should be surprised at the role played by the leader of Algeria, a country that suffered all the humiliations of colonisation and decolonisation. And no one should be surprised that the function was being carried out by Houari Boumediene, who at 13 was present during the massacres at Sétif and Guelma, near where he had lived. He testified that he had suffered greatly in personal terms: '… I aged prematurely. The child I was became a man'.[3] Several months after the Algiers meeting, he was speaking from the podium at the United Nations, at a special session. For 80 minutes, on that 10 April 1974, he set forth a new charter for international militant struggle, calling for a 'new international economic order', called for solidarity from the richest nations, and demanded the right for each nation to have what is under the surface of its territory. He called for a special programme to help the poorest populations, and ended with a prophecy that expressed his anguish, his fury and his desire to awaken people to consciousness: 'One day, millions of men will leave the Southern hemisphere and travel to the Northern hemisphere. They will not go as friends. They will go up there to conquer. And they will conquer with their sons. The wombs of our women will give us victory'.

Thus began an unbroken period of activity for oppositional diplomacy, a new form that disconcerted Western diplomacy, whose ideas remained attached to the Congress of Vienna and what followed it, the old diplomacy, marked by the stamp of power, and by a single competition between powers. The militant intruder was not taken seriously, not in regard to his motivation, nor in regard to the consequences that would follow. Algeria was the forum—but Algeria was interrupted by ten years of civil war. Up to 1989, Algiers was the capital for all the movements of liberation; Abdelaziz Bouteflika, Boumediene's minister for foreign affairs, who presided over the General Assembly of the United Nations following the famous speech of April 1974, was his highly-regarded and secular right arm. After 1989, these initiatives could have been turned into winning strategies: the end of bipolarity could have given the militant opposition even greater magnitude, at the point when it was liberated from the control exercised by the defunct condominium and its written or unwritten rules. The civil war, which began in Algeria at the very moment when the Berlin Wall fell, forced things a different direction, and there began an empty time, a time of erasure. Things returned to this point after the 'black years'. The election of Bouteflika as President of Algeria, as of September 1999, led to two speeches that returned to past themes: before the Organization of African Unity meeting in Algiers, and immediately after, before the General Assembly of the UN, where he denounced foreign interference with the utmost vigour, at the moment when a NATO operation in Kosovo was finishing, and an expedition to East Timor under a UN mandate was beginning. It was to be expected that he would defend the idea of sovereignty, and he confirmed the primacy of that principle in the credo of militant opposition. Equally, he

[3] 'Quand le merle sifflera', *Dakerscomerle.com*, March 2010.

returned to calling for a 'new international economic order', an idea which resurfaced in a speech given at Arzew in February 2012: the oppositional line was still in place, despite a few sour notes from those newly-inclined towards prudence around great powers.

There could never be a question of such nuances with Hugo Chávez, as he took up the banner of oppositional diplomacy and radicalised it, even as he swept to a comfortable electoral victory in Venezuela in December 1998. With Chávez we see the appearance of a "second generation" oppositional diplomacy, subtly mixing social and political claims and policies, and targeting the United States in a deliberate way. The times had changed. We were no longer in the Cold War; we had moved away from Bandung and decolonisation—that of Venezuela dated back more than 170 years. The young Colonel Chávez lived in a different world, with different humiliations and different denials. The continent of South America had barely emerged from an era of dictators that had—to some extent—spared Venezuela, but the country's environment had been severely scarred, and the American supervision stood accused of this crime. Venezuela had been a principal target of the IMF and its merciless policy of adjustment, which violated as many sovereignties as it made victims of the poor. Beginning in 1989, the reforms that President Carlos Andres Perez was forced to accept—a president supported by the left—led to drastic increases in the price of staples and in the price of public transportation: in February, the riots of 'Caracazo' led to significant violence, which led to unprecedented repressive force, officially causing the deaths of several hundred people, a number that unofficially is said to be as high as 3,000 victims. This mixture of social unrest and an accusation levelled at the IMF was ideal for accelerating the internationalisation of slogans, and for opening up a path to the first coup Chávez tried, which he called 'Operation Ezequiel Zamora', after the revolutionary hero who defended the peasants. That first attempt failed and earned him a term in prison. His second attempt also failed; it took place prior to the election of Rafael Caldera, who also had the support of the left, so he could carry out the same neoliberal policies recommended by the same IMF, leading to the same shortages, the same devaluations and the same social austerity.

But Hugo Chávez was eventually elected on a programme that was obviously nationalist, mixing together populism, a social orientation, and the denunciation of international economic organisations. Once in power, he had only to transform his crusade against humiliation into a new foreign policy, assembling, in the best-orchestrated way possible, all the elements that had led to his victory: anti-Americanism, denunciation of the international economic order, sovereigntism, nationalism, and international social justice.

The man had resources. He was born to an Amerindian family, and understood the issue of cultural identities. He was marked by a difficult youth; he had worked as a travelling salesman. He knew the price of social tensions; he was more or less comfortable with religion and even the priesthood. He had all the arguments that he needed for the denunciation of ultra-liberalism. Joining the army, he had acquired a particular knowledge of the history of Bolivar, while moving closer to Marxist ideology, to Castro, Guevara or Allende. He had sympathy for the experience of Omar Torrijos, the 'maximum leader' of Panama (*leader Massimo*) who managed to re-establish the sovereignty of Panama in 1978—including the Canal, which the United States had controlled up to that point.

The rhetoric thus derived allows us to make a first approach to understanding the oppositional diplomacy which is taking shape. We remember the famous speech Chávez gave on 20 September 2006, before the General Assembly of the United Nations, calling George W Bush a tyrant, a liar, and a devil that had left behind at the rostrum, where he (Bush) had spoken a few hours before, 'a whiff of sulphur'. The American president was also called an ass and a drunkard, and accused of having ordered the coup that failed to overthrow the Venezuelan president in 2002. A complaint was even filed, in regard to this accusation, with the Organization of American States (OAS). Thus anti-Americanism becomes something to rally around, as in all militant organisations: Chávez wanted to be friends with Iran, and in particular, with Mahmoud Ahmadinejad, whom he met with several times, both in Caracas and in Tehran. He supported North Korea, Belarus, Zimbabwe and Bashar al-Assad. He fought against 'Israeli fascism'.[4] He was deeply involved in the Palestinian cause, and demanded that Israeli and American leaders be brought before the International Criminal Court. But as proof that even militant opposition is not yet confrontation, still less deviance, commercial relations with the United States were protected, and oil supplies were shipped between the two countries. There are more instances of denunciations than of destruction. The IMF was referred to as a 'Dracula'. But Chávez discovered, to his chagrin, that American influence is everywhere, even in the areas of his loves, Venezuelan music and baseball.

His diplomacy of militant opposition stigmatises, accuses, and then reunites. The latter perspective uses the most readily-available resources, first of all oil, since Venezuela is the fifth largest exporter in the world. An association has been created within OPEC that reaches out to small producers and also poor consumers. Venezuela's 'oil diplomacy' was active in relation to African producer-States, and Venezuela opened embassies in those States.[5] The idea was to project over Africa a policy called 'full

[4] *Libération*, 31 July 2006.

[5] C Forite, 'La diplomatie pétrolière du gouvernement Chávez en Afrique: pour une projection du "socialisme du xxie siècle"?' (2012) 5 *RITA*.

sovereignty' with regard to oil, which Chávez had established in Venezuela in stages, making sure not to draw down his resources too much. The objective was to make this policy an instrument for the emancipation of the countries that had been marginalised and humiliated on the international scene, from Gambia to Equatorial Guinea.[6] For the countries that were non-producers, policies of solidarity and social development were put forward; Venezuelan oil was offered at preferential rates, as in the 'PetroCaribe' programme, which benefited several Central American and island States. PetroCaribe was even able to accelerate the more political process that gave rise to the Bolivarian alliance for the Americas (ALBA) which brought together, around a Venezuelan centre, Bolivia, Cuba, the Dominican Republic, Antigua, Nicaragua and Saint-Vincent. Mischievously, Chávez offered low-price oil for the poorest citizens in the United States, and for victims of Hurricane Katrina.

Now we see the outline of this new oppositional diplomacy, probably further from Bandung and certainly from the twists and turns of the Cold War, and more romantic as well, at a moment when the great ideologies of the past era have almost disappeared. The novel form of foreign policy which goes along with oppositional diplomacy is closely bound up with internal social tensions and with failures of development, both of which are constructed and displayed as if they were the mechanical and harmful effects of misleading international economic regulation. In a world that is no longer bipolar, accusations are hurled at an 'American imperialism' that is cried down, insulted and demonised. Its denunciation is thus more 'populist' than 'scientific', as it once was: now it comes accompanied by mockery and derision, easily grasped figures and images, and often-used themes of conspiracy, misconduct, and even superstition.

Are we saying that oppositional or militant diplomacy is mostly a matter of image or of words? Compared to Boumediene in his day, Chávez appears to be more focused on gestures, signs and language. This could be one feature of oppositional diplomacy, something familiar to all orators who know how to remind victims of the humiliations that put them in the place they are, and delight in mocking those who seem to be their tormentors. At the same time, however, this diplomacy goes further, taking on three characteristics that transform the usual characters of the international game.

First, like all opposition, it does not form a competing coalition that would try to establish a new balance of powers, but rather a front made of small countries, or at least of entities that have their relative weakness in common. We have, therefore, left the world of competition between powers and enter into a quest for autonomy, although that quest is pursued in a game that is from now on asymmetrical. Secondly, this diplomacy has

[6] ibid.

an effect on what is placed on the international agenda: naturally proactive, it tries to direct public attention, raises issues, forces great powers to react to unforeseen subjects, and considers certain situations worth fighting over, even though others may have assumed they were completely settled. 'Petro-diplomacy' is, in all its aspects, archetypal from this point of view, a perpetual source of uncertainty, irritation and anxieties. But other kinds of dispute, which arise out of surprise initiatives, at the WTO or during climate negotiations, are of the same ilk. Oppositional diplomacy puts, within the international public space, the need for the restructuring of the world-scene, its institutions, and its practices: it acts on its legitimacy, displays their weaknesses, and denounces their routines.

The novelty is probably that this kind of diplomacy cannot be handled by any of the conventional control mechanisms. Power feeds it instead of reducing it, while negotiation too often finds itself paralysed. Worse yet, this diplomacy is beginning to look like an antechamber leading to the diplomacy of deviance.

Diplomacies of Deviance

The boundary between these two diplomacies, of opposition and of deviance, is not always quite clear. The latter may appear as the radicalisation of the former, and stand for the art of gaining advantages within the international system by transgressing its rules, norms and values. First of all, there is something deliberately ostentatious in the behaviour of transgression, such that some people deliberately choose to speak of what is provocative. The authors of the behaviour are looking for a demonstrative effect that has overtones of 'payback' and self-affirmation at the same time. The first advantage has to do with showing oneself publicly as being completely outside the existing order—whatever it is—in order to highlight one's difference and personality. The one who transgresses is present, remarked upon, forcing others to define themselves in relation to the transgressor: such a person is proactive, at the centre of the scene, and thereby acquires international status at very little cost.

Transgression does, though, have a cost: in casting doubt upon rules, and sometimes, more seriously, on values that are the subject of a consensus, one exposes oneself to stigmatisation and moral condemnation—leading to exclusion, and often enough, sanctions of some kind. These risks may be minimised by the talents or the radical nature of those who are transgressing; it may be accepted in a spirit of risk-taking, or for the pleasure of shocking those whom one detests: this obviously stands well and truly outside the realist model, even when faced with the opposite and with a model that is really not very Schmittian. In such a context, the vicious circle works perfectly. The more you criticise, punish or condemn, the more you encourage transgression. Transgression can only be overcome through a profound modification of the role, which must bring the transgressor out of his status as a humiliated person.

Transgression can appear in verbal forms that identify it as a continuation of contestation: are the limits of these forms not 'transgressed', when Hugo Chávez starts talking about 'the frigging Yankees'? The transgression can be symbolic, as in 1998 when the president of Belarus, Alexander Lukachenko, decided to expel 20 Western ambassadors from the residential zone of Drozdy, because they were too close to the presidential palace. Here, 'provocation' is stronger because it is a violation of international conventions governing the status of diplomats. It proved to be quite 'profitable', in the sense that the conflict went on for almost a year, and was widely reported on in the West during that time, sometimes making the front pages of newspapers. This is one way to play things, and one way to react to being isolated by Western democracies as the 'last European dictatorship'. But a line had been crossed, leading the European Union and the United States to refuse a visa to the strongman of Minsk and his entourage. The fact remains that this leader managed to gain publicity, and a degree of exposure that he could not otherwise have afforded.

One can go further up the scale of outrages with Mahmoud Ahmadinejad, who supported negationist positions and even reach a high level of violence, such as when Gaddafi 'allowed' his supporters to sack the US Embassy in Tripoli in 1981; one could consider the outrage of support for terrorism, when the Libyan leader revealed and even vaunted his connection to the Ireland's IRA. Those were dark days. Even worse, there was an implication to be read between the lines—a tacit admission that his intelligence services had indeed been involved in the Lockerbie bombing. But without going to such extremes, the 'normal' profile of deviance consists in disturbing an international order that is defined in far too unilateral a fashion: one is not inevitably mired in evil, but rather one is demonstrating that no gain is ever completely secure. Thus Robert Mugabe welcomed Mahmoud Ahmadinejad to Harare, ostensibly to sign eight commercial agreements with Iran, as if to show solidarity between international pariahs, and countries that were both labouring under international sanctions. Or take the example of the president of Ecuador, Rafael Correa, who granted asylum to Julian Assange, who during the summer of 2012 was being pursued by several Western police forces. Each time, it is a norm that comes under attack, or what passes in the West for a norm, in order to show the difference, and reverse the marginalisation of which one's own country is a victim. This is no longer the expression of a fatal superiority of the 'other', but just the result of a free choice, and a distinction maintained in the face of an order of which one disapproves.

The method works when it is handled with care. Saddam Hussein wanted to take it to unaccustomed heights when he decided to destroy the sovereignty of Kuwait and annex the emirate, making it an Iraqi province.

This was the most serious deviance, an attack against the most sacred of international principles, that of sovereignty, which everyone holds on to as tightly as possible, because it can assure their survival. The international community, almost unanimously, made Hussein see reason. However, when the deviant diplomacy knows how not to go too far, it receives much more attention than it might have been given otherwise. The deviant country becomes more visible, it has more influence over the agenda, it can attract support, and sometimes even be asked to mediate.

The Iranian case is worth paying attention to. Humiliation, for Persia, is a constitutive parameter. Embattled amidst peoples who are presumed hostile, this country acquired the habit of regarding other countries with suspicion when they became powerful.[7] In the North, Russia had attempted to overturn the constitutional revolution of 1906, and the Russians had been accustomed to act to suit themselves. When Russia became the USSR, its methods did not change, and Stalin knew how to manipulate Kurds and Iranian Azeris to make them to favour secession. Great Britain, which was not far away as the country then governing India, came to an agreement with the Tsars, that they would occupy the southern part of Iran, and allow the Russians to do as they liked in the North. Britain also knew how to manipulate intrigues at court. Further afield, the European powers still excelled at obtaining and dividing lucrative concessions for customs houses, mail service, tobacco and the police. Turks and Arabs knew how to profit from the smallest weakness, first rectifying borders for profit and, second, getting the Arab-speaking and Kurdish tribes to revolt. Late to the party, the United States proved no less greedy: Morgan Shuster, followed by Arthur Millspaugh, American citizens, were named as secretaries of the treasury by Reza Shah Pahlavi. Officially, it is known, and supported by American excuses, that in Operation Ajax the CIA orchestrated a military coup d'état that overthrew Mossadegh, the architect of the nationalisation of Iranian oil. During the following 25 years the United States moved into Iran like it was a holiday home, eventually sending as many as 30,000 'advisors' to support the administration of the Shah.

A reaction involving deviance was not long in arriving: the occupation of the American Embassy in Tehran at the beginning of the Revolution, and the capture of its personnel by Islamist 'students' and the *pasdaran* were the beginning. The United States became the 'Great Satan', and this identity was built through an entire operation focused on denunciation: marches almost every day, cries of 'Death to America' featured at some marches, posters, exhibitions, all kinds of propaganda, many connections

[7] On the history of Iranian-American relations and the effects of the Islamic revolution, *cf* B Rubin, *Paved with Good Intentions* (Oxford, Oxford University Press, 1980).

with regimes and movements opposed to the United States, solidarity with all those who battled against the superpower. Here too, reactions were not long in coming, and they arrived in the form of sanctions and multiple drone operations beginning in 2003, threats, refusals to issue visas to Iranian officials en route to meetings at the United Nations in New York: everything kept the denunciation of the Great Satan in the public eye, so visible that it could be made the basis for a diplomacy of combat.

Thus there is complete dissonance between an Iranian diplomacy that oscillates between opposition and deviance, and the Western chancelleries who are offended by it. Iran knows very well how to play on its own deviant actions in order to put itself in the position of tribune, a leader of States that have been victimised by foreign domination, placing its voice and abilities at the service of many a crusade.[8] Mahmoud Ahmadinejad went to Niger in April 2013, when its president, Mahamadou Issoufou, had just severely criticised a contract signed between his country and Areva for the management of uranium mines. The Iranian leader presented himself as a defender, but also argued that Iran could be a fair client. In Benin, in Ghana, he mixed together denunciation of imperialism with offers of aid and partnership. This did not prevent him, at Casamance, from supporting the Movement of Democratic Forces, and that support led to a break in diplomatic relations between Iran and Senegal.

Is this confused diplomacy, and is this what always comes from populist demonstrations? Is this diplomacy provocative, rather than constructive? Is there a choice between two extremes, leading to inevitable mutual incomprehension? Radical options leading nowhere, except to more and more unbearable sanctions? All that has its basis in reality, but probably misses the essential point. In our international system, the excluded one is the prisoner of a perpetual dilemma that leads the excluded to choose between alignment and deviance, with, of course, a choice of forms on either side that modify the set of options available. The advantage of alignment is that it guarantees protection, but this can prove uncertain, as Mubarak and the Shah of Iran have been able to attest in the course of their personal destinies. The cost of alignment, on the other hand, is high, causing the Egyptian leader to disappear completely from the diplomatic radar and to lose an essential part of his legitimacy. The diplomacy of deviance offers visibility and a presence on the international scene, well beyond the actual capacity and resources of the country in question: as long as they stay within certain limits, deviant diplomacy may allow a country to exist in a world where the right to exist is the province of a small number of States.

[8] For a doubtful but suggestive interpretation, *cf* M Eisenstadt, 'The strategic culture of the Islamic Republic of Iran' *MES Monographs*, 1, August 2011.

The optimum position between the two consists of a subtle mixture of opposition and restrained deviance, or a well-designed alternation, for which Iran furnished an example, when Ahmadinejad succeeded Khatami and then was replaced by Hassan Rohani. Even more weight, perhaps, should be given to the nature of the political system that has produced all this, whose extreme institutional complexity combines actors who display openness and who are eager to make transactions, and intransigent actors who are usually following the 'Supreme Guide' in that way. Iran, in this situation, takes risks, but lives—thanks to those risks—well above its diplomatic means. In Lebanon, Syria, Iraq, even Afghanistan, in Palestine and in the Gulf, the Islamic Republic has become an actor that cannot be ignored. Iran even acts as a mediator, whose radical nature, and even deviance, allows it to exercise real influence on actors that are not well integrated into the international game. That was what an Iranian diplomat suggested in 2004, making it known that his country was ready to 'help' the United States out of its entanglement with Iraq: 'If they accept our help, they will find advantages, and if they don't we'll pull the rug out from under them.'

This close connection between deviance and affirmation of rights, especially in an area as sensitive as nuclear technology, in fact becomes a mundane moment in international relations, in particular for any country that intends to settle accounts with a past of humiliation. The connection feeds on the institutional weaknesses of the international system, and also on the decision by classical powers to 'show firmness', easily identified with a past they would like to forget. Policies that respond to humiliation must not disappear under the effect of force; they must nourish themselves; and when such policies allow the international status of a State to be raised, they have every chance of being continued.

***

Militant opposition and deviance, poorly separated by vague boundaries, become in reality the current productions of an international system that is still learning, as once nations had to learn about their serious defects in integration. It is no surprise that they should be closely related to humiliations that have been experienced, or that the adept management of those humiliations determines their development. Only a policy of international social integration can stop them, or at least ease them.

9

Uncontrolled Violence

INTERNATIONAL VIOLENCE TODAY does not resemble the violence of the past. It has lost its exceptionality and its ordered nature. It no longer sets two armies against one another, in a disciplined assault, according to centuries-old traditions; it is no longer the result of a combat between equals, and no longer obeys the rules of Clausewitz or Carl Schmitt. What was once marginal, in the days when Faidherbe battled El Hadj Oumar or when Kitchener crossed swords with Al-Mahdi, has become the rule, it has deepened and it has become widespread.

The shock of societies colliding has often replaced a collision between States and their armies. International violence has become social. It no longer has a very close relationship with borders, but rather expresses a troubling continuum between what is internal and what is external. It develops according to shortages and denials, to frustrations and thus humiliations. This is a diffuse and fragmented social violence, which the logic of the State has a great deal of trouble managing or even containing: violence that is felt, almost endemic, similar to social demands that specialised entrepreneurs quickly take charge of, to channel the violence into their own profit, as any businessman would do.

This is to say that these 'new international conflicts' arise more from such a change of political landscape than from practices of violence that were marginalised and poorly identified. These are extreme forms of social alienation stemming from deep and sometimes very old humiliations. They are resistant to military solutions, and make necessary a new effort towards understanding various modes of the construction of peace.

New Conflicts, New Violence

War, in moving around the planet, takes on different shapes. Apart from the last spasms of the Balkan conflicts, Europe no longer fills up martial chronicles. By leaving the Old Continent, war also left the territory of the rich and powerful, and moved towards the territory of the poor and marginal of yesterday. South Asia, the Middle East and Africa account for 75% of all current conflicts, and so we easily understand that today, rich people make war by proxy, or by converting poor people into instruments. Conflicts become essentially a matter handled by poor or weak people, who are in any case the principal victims, the actors on the ground.[1] This is part of the reason for the renewed importance of small arms;[2] it also explains the new social proximity of war, which has lost the professionalisation that characterised it during the entire Westphalian period; it is why humiliation plays the part it does in processes of mobilisation. It is absurd to say that humiliation has become the cause or the main factor in new conflicts, but it does appear that it energises reactions that tend to propagate conflict. In the market-based logic we are describing, offers of violence, more and more, find social situations that are fertile ground. The appeal to violence may be constructed so as to remind people of the humiliations they have suffered. These humiliations often make conflicts more complex, adding a social relevance to the strategies of warlords, to predatory desires, to the windfalls from all kinds of trafficking, that becomes, in its turn, a critical parameter.[3]

This social adhesion is stronger and more meaningful because most new conflicts are closely associated with the collapse of a State. The failure of the State hastens the emergence of conflicts from their Clausewitzian context, but at the same time, it causes them to diverge even more strongly from the rationale of the citizen, deprives the same of political mediation, and gives free rein to social anger and frustration. Since mobilisation is now not made according to one's allegiance as a citizen, it must be replaced by utilitarian appeals and populist formulas. Militias and warlords' armies dispense material goods, feeding and clothing a fighting population, and there are also symbolic gifts, giving that population a semblance of pride in their own existence, all the stronger for being affirmed in connection with the memory of humiliations suffered. This is how private armies and militias so easily recruit child soldiers and even young women, who more and more seek vengeance for the suffering inflicted upon them or their families.[4] Humiliation acts as a social driver of new conflicts that present themselves, in turn, as a means of erasing humiliation. At this point we are seeing the precise inversion of the Westphalian model of war.

[1] On these new conflicts, *cf* M Kaldor, *New and Old Wars* (Cambridge, Polity Press, 1999); H Munkler, *The New Wars* (Polity, 2004); P Wallensteen and M Sollenberg, 'Armed conflict, 1989–1998' (1999) 36(5) *Journal of Peace Research* 243–257. For a contrary view, that rejects the idea of 'new conflicts', *cf* C Gray, *Another Bloody Century: Future Warfare* (London, Weidenfeld and Nicolson, 2005).

[2] *cf* the report of the Secretary-General of the UN to the Security Council concerning small arms, 17 April 2008.

[3] On warlords, *cf* W Reno, *Warlords and African States* (Boulder (Colorado), Lynne Rienner Publishers, 1999); P Rich (ed), *Warlords in International Relations* (London, Macmillan, 1999); R Malejacq, *Warlords and the State System*, PhD thesis (IEP de Paris and Northwestern University, 2012).

[4] Concerning child soldiers, *cf* the testimony of someone who was a child soldier in Sierra Leone, I Beah, *A Long Way Gone: Memoirs of a Boy Soldier* (London, Sarah Crichton Books, 2007).

Of course, this 'resocialisation of war' began with the process of decolonisation. This no longer placed two States against each other, but rather set the colonial State against societies—or fragments of societies—that were originally motivated and mobilised because of the desire to defeat and overcome humiliation. This is probably the source of the unrest and the difficulties the colonial State had in negotiating during a conflict that did not correspond to its experience of wars, in which the combatants on the other side did not have, in its eyes, a status worthy of a partnership. We find the same recurrent effect of this systematic humiliation in what is left today of colonial war, especially through the war between Israel and Palestine.

There is a certain similarity between these wars of liberation and the newest forms of conflict. Examples, unfortunately, are plentiful. Most of the bloody conflicts in Africa confirm these orientations: often correlated with the collapse of a State, as in Sierra Leone or Liberia yesterday, in the Democratic Republic of Congo or the Central African Republic today, they substitute militias for armies, and warlords for heads of government. They thus aggravate the lack of differentiation between societies and fighting forces, between social incitement to mobilise and military strategy, between civil victims and military victims. In the absence of confrontating States, the symbols deployed are strongly sub-political, religious, ethnic, racial. The *hostis* has been replaced by the *inimicus:* the enemy no longer possesses that public virtue, upon which classical war was founded, but becomes instead the object of absolute hate:there is no more discourse and no more compromise; negotiation becomes almost impossible.

The example of Sierra Leone is particularly remarkable. This former British colony, independent since April 1961, was highly institutionalised, but had suffered a string of coups d'état. The first coup occurred only six years after independence, and there were about ten more, some successful, some not. In the last case, capital executions radicalised the situation, to the point that the Revolutionary United Front (RUF) launched guerrilla actions in March 1991, upon the initiative of the RUF leader, Foday Saybana Sankoh. He had been a corporal in the army, and had participated in the very first coup, in 1967. Following this, Sankoh worked actively to support other coup attempts, and was eventually sentenced to six years in prison. Following his release, living on the margins of society, he was drawn into the orbit of Muammar Gaddafi, as was Charles Taylor, his future associate in Liberia. Marginality and deviance brought him back to the pathways of the guerrilla fighter, with one objective in his mind: to take over the diamond mines, located in the interior of a country that had always concentrated its wealth along the coast, as had a string of other States situated on the Gulf of Guinea.

Since independence, in fact, the power has been at Freetown, the capital of Sierra Leone, which lies on the Atlantic coast. The coastal zone population is largely Creole, and they hold not only the State or what is left of it, but also the economic power, traditionally held by merchants who trade directly with foreigners near and far. The interior area of the country has subsoil that is rich in diamond ore, something that does not benefit the extremely poor population of the area.[5] It is easy to understand how any act of rebellion, such as the one committed by Foday Sankoh, might seek to assume the role of the opposition, and make an appeal to the impoverished population, who might—by rebelling—have enough food to eat, have clothes to wear, and thus survive. The machete, in its cruelty, offers a semblance of affirmation and existence.

The case of Sierra Leone is, as we noted, evocative, since it shows the new type of conflict that no longer is based on a rivalry between equal forces, but upon disorder and disequilibrium, bringing into opposition zones of extreme social pathology and fragile and illusory centres of power. The conflicts magnify the failures of an authority that was never properly acquired, but the parties to the conflicts themselves employ all available means of domination. In Freetown, we can observe a succession of presidents: Major General Joseph Saidu Momoh (until 1992), Captain Valentine Strasser (1992–1996), General Julius Bio (1996), Ahmad Kabbah (1996–1997 and after 1998), and Commandant Johnny Paul Koroma (1997–1998). We can also see the activity of the United Nations, led by the US and Great Britain, plus ECOMOG, the intervention force of the Economic Community of West African States (ECOWAS), itself led by Nigeria, along with representatives of most neighbouring States and major commercial interests, all attracted by the trade in diamonds. On the other side, there was an assembled group of frustrated intellectuals, officers or sub-officers at odds with authority and militias clothed in rags, compensating for isolation and inferiority by resorting to extreme violence. Deviant diplomacy would become part of the conflict, would be engaged in by the rebellion, and then inevitably supported by Colonel Gaddafi, and by the Burkina Faso of Captain Blaise Compaoré, who had just overthrown Captain Thomas Sankara, father of the Burkinabé revolution, and whose legacy Compaoré was still trying to exploit.

Thus humiliation figured three times in the very construction of the conflict. First at the level of actors: the new type of conflict does not focus on States in competition, representing interests that are opposed to one another, but rather on failed States opposed to military and intellectual sub-elites, which they have not been able to integrate. On one hand, these failed States have not always had the means to bring integration about, and on the other, their extremely precarious situation offered entrepreneurs

[5] S Brunel, *Géopolitique de la faim* (Paris, PUF, 2000) 65.

of violence an ongoing opportunity for the conquest of power by force; and such attempts, when not successful, lead into a well-known cycle of repression, marginalisation, and thence to humiliation again. This vicious circle has affected the paths of many people who have been involved in the principal African conflicts. It illustrates the course of Laurent-Désiré Kabila in the Democratic Republic of Congo, stagnating hopelessly during a long guerrilla struggle in Lumumba's forces before gaining power in 1997, and also the career of Idris Deby, who changed roles, going back and forth between his training as a fighter pilot in France, his shaky appointments in the entourages of several Chadian presidents, and his role as a leader of guerrilla forces in the North, on the borders of Gaddafi's Libya. Paul Kagamé belonged to the Tutsi tribe of Rwanda, and for this reason his family had to leave that country when he was four years old. He went to Uganda, and when he came of age he fought in the rebel army of Yoweri Museveni, who would become president of Uganda. Eventually fought to reconquer the Rwandan state, and he completed this aim in March 2000. The degree of humiliation was so strong that Kagamé's forces even fought in the Congolese civil wars, in the former Zaire. Without there having been a war, the memory of Congo-Brazzaville retains the image of Captain Marien Ngouabi, who was a respected officer until, in 1966, he entered the arena of political protects, and was eventually demoted to the rank of a first-class private by President Massamba-Débat, whom he then disposed of in a coup d'état in January 1969. This incapacity—systematic and sometimes strategic—to integrate elites into the political order leads most directly to war. It creates humiliation by relegation, which in the long run can only be remedied through force, at least in the eyes of those who have been its victims.

In Sierra Leone, where wealth and power are concentrated in the capital, on the Atlantic coast, and the interior of the country is only considered good for supporting church-sponsored prebendaries or rent-collecting landlords, humiliation is an integral part of the political system. The effect of the contrast is all the more glaring, since many profit from it. A small, compact local elite is a cheap proxy for outside actors, powers from the North, international institutions, or giant commercial companies. Internal imbalances are a source of all kinds of humiliations, which are accentuated and symbolised through connection with religious or tribal identities. Long term, they may be catastrophic, but in the short term they appear profitable and they provide external powers with distinct advantages.

We find them again in the Democratic Republic of Congo, where the exclusion of the Banyamulenge was the cause of war beginning again in 1996 in Sudan, where the British administration had already imposed a strict separation between the Muslim North and the Christian South. This was the source of all inequalities, which then matured, until they contributed to the conflict between the two parties, a conflict that essentially began on the day of independence, in 1956. Following this, all that was required to turn this separation into a cause of war was the refusal, in June 1958, on the part of the Parliament of Khartoum to grant autonomy to the southern region, which had demanded it. As in Sierra Leone, the dominated party was in a situation of political, economic, social and cultural marginalisation, particularly remarkable through its elites. John Garang, who was the unquestioned leader of the Southerners' rebellion for more than 20 years, rejoined the mutineers in 1983, when he was a colonel with no future in the Sudanese Army, although he had diplomas from schools in the United States. His successor, Salva Kiir, the first president of South Sudan, chose to follow him, measuring, from 1983, the impasse that his very low rank in the army of Khartoum left him in. As in Sierra Leone, this humiliation is made worse by the riches that lie underneath the ground—oil, copper and zinc—from which the South Sudanese derived no profit.

The same analysis is valid for Mali. The circumstances that accompanied colonisation divided and closed the borders of a Sahara and a Sahel whose people up to that moment had lived by mobility, ignoring borders. At the same time a French Sudan was created that became Mali, made of the Southern part of a country, created near centres of power and decision; and then there was a North that was far away and thinly populated, and thus relegated to the status of a periphery.[6] This region, at independence and even before, experienced inferiority through its ethnic particularity, marked by indecision about the status of Tuaregs and Arabs, excluded de facto from political and economic life. The region resented this more and more because of the worsening economic situation, hit by drought in 1972, 1974 and 1984–1986. This deterioration led rural people to migrate to cities, causing just as many social ills; it gave free rein to an informal economy, which was obviously Mafia-like. It accelerated the mobility of people who were then able to think about going to Libya or Algeria: their return, later, could only increase tensions. The borders, which had been hindrances, became shelters, giving a raison d'etre to contraband operations, and providing food for a population and quickly becoming its principal resource. The State was of little use; people learned to work around it and to patch together arrangements that were mutually beneficial for everyone.[7] As for the Tuaregs, not assimilated, harassed by paramilitary militias who also destroyed their cattle, and hunted, especially in neighbouring Niger, by mining companies, over time they accumulated certain attributes that led

[6] G Giraud, 'Cinquante ans de tensions dans la zone sahélosaharienne' in M Galy (ed), *La Guerre au Mali* (Paris, La Découverte, 2013) 29.

[7] J-L Sagot-Duvauroux, 'Quelques traits du Mali en crise', ibid 93–95.

the American Department of State to describe the area where they lived as a 'terrorist area'.[8] The circle is complete.

The third level of humiliation places the international at centre stage. Certain inescapable conclusions follow from statistics kept by international institutions. Sierra Leone ranks 180th in terms of the Human Development Index (HDI—calculated by the United Nations Development Programme and combining indicators of economic, sanitary and educational quality of life); Mali ranks 182nd, ahead of the Democratic Republic of the Congo and Niger, which are 186th *ex-aequo*. Unicef says the latter country suffered 2,500 cases of infant mortality during the first eight months of 2013. But this inequality becomes humiliating to the extent that the higher rank occupied by international powers becomes directly visible on the ground, and directly associated with felt injustices. So it is with the diamond mines of Sierra Leone, which can send the riches they uncover to Europe, in exchange for money that fuels the conflicts and pays for the weapons they require. So it is with the exploitation of underground riches in Niger (uranium), Congo, Sierra Leone, and Sudan (oil). Thus it is with the conflicts themselves, in which Northern powers risk something, with good or bad intentions, but always putting up the old laws of war against the newly-invented mechanisms on display in many conflicts. Whether they are willing or unwilling participants in these conflicts born out of the pathologies that African societies suffer from, the powers of the old era are quickly perceived as manipulators, whether at a distance or at close range, and it is suspected that they manage to profit from the conflict. This is why such conflicts tend to lend credence to anti-Western suspicions, as long as the ill-fated initiatives of the North do little, other than helping along the gradual transformation of Africa into an immense warlike society.

The phenomenon is all the more serious because effect of the system is undeniable. The mobility of mercenary soldiers is one factor, something that the hardening of national borders quickly erased in Europe, even if it was still not rare, up to the time of the Napoleonic wars, to see mercenary forces take advantage of boundary lines in order to commit crimes, often following humiliations. Opposition from a nation-state to such practices would have quickly eliminated them, as Europe gradually entered modernity. Here, the reverse is true: the movement of fighters in Africa and Asia, and often from one continent to another, from Afghanistan to Mali, from Libya to Chechenya, or from Yemen to Syria has created a real community of fighters whose reach extends to the fringes of European cities. The feeling of humiliation becomes a remarkable cohesive factor, which can give this particular 'international' a collective awareness that seeks only to grow. The entrepreneurs of violence have made this an essential element in a

[8] H Claudot-Hawad, 'La question touarègue, quels enjeux', ibid 139.

strategy of mobility that puts States, armies and classical diplomacy on the back foot, but which is well suited to the Muslim idea of the Umma, and the project of substituting a different configuration of global space than the system of relations between States that we have.

The speed with which the conflict between Christians and Muslims was able to structure the political system in the Central African Republic, as the conflict dragged on through 2013, was particularly remarkable. Everything happened as if the weight of the social crisis in that country could only crystallise the felt humiliation, and thus empower opposition groups at the intercommunity or—in some cases—interfaith level. Struggles for power become more frequent when failures of integration become public knowledge. It was suddenly discovered, at the moment of the coup d'état of March 2013, that the armed 'allied' group, 'la Seleka', which had permitted Michel Djotodia to take power, was Muslim, in a situation where Islam had previously played almost no role.

The marginalisation of the Muslim minority, something that had persisted since independence, thus became an argument for mobilisation, giving a social meaning to the coup and to the overthrow of the old president Bozizé, and even offering an argument in favour of retaliatory destruction, which could be hidden behind vendetta-like behaviour. Throughout the summer of 2013, people robbing and destroying churches was a fact of daily life, especially around the geographical border where the Christian and Muslim communities met. If Christians were murdered, then mechanically Muslims were murdered. The humiliation of people who were once marginalised becomes a driver, feeding the quest for power.

Violence and Social Integration

One of the most remarkable aspects of the contemporary international system has to do with the extreme decentralisation of the violence that plagues it. This violence is diffuse and fragmented, taking on the shape of a network, which corresponds to the profound reality of globalisation. Distancing itself more and more from direct war, the war of Clausewitz, this new form of international violence found itself rapidly described as 'terrorism', which simplifies it into a composite whole, in which different types coexist, which some perceive as acts of resistance, others as 'acts of despair', 'displays' or 'fanaticism'. In reality this new international violence presents two characteristics: on one hand it is handled and produced by specialised entrepreneurs who are only sometimes, very indirectly, connected to States; on the other hand, this violence is part of a social situation that fosters its extension, giving rise to diverse forms and varying degrees of intensity of commitment. Thus, this violence acquires a meaning in the opinion of a certain public, made up of people who may respond to the discourse of the entrepreneurs, or sympathise with them to some extent.

That sympathy, which is surprising and disturbing, might turn out to be connected to different systems of attitudes that are the product of crises of identity, perhaps severe, failed integration, painful marginalisation, disappointed hopes for advancement in society. Here we recognise different symptoms of humiliation, activated by traits that have become classical and familiar when it comes to describing globalisation.

The actors of this new violence demonstrate it in their own careers. Mohammed Atta, who was in some sense the leader of the terrorists of 9/11, reflected this mix of anomie and unrealised hopes. He was born in the Nile delta, the son of a lawyer. He grew up in Giza; he studied in Egypt and received a degree in architecture. He went to Germany to complete his training and studied in Hamburg, but ended up working as a car salesman while he finished a dissertation. He reacted with increasing anger at the continued failure of any resolution to the Palestinian crisis, and became enraged over Israel's bombing of Cana in 1996.

There are great similarities in the personal histories of many of the hijackers of 9/11. Several of them are marked out by their wandering lifestyles. Fayez Banihammad went to live in Orlando; Ahmed al-Ghamdi lived in Chechnya before moving to America. Hani Hanjour moved to San Diego; Ziad Jarrah, Lebanese and a member of a well-to-do Sunni family, first went to Germany to study German, and then went to engineering school in Hamburg as well. He then subsequently went to Chechnya and Afghanistan before moving to America. In Chechnya he encountered Saïd al-Ghamdi, another of the hijackers.

The same wandering route can be seen with Ayman al-Zaouahiri. He was the lieutenant of—and successor to—Bin Laden as head of al-Qaeda. He was the son of a reputable pharmacist, and himself a doctor and surgeon who left his native Egypt and went to Afghanistan, and then Chechnya. Ramzi Bin al-Shibh, the treasurer of al-Qaeda, a Yemeni, went to Karachi, where he was arrested. One of the organisation's recruiters, Mohammed Haydar Zammar, born in Syria, went to live in Germany at the age of 10. He was trained as a metallurgist, and earned a living as a truck driver. Abu Moussab al-Zarqawi, who led al-Qaeda in Iraq, started in Jordan with a life of debauchery, a drunkard, tattooed, convicted of rape and theft. He went to Afghanistan before returning to Mesopotamia. Zacarias Moussaoui, part French and part Moroccan, presumed to have been an accomplice in the attacks of 9/11, went to college in Perpignan, and then went to London before going to Chechnya and then Afghanistan.

These actors represent a phenomenon that has been commented on: they are both attracted to and repelled by the West. In their career paths, we see a desire to fit in to a globalised world, but also a desire to stand on an Islamist field of battle. Hopes of greatness are raised but not achieved, and the identities one attempts to construct become victims of mobility and transnationality, as if these were a trap. Gilles Kepel thought he saw a similar logic operating when he studied the terror killings in Toulouse and Boston.[9] The first of these, in March 2012, cost the lives of several French soldiers, some students, and a professor from the Jewish school, Ozar-Hatorah; the second occurred a year later. Three bystanders were killed and many people watching the Boston Marathon were wounded.

Kepel underlines the fact that this kind of attack is a reconstruction, on a small scale, and in a decentralised form, of a jihad that can no longer conform to the 'massive' model of 9/11, and finds in the career paths of these actors similar symptoms of failed integration relative to globalisation and the West, and the same sort of social instability and anomie. Mohamed Merah carries all the marks of a failed integration between Algeria, where his father lived, and France, where he grew up; between multiple foster homes where he failed to settle; between civilian life and chronic delinquency of assault and battery, throwing rocks at a bus, injuring several people; between failing academically and small jobs that never lasted long; between freedom and prison, where he had nothing to do but read the Koran. The two Tsarnaev brothers presented these signs as well, at a higher social level: the same failed integration in the United States; the older brother went from training as a boxer, to debauchery, to discovering rigorous Islam. Merah travelled to Pakistan and Afghanistan; the Tsarnaev brothers were torn between North America and the Caucasus, and obviously Chechnya. They were all exposed to an Islamophobic society that weighed upon their daily lives, a recurrent humiliation.

The constant reference to Afghanistan and Pakistan ('Afpak') is emblematic. This is not just because the Afghan conflict, and its effect on neighbouring Pakistan, constitutes a field of battle where Islamism has raised its banner in varying forms for a third of a century; also and above all it is because Pakistan is the perfect role model of a suffering society. An atomic power, it ranks only at #141 in the world ranking of the Human Development Index. Its involvement in the Afghan War has cost 35,000 lives, including 10,000 civilian non-combatants. Terrorist attacks alone have killed almost 5,000. There are hundreds of thousands of displaced people, and the financial cost is estimated at €35 billion, in a country where the annual GDP is €165 billion.

A population uprooted by the exodus, fleeing towards cities that are overcrowded and poorly equipped to handle refugees; victims of the low level of social integration, bringing their poverty and malnutrition into an urban setting; living in the middle of a never-ending war that is sometimes visible and sometimes invisible, under the twin pressures of India, its neighbour, and the interminable Afghan conflict; accumulating the most frightening scores in terms of various development indices, notably in the

[9] G Kepel, 'Merah et Tsarnaev, même combat', *Le Monde*, 30 April 2013, p 17.

rate of youth suicides: Pakistan has become a symbol of suffering, even of social pathology. Pakistan is suspected by almost everyone of supporting terror and, stigmatised in this regard, is condemned by those who are intolerant of radical Islam, accused of having 'invented' the Taliban schools and of having supported Bin Laden, the hallmark of its international status is that it is afflicted by constant humiliation. It is, as if in response, the main flashpoint in the world.

Pakistan occupies a theoretically interesting position in a typology that reflects the things that are made weaker by globalisation, and the failures of integration that are the consequence. The failure of integration potentiates the feeling of humiliation: in a system that is globalised and dominated, there is necessarily an international dimension to feelings of frustration. Every poorly-integrated society acts as a filter between the individual in an suburb of Karachi or a village in the Sahel and the international system. This filter pushes people towards radicalism and a denunciation of the external and distant other who nonetheless occupies the place of a superior.

This lack of integration affects societies in unequal ways in the world space, but it is clearly noticeable where the new battlefields are being created. We can distinguish various forms: failure of national integration, failure of political integration, failure of social integration. Even in a context of globalisation, a lack of national integration functions as a machine for humiliation: not to be recognised as a nation, like the Palestinians (who are admitted to nationhood on paper but not in reality), like the Kurds, the Sahrawi or the Tuaregs, is the pinnacle of social humiliation; it is in fact the negation of the idea of status. On the same spectrum, living as a minority, where the chances of rising to political power are limited, is another social factor that potentiates humiliation, as with the Moro Muslims in the Philippines; Muslims in India, socially relegated and probable flashpoints of instability for tomorrow; Uyghurs in China, converted into a minority on their own territory, more and more attentive to fundamentalist messages; and finally, until 2011 at any rate, the Christians of South Sudan. One could say the same about heavily tribalised societies that block access to decision-making for all those who are not tribal members, thus creating a lasting feeling of exclusion, something that also happened in Yemen and Afghanistan.

A failure of political integration marks failed States that are lacking a community of citizens, such as Somalia since 1991, Iraq since 2003, and the Central African Republic or the Democratic Republic of the Congo today: not only is an organised political community lacking, which gives rise to behaviour affected by alienation and anomie, but this lack also intensifies differences, inequalities of status or individual resentments. The situation has oriented individual attitudes towards denouncing an international order in which people are not represented, and in regard to which they must stand as victims. There is yet another form of failed political integration, which is based on a different kind of exclusion: one based on the absence of any chance to participate in politics, and thus upon a vision of politics as external, even foreign. For this viewpoint, authoritarianism is normal, and this explains why entrepreneurs of violence recruit so easily in countries that are governed by the most entrenched dictatorships, and why they can so easily capitalise on the humiliations of those who are perpetually excluded. This explains some of the success of Islamist disputes in Syria, as well as the progress of active jihadism in Sudan and Sunni regions of Iran, such as Baluchistan. The one who is relegated and who is still in the city follows the same series of stages as the States who are victimised by relegation within the international system; in the end these people come to the same deviant behaviours, even in the 'suburbs of Islam' in Western Europe.[10]

Finally, a failure of *social integration* leads inevitably to the same results. Failure occurs due to massive gaps between social developments that normalise globalisation and that are becoming more visible. There is a rift, within the societies of the South, between rich and poor, which is becoming more and more perceptible. It separates those who look to the North to make Western-style consumption possible, from those who lack all kinds of security, and who identify their miserable condition with their humiliating inability to keep up with a Western standard of consumption.

The great mistake has been to think that these pathologies could be healed by actions that belonged to the bygone age of Westphalian Europe, by force that opposes a strategist enemy. Disoriented by the illusions that the idea of menace produces, governments from the old world are relying on a policy of smoke and mirrors: thinking that for any risk of destabilisation, there was an effective remedy to be found among the classical instruments of power. If a menace is a threatened attack on the integrity of persons and goods, it is false to believe that it will be extinguished by the same means. Will we one day try to go to war against climate change, or against the things that menace our economy? Or against our benefit system?

Providing the wrong treatment renders the remedy worse than the original illness. Defects in integration presuppose a social treatment and a political surplus, in fact sacrificed to an excessive personalisation of power, which is to the detriment of institutions, and which stands in the way of remedying failures in innovation. Using force as a recourse against enterprises of violence that attempt to gain a foothold in Mali allows us to overlook the real causes of the despair that affects the Sahel. To 'destroy' the fighters, many of them child soldiers, only normalises a warrior game that inflames resentment and humiliation. Using drones in Pakistan is a way of reinventing

[10] To appropriate the title of G Kepel, *Les Banlieues de l'islam* (Paris, Seuil, 1987).

war so that one side has no casualties at all, but it leads to the same result, especially when the drones kill civilians. Even if it is difficult to obtain credible statistics, and even if the US government denies it, major humanitarian NGOs such as Amnesty International have already verified the deaths of many civilians in drone strikes in Yemen and especially in Pakistan; the strikes have hit targets among refugee populations fleeing combat. It has been estimated that between 350 and 900 innocent people have been killed by drones.[11] It is a supreme humiliation to see your loved ones killed by a remote-controlled machine, operated by an agent sitting thousands of miles away, and who runs no risk whatsoever.

***

Social movements of every kind, oppositional and deviant diplomacies, new conflicts whose violence and cruelty have not been condemned or countered over the years: humiliation, to the extent that it is normalised within the international game, has overturned the rules, created new dangers, and given rise to new dysfunctions that are often difficult to overcome. The process, once begun, is fearful: this time there is no cold-hearted monster, but a rational strategist at the controls. He may intend to stay there, but an essential part of the international dynamic escapes him, because this massive invasion of emotion profoundly changes the situation.[12]

These tendencies, which are constantly giving strength to all kinds of racism, or contributing to the distressing wave of Islamophobia,[13] or simply reinforcing the trend towards fear of the 'other',[14] are worrisome because they can easily fall into a vicious circle. This is a case of a doubly vicious circle, because humiliation is only made more painful by the falsified response one may make to it, as well as the game of oneupmanship played by anyone humiliated, who often dreams of gaining revenge by becoming someone who humiliates sometime else at some point. This is what Esther Benbassa noted regarding the derivations from Zionism,[15] and it is what we observe today in the discourses and practices of radical Islam. Humiliation never stops being reborn under the influence of the errors it inspires.

[11] 'Will I Be the Next?', report from Amnesty International, October 2013, about 45 drone attacks launched between January 2012 and August 2013 in Pakistan; the lower estimate (350) comes from the New American Foundation, the higher (475–900) from the Bureau of Investigative Journalism.

[12] D Moïsi, *La Géopolitique de l'émotion* (Paris, Flammarion, 2009).

[13] A Hojjat and M Mohamed, *Islamophobie* (Paris, La Découverte, 2013).

[14] Fear of the other, including hatred of the other for being different to you, is particularly likely to cause violence in the context of globalisation.

[15] E Benbassa, *Être juif après Gaza* (Paris, CNRS Éditions, 2009) 46.

Conclusion

WHAT ARE THE prospects for action or change? The simplest response has often been to turn towards fatalism: humiliation being a universal social trait, we are fated to find it everywhere and always, in all international scenes just as much as in social ones. It can hardly be softened or disguised. After all, that is also why the rules of diplomatic protocol were invented, formalising politeness and respect, partly to civilise international mores, but mostly in order to erase the distorting effect of power itself.

Nevertheless, we made another argument: linked to the failures people encounter in the quest for status, humiliation is to be considered as an effect of the system, which derived from the breakup of the Westphalian order, which had cultivated a sort of quiet equality in which any founding State might pursue a rivalry with a comparable State. With the socialisation of international life and with globalisation, things have gone differently. People have not only given an affective dimension to revenge; they have conferred upon it a social context that quickly led to the construction of many new mediations between those at war, ending up with ideologies whose main substance was humiliation. As for globalisation, it has given rise to many actors who are quickly judged to be implausible, and just as spontaneously regarded as intruders: small States; people from cultures considered 'distant' or exotic, and often thought of as primitive, having only recently 'awakened to History'; emergent citizens seen as nouveau riches, or worse, non-State actors who have no business in the inner sanctum of diplomacy.

These symptoms are well known to sociology: globalisation creates new inequalities and, if these are not controlled, there is an increased loss of status, denial of equality and stigmatisation. The greater the tension, the more violent the reaction in the opposite direction. The vicious circle is formed, and evil is fought by evil.

So we come to the heart of the matter: the Westphalian system was too highly structured, too functional, and too exclusive to be able to adapt itself, spontaneously, to globalisation. It offered too many advantages to regular players for them to easily change the rules. The great inconvenience was of a classical nature, too familiar and well-loved to be stored away for the benefit of a new global order that one does not understand, that one does not know, something the traditional powers take into account only to the extent that it serves as a bogeyman. Multilateralism was invented, in part at least, to move beyond this old order; in reality it was obliged to pledge allegiance to it and to bend to its old fashioned discipline. Those who were not admitted to the Westphalian inner sanctum and who now edge closer to it are pleased to pay homage to it in their turn and to adopt its mores. Each time, the strategy of humiliation repeats its work.

But this, after all, is a policy like any other, produced by States that can measure its failure day by day, thus measuring the price of such deliberate blindness in the face of new realities. These realities can be analysed, whatever may be the costs of adjustment that must be paid.

Humiliation and its dysfunctional effects on the international system can be remedied in some measure if the status of States is rethought as a function of globalisation. The ignorance that prevails concerning this matter is intolerable. Outside the West, the 'rest of the world' can no longer be considered as a mere afterthought. The cultural homogeneity of the Westphalian system has expired. Europe is no longer the battlefield of the world, as it was for 400 years. Even the weak today know that globalisation has conferred new resources on them, that they have some weight in the grand balancing act of the great powers. They can suffer, but they can also harm. The entente is no longer an all-powerful inner sanctum. Force can no longer resolve everything. Governance can no longer be based primarily on exclusion.

We see then, instead of the powers of yesterday, the choice of a new foreign policy that must, if it is to be successful, accomplish at least three transformations. First, it must establish itself as a policy of diversity. Today the best way of serving the national interest is to rethink it in relation to the other, no longer conceived of as some eternal rival one wishes to outclass, or the occasional vassal who needs guidance, but a partner who will prove all the more useful with the status of an equal, who is spoken to, admitted, included, and not made a recipient of all one's mistrust. This is a necessary stance the bourgeois class of many States had to resign themselves to, admitting the full citizenship of the working class they had so long despised, so that they were obsessed with the danger they supposedly represented. The guardian does not exist anymore, and neither really does the self-proclaimed policeman; a power cannot claim to be a model anymore, at the risk of being denigrated.

Foreign policy also has to be social, taking into account these complex new realities that go beyond pure strategic deliberations. The world is no longer the result of a game played by members of a club of cold-hearted monsters; it is a tangle of social facts that can no longer be reduced to bad guys, nor to puppet masters. It is more urgent to imagine and promote international social policies and working for the social integration of seven billion human beings, as a response to demands for a new kind of security, than to hound each other in outdated politico-military agendas.

At the end of the day this policy can only live if it is set free of Westphalian chimeras, and of mirages of a power that has grown too old to be effective and attractive. This power can only regain its potency through *multilateralism* that has been rethought and regenerated, finally freed from the distortion caused by the Cold War. In an interdependent world, it is appropriate to do more and more in other countries: to do this usefully and legitimately, it must be done in the name of everyone, not simply for a group that stands for the powerful.

In fact international relations, which have become global and intersocial, have finally begun to discover the effects of a system that nations were forced to perceive and finally accept as part of their domestic situations almost a century ago. A winning foreign policy is probably one which, in this new wide dimension and with this new logic, the resources to make further gains. In the meantime, humiliation remains the primary mark of the defeat of all conservatisms. It testifies to the difficulty in conceiving of otherness in the post-Westphalian world.

www.ingramcontent.com/pod-product-compliance
Lightning Source LLC
LaVergne TN
LVHW022043200926
848481LV00003B/761